791.40979 ASP

Aspen, Nelson.
Hollywood insider :
exposed! /
FRSN 1078675301

HOLLYWOOD INSIDER EXPOSED!

Nelson Aspen

To Mother and Dad, for their
unwavering support, guidance,
enthusiasm and encouragement.
And most especially for their gift
of good humor.

Acknowledgements

A great debt of thanks to Linda, Fiona and Diane at New Holland Publishers for their interest and assistance. A big 'good on ya' of appreciation also to my Aussie manager Matt Clarke, longtime friend Lou Ann Pavelin and US agent John Derr, as well as to Maura Teitelbaum and Jonathan Sichel for their counsel.

Contents

Who's Where	4
Introduction: The G-Word	7
Brangelina	27
My Mentor, Mary Stuart	31
How Hugh Grant Hiring a Hooker Helped my Hollywood Career	38
Facing the Prada-Wearing Devils	40
Comic Geeks	44
Ellen, Anne, Portia and a Coupla Dogs	50
9–11	55
Uncle Nelson	58
Hangin' with Leo	64
Mr and Mrs Douglas	69
Mr and Mrs Urban	74
Famous Persons' Disease	80
Too Hot to Handle	85
Ships Ahoy!	92
Quirks, Foibles and Foul-Ups	99
Aspiring Actor	112
My Favorite Movie Star	125
Marathon Mania	138
On the Campaign Trail	148
The Guy of 100 Lists	153
Dishing Up Homemade Fun	163
My Best Friend	180
A Day in the Life	185
On Location	195
Beauty & the Blogs	209
Friends On-Camera and Off	213
Turning Points	220
The Right Place at the Right Time	225
There is Nothing Like a Dame	231
So Long for Now	255

Who's Where

Affleck, Ben 153, 154
Alba, Jessica 157-8, 160, 199
Allen, Irwin 126, 134
Allen, Steve 9, 19, 61
Amor, Mike and Tracey 78, 215
Anderson, Pamela 12, 154, 203
Andrews, Dame Julie 42, 156, 193, 203, 244-54
Andrews, Naveen 117, 118
Aniston, Jennifer 27, 60, 142, 199, 241
Aniston, John 27, 32
Astaire, Fred 137, 239
Baker, Carroll 127, 133
Baldwin, Alec 157, 158
Bana, Eric 74, 82, 154, 193
Bancroft, Anne 115, 220
Banderas, Antonio 16, 199
Barr, Natalie 76, 214
Beatty, Warren 116, 157
Beckham, David 52, 157, 158, 159, 211, 217
Beckham, Victoria 12, 176
Beechman, Laurie 236-7
Begley Jr, Ed 21, 198
Beretta, Mark 'Beretts' 208, 214
Blanchett, Cate 40, 74, 82-3, 156, 157
Boland, Adam 202, 205
Borgnine, Ernest 134, 136
Brown, Divine 38, 220
Burnett, Carol 14, 32, 236, 251
Burton, Richard 250
Buttons, Red 134, 136, 137

Cage, Nicholas 48, 193
Caine, Sir Michael 84, 193
Cameron, James 64, 96-7, 98
Carey, Mariah 99, 201
Carrey, Jim 13, 45, 60
Carter, Lynda 49, 154
Charlton, Janet 65, 218
Clift, Montgomery 12, 156
Clinton, Hillary 151, 152
Clinton, President 51
Clooney, George 29, 46, 157, 158
Close, Glenn 156
Collins, Jackie 23, 24
Collins, Joan 23
Connery, Sir Sean 160
Couric, Katie 56, 184
Crawford, Joan 156, 211
Crouch, Jared 154, 208
Crowe, Russell 74, 155
Cruise, Tom 14, 74, 102, 109, 158, 192, 193, 197
Csortan, Laura 217-18
Day, Doris 156
Damon, Matt 30, 72, 153, 156
Davis, Kristin 159, 196
Day-Lewis, Daniel 9, 84, 136
De Niro, Robert 99, 155
De Rossi, Portia 50, 54
Degeneres, Ellen 9, 50-4
Dempsey, Patrick 13, 153
Denton, James 149, 151, 193
Depp, Johnny 136, 153, 156, 197
Dey, Susan 139, 155

DiCaprio, Irmelin 66-8, 97, 156
DiCaprio, Leonardo 8, 18, 39, 64-8, 211
De Havilland, Olivia 92
Dench, Dame Judi 115
Diaz, Cameron 159
Douglas, Kirk 71, 126
Douglas, Michael 14, 69-71
Doyle, Melissa 75, 200, 202, 203, 213-14
Dunaway, Faye 12, 127, 158
Eden, Barbara 154, 155, 201, 242-3
Edwards, Senator John 149, 150-2, 154
Fergie 104, 136
Ferrara, America 13, 55
Ferrell, Will 138, 139
Ford, Glenn 92, 137
Foster, Jodie 18, 82, 121
Foxx, Jamie 14, 157
Frost, David 130, 137
Garland, Judy 137, 156
Gibson, Mel 74, 158
Gillespie, Bonnie 122-4
Goldblum, Jeff 51-2, 54, 62
Grant, Hugh 38-9, 220
Griffith, Melanie 16, 158, 204
Gyllenhall, Jake 145, 197, 211
Heche, Anne 50-4
Hedren, Tippi 159, 204
Hefner, Hugh 22, 178
Heigl, Katherine 22-3, 154
Hilton, Paris 14, 62, 148, 187, 230
Hoffman, Dustin 116,

156, 181
Holmes, Katie 138, 229–30
Hopkins, Sir Anthony 18, 115, 156
Hudson, Rock 12, 126
Hunter, Tab 12, 15
Jackman, Hugh 30, 47, 74, 78, 83, 154
Jackson, Michael 78, 85, 103
John, Sir Elton 50
Jolie, Angelina 27, 28–9, 159
Karnazes, Dean 24, 144, 145
Keane, Sheana 216–17
Kelly, Gene 239
Kelly, Lorraine 16, 102, 215–16
Kerr, Deborah 16
Kidman, Nicole 40, 74–9, 157
Kirkland, Sally 156, 237–8
Knightley, Keira 121, 136, 155
Koch, David 76, 202, 203, 214
Lancaster, Burt 17, 239
Lang, kd 162, 197
Lapson, Charlie 157, 199
Lauer, Matt 25, 56
Law, Jude 83–4, 156, 160
Ledger, Heath 9, 74, 146, 205
Liberace 12, 204
Liu, Lucy 154, 241
Locklear, Heather 154, 242
Long Jr, Milton Clyde 95, 97, 98
Longoria, Eva 100, 154, 160
Loos, Rebecca 52, 217
Lynley, Carol 125–37
McCabe, Marcia 33, 35, 37
McClure, Marc 45, 166
McDowall, Roddy 126, 134

MacLaine, Shirley 156, 220
Madonna 157
Margolis, Cindy 22, 178–9
Marsden, James 13, 46–7, 154
Miller, Wentworth 83, 154, 193
Montgomery, Elizabeth 154
Mortensen, Viggo 32, 154
Neame, Ronald 133, 134
Newman, Paul 102, 159
Newmar, Julie 45, 155
Obama, Barack 151, 152
O'Brien, Conan 9, 190
O'Brien, Erin 149, 151
O'Donnell, Rosie 44, 50
Olivier, Sir Laurence 31, 126
Olmos, Edward James 133, 226
Paltrow, Gwyneth 27, 65
Paul, Alexandra 138, 198
Pennell, Louise 149, 151
Philbin, Regis 19, 113
Phillips, Michelle 21, 196
Pitt, Brad 26, 27–30, 65, 102, 153, 157, 158, 159
Polanski, Roman 127, 135
Posey, Parker 11, 46
Potts, Annie 55, 56
Princess Diana 14, 21, 200, 222
Quest, Richard 218, 245
Redford, Robert 102, 158
Reeve, Christopher 45, 47, 200
Reeve, Simon 76, 214
Reynolds, Debbie 14–15
Reynolds, Ryan 48, 153
Roberts, Doris 193, 224
Roberts, Julia 81, 102
Rush, Geoffrey 77, 193
Santana, Carlos 226–7

Sawyer, Diane 25, 190
Seymour, Carolyn 66, 67
Sheldon, Sidney 243–4
Simpson, OJ 82, 183
Sinatra, Frank 137, 232
Singer, Bryan 46, 48
Smith, Anna Nicole 78, 238
Smith, Liz 8, 12
Smith, Will 9, 153, 157
Spacey, Kevin 11, 46
Spears, Britney 62, 63, 102, 148
Stallone, Sylvester 135, 158, 227
Stevens, Stella 126, 132, 134, 136
Stewart, Martha 163, 184
Stewart, Rod 157, 199
Streep, Meryl 9, 40–3, 156
Stuart, Mary 31–7, 255
Taylor, Elizabeth 15, 32, 157
Thayer, Jack 94, 97
Timberlake, Justin 153, 160
Urban, Keith 74–9, 201
Van Dyke, Dick 223–4, 247, 251
Verdon, Gwen 233–5, 239
Wahlberg, Mark 30, 159, 160
Watts, Naomi 74, 78, 110–11
Weld, Tuesday 126, 127
White, Betty 21, 196
Williams, Robin 60, 114, 142
Winfrey, Oprah 138, 151
Winters, Shelley 126, 237
Witherspoon, Reese 11, 136
Zanuck, Daryl F 113, 201
Zellweger, Renée 39, 233
Zeta Jones, Catherine 14, 32, 69–73, 157, 193

Introduction: The G-Word

'gossip'/noun. 1. conversation about personal or intimate rumors of facts, especially when malicious. 2. informal and chatty conversation about recent and often personal events. 3. someone given to spreading personal or intimate information about other people.

Unlike many of my showbiz peers, I rarely use the G-word unless it's in relation to a particularly salacious item that is making news, courtesy of a tabloid outlet. That kind of sadistic media is outright schadenfreude: enjoyment obtained over someone else's misfortunes. And it couldn't be further from my outlook on life, let alone my approach to reporting. As it is there's already too little civility in our culture. I will, however, use the G-word whenever I'm debunking a false claim. It's almost like hosting a game show called 'Truth or Trash'! Even though most people will gleefully acknowledge that they get a kick out of that kind of lighthearted entertainment, I've always been instinctively wary of it. I once worked for popular Los Angeles radio station Groove 103.1 FM's morning show and they bestowed upon me the unfortunate nickname of 'The Groovy Gossip Guy'. It took a while to let that die down.

I'm proud to say that in all my years of daily reportage, the only celebrity who ever took umbrage at something I said was Carmen

Electra. She denied my contention that she was, at the time, dating former basketball star Dennis Rodman. I was proven right a very short time later when she eloped with him for that now-famous frenetic and fast marriage. Carmen's a doll and one heck of a pole dancer, so no hard feelings and I'm glad she's moved on. *New York Post* maven Liz Smith once said, 'Gossip is news running ahead of itself in a red satin dress'. Nice imagery, but I disagree. Isn't the line between news and innuendo already too blurred? I don't deal in mean-spirited chatter. I log an awful lot of hours talking on live television and radio…no scripts or censors…just what I call info-tainment.

Of course, I want to be cheeky…and funny. I'm a comedian. But I'm also a journalist. So I take a very personal responsibility to be fair, accurate and always err on the side of caution and give folks the benefit of the doubt. I source my material and communicate with my audience what is fact, what is fiction, what is supposition and what may be a combination of all three. I don't pretend to know everything, but I'm pleased to be a pundit on the subject matter at hand. Maybe that's not as lip-smackingly scandalous as the gleeful bitch-fests from some of my colleagues, but I prefer cat-fights on *Desperate Housewives* or *Melrose Place* reruns, not on broadcast outlets where people happen to also turn for weather, news and other relevant information they can trust. Why should entertainment news be exempted from the same standards or decency? Unlike many corporately controlled talking heads on some of the popular magazine-style shows, I am not under any obligation or pressure to promote a particular agenda. If I think a movie is awful or boring, I can say so without fear of studio reprisal. (Of course, they get very excited when I have a rave, and I learned to predicate which of my comments are available for promotional purposes after I saw a full page newspaper ad for Leonardo DiCaprio's 2006 *Blood Diamond*, splashed with a colorful quote from me that read, 'The Best Movie of the Year!—Nelson Aspen'. I did approve 'A lightning paced thriller from beginning to end', for Will Smith's exciting *I Am Legend*.)

I'm hired to opine. To me, being sought after as a raconteur is an honor and a responsibility. Being a good one is a lost art, so I work diligently to hone those chat skills every day. I strive to live up to the likes of Merv Griffin, Johnny Carson, Tom Snyder and Steve Allen…these late, great talk show hosts would be sorely disappointed with most of their showbiz successors. Ellen Degeneres and Conan O'Brien are two contemporary examples of hosts who 'get it'.

I'm not an overly religious person, but I'm a big believer in The Golden Rule: do unto others as you would have them do unto you. And the karmic idea that what goes around comes around. Words are a journalist's tool. 'The pen is mightier than the sword', and all that. Words can be used as weapons…sometimes as weapons of mass destruction.

✯ ✯ ✯ ✯ ✯ ✯ ✯ ✯ ✯ ✯ ✯ ✯ ✯ ✯ ✯ ✯

In the days after Heath Ledger's death, pundits were desperate to fill air time discussing all the various theories that could have led up to his untimely demise. One noteworthy hypothesis offered up by a medical doctor was that the young star could have benefited from professional acting training as a way to more ably cope with the emotional and physical stresses of such a demanding role as the psychotic comic book villain, The Joker. As you'll read in my chapter, Aspiring Actor, I am a big believer in actors taking classes, but I seriously doubt it will make much of a MEDICAL difference. If acting were that dangerous, leading players would have stunt men reading their lines too! The old 'method' style of acting is pretty rare these days and most talented people are able to turn it off when the director yells 'Cut!'. Can you imagine Meryl Streep taking home *Sophie's Choice* to the dinner table? Or Daniel Day-Lewis frightening his kids over milkshakes after a rough week on *There Will Be Blood*?

✯ ✯ ✯ ✯ ✯ ✯ ✯ ✯ ✯ ✯ ✯ ✯ ✯ ✯ ✯ ✯

HOLLYWOOD INSIDER
EXPOSED!

For public speakers as much as for anyone else, telling the truth shouldn't mean sacrificing tact and good manners. I wish somebody would get some of those tabloid TV talking heads to understand that, and knock off the sing-songy salacious style with which they seem to gleefully relate every iota of info.

Especially in the internet age, gossip is rife and easy to gather and disseminate at lightning speed. Particularly the unreliable kind. Maybe it's fun to talk about around the water cooler, but it's not news.

Unlike so many self-proclaimed gossip gurus, I actually live and work in Hollywood. It's an industry town. The stars are my friends, my neighbors, my gym buddies. Even if I were so inclined, why would I risk turning myself into a pariah within my own community? Instead, I've become the go-to guy on the red carpet and press conferences. Rather than duck for cover, celebs and their reps actually smile when they see me because they know me, they remember me and, most importantly to all concerned, they trust me. The guy who will give them a fair shake…be polite and respectful. Unlike the relentless paparazzi who often hurl abuse at celebrities to incite a more interesting photo op, I prefer to be an observer and questioner, not an instigator. That's why I have never used the camera on my phone, no matter what celebrity scene I've stumbled upon. Seeing Dominic Monaghan in tears with a mystery woman while waiting at the valet parking is a dramatic enough anecdote. I'd never be crass enough to whip out a gadget to snap a picture of it. With apologies to host Ashton Kutcher, nobody wants to actually be the victim of *Candid Camera*. I want the stars to look good, coming off as smart, easy-going and genuine. Because that's the same courtesy I'd like extended to me. Plus, as a TV host, it's my job to make my guests feel relaxed and comfortable. It doesn't always work, admittedly.

Some stars have been so burned by members of the press that they're immediately defensive, evasive and/or quick tempered. Kevin

Spacey is so mistrustful of journos that he seems to have lost every bit of pleasantry he may have ever possessed. How ironic that he chooses to do light fare like *Superman Returns* or *Fred Claus*, but then can't deliver some lively banter about his work on them. Would you believe I actually shaved my head to 'become' Superman's evil nemesis, Lex Luthor, before sitting down to interview Spacey? He wasn't impressed. The least he could have done was get a kick out of my dedication to comic book fandom. After all, isn't that what playing a pop culture icon is all about? He was so contrary about anything and everything. If I said having a bald head was cold, he'd say his was hot. When I asked him about living in London and being a Hollywood expatriate, he replied in a surly manner, 'I never lived in Hollywood, so how could I be an ex-pat?' Then I really went out on a limb and was hoping I could somehow uncover a lighter side to him by asking if he wouldn't mind using my electric razor to give my bald pate a little touch-up, for luck. He froze. He could barely manage to utter, 'I'm really not comfortable with that'. Loosen up, Lex. I could only assume he didn't want videotape of himself shaving the head of another man. Especially after the huge ruckus that was caused a few years back when photos were circulating of a man, presumed to be him, cuddling on a canyon outing with a much younger fellow. At least his co-star, adorable Parker Posey, got into the spirit of the fantasy film and played along…even using my razor to give her legs a little touch up!

Like Spacey, Reese Witherspoon is an icy one, too. Whatever sweetness or smarts she may possess is buried deep beneath her justifiable distrust of journalists. Another A-lister who pays a fortune for a personal publicist but doesn't always have a handle on basic interview essentials. Sometimes I think PR people are either scared of their own clients or are just out to take the money and be sycophants for the celebrity's own egomania. And *without* their

HOLLYWOOD INSIDER
EXPOSED!

'people' around, they can be even more frightening! (Faye Dunaway, are you listening?)

You have to look no further than cases like those of former matinee idols Rock Hudson, Tab Hunter, Sal Mineo, Anthony Perkins, James Dean or Montgomery Clift. So dogged by tabloid whisperings of their sexuality, it cost a few of them their careers and, for others, a life of forced exile inside 'the celluloid closet'. *Confidential* magazine, founded in 1952 by publisher Robert Harrison, forever changed the tone of celebrity journalism. Goodbye, legendary gossip columnists Hedda Hopper and Louella Parsons with their studio-manufactured, publicity-driven sob stories. Hello, shock and titillation! Stars themselves would never admit to buying the top-selling mag, but they all read it just the same. Even now, stars-of-the-moment will have staffers whose job it is to go through all the press and keep an eye on what's being said about them (or, God forbid, what's *not* being said). Victoria Beckham and Pamela Anderson are believed to have tabloid editors on speed dial to tip them off to PR-friendly photo opportunities. ('Hi, it's Posh. I just got a ma-jah new haircut and I'll be showing it off at Spago this afternoon if you want to check it out.' 'Paris, here. I have a hot new outfit I'm wearing to Hyde tonight. I'd love you to come by and see me. Knickers optional. Mwah!') Tab Hunter and Liberace famously took on *Confidential* in the courts, ultimately effecting little change. How different life could have been for later celebs like sweetheart-of-a-guy Robert Reed or hysterical, witty comedian and actor Paul Lynde (who once signed an autograph for me, 'Love & Laughter…Paul Lynde'. I thought it was such a fantastic wish to write that I use it myself, often).

The day after 9/11, Liz Smith theatrically proclaimed, 'Gossip is Dead!', but she was back writing her usual column in the *New York Post* a short time later. Like Frankenstein's monster, the G-word never really dies. It just waits for a new incarnation to inhabit. Times change, people don't! From rag sheets to supermarket tabloids to blog sites, it will always manifest itself in inventive ways because there is always a public hunger for it. For all its ubiquitous and thorough coverage of showbiz minutiae, I am still baffled by the startling popularity of TMZ's entertainment gossip website and syndicated television show...not because of the subject matter—we all love entertainment, but because of the downright nasty approach they take when reporting it. I don't know when it's going to come, but I am concerned for their sakes that one of these days payback is gonna be a bitch. Meanwhile, they actually have a large portion of the celebrity community quaking with fear and/or sucking up for favorable coverage.

How many times have you read 'A rep for *Celebrity X* has not returned calls for a comment?' Rarely (and wisely) will a star address the fodder, preferring to let it quickly die down so that somebody else's supposed scandal can take its place on the headline banner. If there's so much as a grain of truth in an item, it's often best to turn the other cheek and let it pass. This is why you don't see stars such as Julianne Moore, Brendan Fraser, America Ferrara or James Marsden appear in the gossip columns...they stay out of trouble. They're working professionals who get up in the morning, go to work, and come home at night to their families. When was the last time you heard a negative remark about Patrick Dempsey, Donny Osmond or Jim Carrey? They're gentlemen! Ho-hum, maybe, but you don't see them splashed across the pages of the glossies or mug-shots posted on every website. Frankly, these folks fascinate me the most, because their personal lives are actually rich and fulfilling enough, and psyches secure enough, that they don't need to search out the spotlight in their spare time.

Blatant lies are another story, though, and must be confronted and dealt with swiftly, lest the court of pubic opinion allow unsubstantiated allegations to spin out of control until they become perceived truths. Funny lady Carol Burnett wasn't laughing when she hit out at *The National Enquirer* with a libel suit in 1981 against claims of her public drunkenness. She not only won an unprecedented $1.6 million dollars, she proceeded to donate the monies to a university's journalism department to fund law and ethics courses.

In the modern era of big-bucks photo deals, stars carefully negotiate major exclusives with top outlets for shots of their weddings, honeymoons, new babies or inner sanctums. No wonder Catherine Zeta Jones and Michael Douglas took on Britain's *Hello!* magazine when they printed unapproved shots of their lavish November 2000, nuptials at New York City's Plaza Hotel. The Oscar-winning power couple emerged victorious, claiming that the pirated pics were such an invasion of privacy, and unflattering, that it could damage their careers. The High Court decided the damage was minimal and fined the mag just under $25,000 to be paid in restitution, but a precedent was set nonetheless. And remember David Hans Schmidt, who was facing hard prison time for trying to extort a million dollars from Tom Cruise for his stolen shots of the TomKat wedding? It hadn't been his first brush with brokering salacious pics (Colin Farrell, Jamie Foxx and Paris Hilton were also on his résumé) and he apparently opted to end his life by suicide rather than be incarcerated. Whether or not you blame the frenzied paparazzi pursuit for Princess Diana's tragic death in 1997, there is no doubt that the wild world of tabloid journalism can often be described as bloodthirsty.

One of my biggest rants is the lack of media training modern celebrities receive. Back in the old days, the famous were properly prepared for what the media had in store for them. Debbie Reynolds, like other young stars of her day, signed her MGM contract and was immediately thrust into a rigorous schedule of classes in singing, dancing, dialects, even stage fighting! Being a star meant more than just saying lines on a soundstage. It also included being gracious with interviews, fan-mail, charitable works and personal appearances. It was, and still should be in my opinion, hard work! Any sense of entitlement the great stars of the silver screen may have assumed was because they had earned it. Debbie is a great example of that work-ethic of another era. She's still hard at it and one of the most diligent divas in the biz. Not only does she still perform and share her enormous gifts with audiences all around the world, she always has time to sign autographs and reminisce about the Golden Age of Hollywood. She's one of its history's great curators, being a forerunner in the mission to preserve artifacts from the silver screen. At one point she even had her own memorabilia museum in Las Vegas (with her own signature slot machines in the lobby: three 'Debbies' and you were a winner). That's where I asked her, of all the stars who'd passed on, whom she missed the most and she answered with tears in her eyes, 'Agnes Moorehead and George Peppard'. Of course, Debbie knows all about being splashed across the pages of gossip magazines after the infamous love triangle of the 1950s between her then-husband, Eddie Fisher, and film fatale Elizabeth Taylor. Still, Debbie never complained or wallowed in self-pity or had a tail-spin into rehab. She bounced back better than ever—which is why she continues to thrive and enjoy such longevity to this day. 'Hold no grudges and keep working' seems to be her credo. Wouldn't it be refreshing if she could conduct a class on that for some of Hollywood's current crop?

Tab Hunter, in his fascinating 2005 autobiography, *Tab Hunter Confidential*, shared what he said was the best advice he'd ever been given on fame…written to him by his friend and co-star, popular 1950's screen siren Linda Darnell: 'Things happen fast in Hollywood and for as long as you're in the spotlight you remain a target for gossip…No matter how hard you try you can't please everyone… Just concentrate on learning to live with yourself in peace—for that is the greatest goal of all'. How many millions of bucks do you suppose today's stars spend on psychiatrists, life coaches and rehab trying to find that elusive peace she's referring to?

After a lifetime in the business and the last two decades in Hollywood, first-hand experience wins out every time. Fortunately, I have significantly more stories to tell about who is nice (Antonio Banderas) as opposed to who's naughty (*Mrs* Antonio Banderas). I enjoy sharing tales of who is interesting. Kind and silly. Any reporter who can only resort to dishing out daily doses of dubious dirt is either very lazy or poorly connected. There are more quirky and compelling stories coming out of Hollywood every day than I could ever use; why should I lower myself to be a mud-monger?

My darling *GMTV* crony, Lorraine Kelly, is the United Kingdom's yummiest mummy and a great fan of offbeat news. We used to do a regular OILA segment (which stood for 'Only In LA'), talking toilet paper rolls, fairy school, boob jobs for men, personal trainers for pooches…it's a bottomless well of madcap merriment!

I'll give you an example about making a simple choice to opt for the high road. When news broke about the death of silver screen legend Deborah Kerr, I was already about to go on the air with the latest update on the legal woes of one of those girls whose names end in 'y' or 'I' or 'ee'. Ashlee…Britney…Lindsay, one of 'em, I don't recall now. I said, 'Let's drop that and let me give a tribute to Deborah Kerr'. 'Deborah who?' asked my producer. I know, I know… I'm an old fogey, sometimes. As the youngest of five kids, I have older parents and all my life I've been accused of being born twenty years too late. But I knew this news was important. Fortunately, my wonderful producer trusted my instincts and let me lead with an obit for the marvelous titian-haired actress.

Certain that most of our viewers, like the young producer, had no idea who I was talking about, I simply acknowledged that. 'Sad news this morning for fans of classic films', I began. I went on to explain the details of her passing with a quick lesson on *why* her death was significant and why everyone interested in entertainment should be informed of it. Her now-iconic lip lock with Burt Lancaster in the crashing waves in *From Here to Eternity* raised the bar for on-screen love scenes. Her grace and talent displayed so magnificently in classics such as *An Affair to Remember*, *The King and I* and *Black Narcissus* spawned new genres and endless imitations for generations to come. And, on a personal note, how her performance in *Tea and Sympathy* so impacted an important stage production of the drama in which I co-starred as a teenager. I managed to get all that broadcast (plus film clips!) in under two minutes, and I was proud that I gave that great lady a respectful goodbye.

And guess what? In the hours and days that followed, I began to receive appreciative mail from viewers—even from a longtime friend of Ms Kerr herself. That is the very best part of my job: to be able to touch someone on the other side of the world and give them a smile, some reassurance or a new idea…just by having a chat about something that is meaningful to me. If you'd asked me at the time I went on the air, I'd've settled for maybe inspiring one person to rent a DVD of an old Kerr classic. Could I possibly have a better job? Communication is what it's all about for me.

It's not as one-sided as you might suspect. I'm not just talking into a microphone, camera lens or to my co-presenters. I love meeting people from the audience and whenever they send me photos of themselves, their families, their pets, etcetera, I keep them at my desk to remind me exactly who I'm talking to, before I go on the air. Australia's *Sunrise*, in particular, is excellent about connectivity with viewers…which inspires such loyalty and camaraderie between both sides of the camera. A big part of my daily routine is keeping up with my audience correspondence. Even with the ease of e-mail, I'm a

HOLLYWOOD INSIDER
EXPOSED!

firm believer that anyone who goes to the time and effort to write to me deserves a note back! I admit to being such an avid e-mailer that my once-immaculate penmanship has suffered horribly! Sir Anthony Hopkins, who's even more of a Luddite than I, admonished me to get back in touch with my stationery and fountain pen…and I've made a point of it.

Many stars are environmentally friendly and I always encourage fans to write to them through their official websites. A pal of mine, eco-warrioress Alexandra Boyd, now starring in the popular UK soapie *Coronation Street*, ended up becoming Leo DiCaprio's 'friend' through Facebook, so they could exchange green-ideas.

Legendary German filmmaker Leni Riefenstahl, who passed away in 2003 at the age of 101, corresponded with me over the course of her final years and that eventually led to what I believe was the final interview she ever gave (about what else: her amazing longevity and near-century of controversy). Even savvy Jodie Foster was impressed when I told her about that…the Oscar-winner has been trying to get a biopic about Riefenstahl off the ground for years. I hope it happens; Jodie isn't just one of my all-time favorite actor/directors, she would be *perfect* casting in the starring role.

This is a business of relationships…and e-mail is as good a way as any to start establishing them, friends! And before you start asking me for personal contact information or addresses, I will tell you right now: hit the internet for official sites, and the Screen Actors Guild can also provide you with agency representation contacts. Don't try and be sneaky, circumventing the proper avenues…that will work against you in the long run.

Many assume that the entertainment industry operates and thrives on nepotism…that power and privilege is reserved only for the well connected. I have learned that the more years I log as a member of the show-business community, the more opportunities arise. It really *is* all about who you know, and that's not a bad thing in any industry. Why wouldn't you want to hire/surround yourself with other people whom you know and trust to do a good job? That's just good business. If you have a choice between hiring a doctor, lawyer, landscaper or tutor that you already respect and feel comfortable with…why risk it on a completely unknown entity? This is why I tell newbies to Tinseltown to definitely stick it out for at least eighteen months before getting discouraged. Only one in a million will ever be discovered while sipping a milkshake at the drug store soda fountain or window-shopping on a stroll down Rodeo Drive. The rest of us gotta work for it!

Certainly my own Road to Hollywood was far from yellow brick or strewn with stardust. Home movies of me from age three (I was obsessed with the Wicked Witch of the West…she was MUCH more interesting a character than her fellow Emerald City citizens. Just ask the smashing Idina Menzel, who originated the role of Elfaba in the Broadway hit *Wicked*. I convinced her it's perfectly okay to celebrate your 'inner witch'), show a big ham waiting for a stage to tread upon. My mother wisely guided me into a local theatrical production of *The House at Pooh Corner* in which, by all reports, I stole the show. A little talent, a lot of extra weight and a pink Piglet costume will do it every time. From there, it was on to more local amateur and semi-professional work as a child actor until I graduated high school and moved to New York, where I enjoyed the heady times of the 1980s. Ten years in the Big Apple, primarily working alternately in daytime television and the fitness industry (had to shed those Piglet pounds!) prepared me for a full-time relocation to Tinseltown in 1990. It was a couple of years of living on sofa-beds and futons, with cinder blocks and milk crates for furniture, but the dream was in sight: I wanted to be the next Regis Philbin, Steve Allen or Mike Douglas (American presenters I grew up watching on daily talk shows…masters of not only chat but of the technical skills needed behind the scenes to make it all appear effortless to the audience).

A recent acknowledgement that I was well on my way along the Road-to-Regis came quite unexpectedly while shooting on the cobblestone streets of a tiny town in the southern part of Ireland. Bundled up against the weather, surrounded by a small film crew in front of the magnificent statue in memoriam to lives lost on the *Lusitania*, a little car puttered by and came to a sudden stop. The driver, a young woman, rolled down her window and called out merrily, 'Hi, Nelson! I hate Faye Dunaway, too!' I burst out laughing and waved back. She not only recognized me from telly, but had been paying attention and, best of all, felt comfortable enough to pause and extend a friendly hello. Lots of Irish folks were that way. How many times beautiful strangers greeted me with a 'You are very welcome!' I may not have any golden statuettes on my mantle (yet!), but there is no greater award than being warmly welcomed by nice people.

Who could have dreamed—certainly not I—that it would be a purple piece of plastic that would jettison me directly into my desired career path. I'm referring to the great exercise fad of the late 80s/early 90s: the Reebok Step. I was one of the first certified instructors in the gimmicky new workout, personally trained by its inventor Gin Miller. This will never last, I remember thinking as I stepped up, up, down, down to the disco rhythms of the low-impact aerobics class. A year later, my classes were sell-outs and I was performing combinations on that platform that would make iconic choreographer Twyla Tharp look twice. The fitness studio where I taught was around the corner from a hotel where lots of flight attendants stayed on layover, so not only did I get a lot of dates, but my classes were packed with fit Brits. Somehow or another, I don't even recall now, I was offered the opportunity to be flown to the UK to train Princess Diana in this hot new workout craze. A longtime Anglophile and Diana devotee, I leapt at the chance.

Once I arrived in Merry Olde England, I was only engaged to instruct Di's personal trainer and conduct master classes…the Princess herself was probably locked away in a tower somewhere. Oh well…she'd learn how to walk up and down the Step second-hand, but at least I was making some money and taking a free vacation.

One of the big British breakfast programs, *This Morning with Richard and Judy*, asked me to be a guest and show off Step techniques, so I was flown to their studio in Liverpool where I dutifully demonstrated my moves while stationed on a floating 'island' in the river which was shaped to resemble the map of England (it was where the weather man was usually positioned for his forecasts). I guess I was a hit with the audience, because the next day one of the newspapers ran an item insisting, 'Don't let the long-haired American go home!' (Yes, it was 1991 and I was sporting a mullet) So Richard and Judy tested me out the very next day by sending me to an old folks' home to teach them get-fit exercises for a lighthearted segment. There may not have been a princess among them, but I was in my element. The producers loved it and I was hired to become their LA-based celebrity fitness correspondent. Before long, I was bringing stories like 'Boxing with [singer] Michelle Phillips' and 'Fitness for Pets with [comedy actress] Betty White' to millions of people in the United Kingdom. I've been working in morning television ever since. Thanks, Reebok!

Prior to becoming the full-time entertainment correspondent for *Sunrise*, the bulk of my reporting focus was on health and fitness. All celebs seem to love discussing their diet and exercise regimens—even when the subject doesn't start off there. Eco-mad actor Ed Begley Jr. started talking to me about riding his bike for transportation, but it turned into him explaining that it enables him to turn the world into his gym! His personal key to good health, he then explained, is 'finding serenity in the everyday world. Not waiting for it to occur on some vacation or after some personal success. Living in the moment!' Maria Conchita Alonso likes to worry less about numbers and more about the feeling of being in shape. 'I don't know how much I weigh', she confessed to me. 'I go by the mirror, not the scales.'

My fab friend Cindy Margolis went from nine months pregnant back to supermodel shape in seemingly no time, shedding the nearly 60 pounds she'd gained in between. 'The hardest challenge was accepting that my body didn't get out of shape overnight, so I had to stop expecting it to get back into shape overnight. I hung up a little sexy bikini in my gym as my motivation.' She also wisely perceives that 'Being healthy is not just for you, it's also a gift you give your family. If you do things you like to do anyway and incorporate them into your daily routine then being fit and healthy becomes a part of who you are.' I should point out that it was after this, and turning 40, that Cindy finally relented and obliged Hugh Hefner's request to pose nude for *Playboy*. She wanted to inspire mature gals to love their bodies, and obviously plenty of people loved Cindy's: it was one of their best-selling issues ever.

The longer you persist, the more people you meet and contacts you make, and the smaller the world will become. To this day, some of my closest friends and most important colleagues and sources are the people I met years and years ago while climbing up the ladder. Any honest work is an opportunity to network with those who can potentially help you further down the line.

Those pay-offs come in large ways and small, always happy surprises. Being courteous to the camera crew should be the norm, but you'd be surprised how much 'talent' can tend to ignore that. And when it's other journalists who act all high and mighty it never ceases to amaze me. We're all in this together, folks! Case in point: I was doing a television interview with actress Katherine Heigl which was running way behind schedule but when I was wrapping it up, the kindly cameraman spoke up that there had been an audio problem and I should re-ask my first few questions. Katherine had no choice but to oblige. Had he not been a professional pal of mine, I would never have known until I got the tape back to an editing bay and it would have been too late. Nice people look out for each other.

I have a game I call 'Two Degrees of Nelson Aspen'. The challenge: any celebrity you can name, I can connect to either personally or professionally by two degrees of separation or less. I've learned to predicate that, on the condition that the celeb of note be someone who hasn't been dead for more than 20 years and it must be a human being…sorry, no Rudolph Valentino or Yogi Bear. For example, although I've never met Joan Collins, I know several of her former *Dynasty* and *Guiding Light* co-stars and also had a boffo interview with her charming sister, Jackie.

I often applaud Jackie for being one of the most hands-on business women I've ever encountered. Not only is she fantastic at working plugs for her latest steamy bestsellers into every interview she ever gives, I've witnessed her pull up to a bookstore—in a limousine, of course, dahhling—and go the fiction section to check their current stock of her inventory. Any shortcomings were immediately reported to the manager, then back into the limo and off to the next store…

Making lots of diverse allies and keeping them by *being* a good friend in return, is a not-so-secret way to succeed and enjoy a long and prosperous career in any profession. A few years ago, I was in between jobs and had just ended a long-term relationship. I was bored, bills were piling up and I needed some extra money and a reason to get out of the house. A firm believer that there is no shame in working for an honest buck, I took a part-time position as a bookseller at my local Borders Books & Music outlet. Not only did I enjoy the employee discount, I made several new friends I'd never

EXPOSED!

have met otherwise. A year or so later, I was back on my feet with a new book out, *Let's Dish Up A Dinner Party!*, and my Borders buddies set me up with lavish book signing events all across the country. They loved that I was one of their own, and so did I. That's friendship, not nepotism. Everybody wins.

★ ★ ★ ★ ★ ★ ★ ★ ★ ★ ★ ★ ★ ★

>On her ability to be an endless font of Hollywood information, Jackie told me with a robust laugh, 'I do know where everybody is buried. And I go to a lot of parties and know most of the players. People are also inclined to tell me plenty. I don't really have spies, but you know...limo drivers, hairdressers, manicurists, they all want to reveal things to me. And I do hear the most incredible information, but I also hear it from the stars themselves. And famous directors and producers and people in the business. So when you read one of my books, you are getting the real truth and not the front page of one of the tabloids. My characters are a compilation of people I have met and observed. Men love me to write about them, only they want to be portrayed as great lovers and incredible studs! When I'm 106, I'll still be scribbling raunchy stories for your enjoyment!' And for the record, glam Jackie's favorite junk food is Reese's Peanut Butter Cups.

★ ★ ★ ★ ★ ★ ★ ★ ★ ★ ★ ★ ★ ★

So the next time you read a book or article about someone you admire, or see a performance or interview that touches you, drop that person a line and let them know. I became a pen-pal with Monty Python's brilliant Michael Palin after writing to commend him on his phenomenal documentary TV series and companion book, *Michael Palin's Hemingway Adventures*. Two of my sports idols, ultra-marathon man Dean Karnazes and Olympian/writer Kenny Moore became e-friends similarly, thanks to the internet.

And it works both ways. After reading an article I wrote in *Running Times* magazine, author Marlin Keesler Googled me until he tracked down my contact info. A dozen e-mails later, we actually met face to face while running across the famous Golden Gate Bridge! It was Mile 7 of the San Francisco Marathon…we literally ran into each other. A memorable moment (and way to be introduced), for sure!

You might not always get a personal response, but you'll probably make someone's day. Or…you'll get lucky and, as I say, 'make a new friend you've yet to meet'.

My mother, a cunning combo of Morticia Addams, Krystal Carrington and Carol Brady, used to say she loved going to bed because she was so excited to wake up and seize the new day. I'm exactly the same way…being an unapologetic morning person is a way of life for me, especially with the anticipation of a fresh day to enjoy. It may wreak havoc with my social life, but I'd much rather wake up at 3am than *stay* up 'til 3am. For a long time, I went to a 24-hour health club so I could get a workout in at any hour. Only in Hollywood could you work up a sweat with drag artist RuPaul on the Stairmaster in front of you, actor Jesse Metcalfe on the treadmill behind you and Jason Priestley in the weight room across from you… all before the sun comes up!

I always considered my off-kilter schedule to be good training for a career in morning television. TV anchors Matt Lauer and Diane Sawyer always talk about getting up at ungodly hours for *The Today Show* and *Good Morning America*. There seems to be a magic to that time before day break…making your way to the studio while the city sleeps. Knocking back those first cups of coffee while prepping your scripts and getting the knot in your tie just right.

It's accurate to say that millions of people wake up with me every morning. (Ooh!) Ironically, most of my international reportage starts with a greeting of 'Good Morning', even though it's not so early for *me*.

HOLLYWOOD INSIDER
EXPOSED!

England's *GMTV* had me in the studio 11pm–2am Los Angeles local time. Yawn! That's a killer! *The Bermuda Sunrise Show*, our own US's *Daily Buzz*, *Sunrise* for both New Zealand and Oz…all live morning shows, but not morning for me. The only early am outlet I have is for Ireland's *The Afternoon Show*, and obviously that's one time I *can't* say 'Good morning!' You can imagine how confusing it gets when we all start changing the clocks for daylight savings time. Live TV is one job where lateness is strictly *verboten*. Especially in the wireless world, I can work around the clock with my various production teams. Sometimes I just have to put on my sneakers and head out for a few miles of running just to get a respite from the endless stream of breaking showbiz news. Believe me, unless I bump into a star while on my run (like the time Brad Pitt ran a stop sign and literally almost ran me over with his truck! 'Stop' means stop, Brad!), that's the one time I hit the Hollywood pause button on my brain.

But in the pages that follow is a taste of what went on behind the scenes…some of my own favorite memorable moments with the stars I'm asked about most often. It's not a kiss and tell…more like a show and tell!

Reading this far, you should also have a little window into my philosophy of the G-word. A little dirt goes a long way, so while I'll occasionally offer up an acknowledged tabloid tidbit, I won't make a steady diet of it. Those who do devour it and regurgitate it to the masses tend to bounce from place to place pretty quickly before eventually disappearing altogether. My transition from acting to presenting occurred in 1991. There aren't many of us who've been at it that long. Admittedly, Hollywood is a town that chews up folks, but for me it is home.

So…welcome to my home. I love showing you around.

Brangelina

I already told you about my near-fatal hit-and-run encounter with Brad Pitt, but I still love him as half of my best-ever Hollywood power couple, Brangelina. I mean, these two are as close to superheroes as we're likely to see in our lifetime! Beautiful, talented, philanthropic and great with kids! It's hard to remember either one of them pre-Brangelina. Jennifer and Billy Bob Who??

But there was a Brad Pitt before he met his soul mate, Angie. His arrival in California, from rural Missouri, back in the '80s landed him in the household of my friend, writer Thom Racina (most famous for creating the brilliant Ice Princess storyline and subsequent wedding episode of *General Hospital*'s own super couple, Luke and Laura Spencer). Brad worked as Thom's houseboy for two years while he was trying to get discovered as an actor. Thom has wonderful memories of their friendship and the poetry-writing, good-humored kid whom he helped start out in TV with a bit part on the soap opera *Another World*.

In spite of the mega star he's become since then, that small-town sensibility has remained a constant for Pitt. When he dated Gwyneth Paltrow in 1998, a friend of mine who worked with her on her film *Hush* told me she'd rush home from the set every night to make Brad dinner. Imagine Gwyneth frying up chicken and mashing potatoes! Even while on the dating scene, Brad wanted to play house. The personal chef who worked for him while he was married to Jennifer Aniston (whose wonderful, gentlemanly dad John, I worked with in my own soap opera days) told me that Brad and Jen were total

HOLLYWOOD INSIDER
EXPOSED!

homebodies—preferring to nestle into their Hollywood Hills home (next door to Danny Devito and Rhea Perlman). The most demanding part of the chef's job was catering to their late-night munchies, but otherwise a perfectly average couple. Brad once said in an interview that his big dream was to sit on the front porch, chatting with friends and locals while he watched his kids playing in the yard. It may be on a much larger, more glamorous scale than he ever imagined, but he seems to have made that dream come true.

I interviewed Angelina a few months before I met Brad. It may sound absurd, but after her publicity people approved me—I was flown to Manhattan to have a three(!)-minute interview with her. I was asked to sign a release form, agreeing not to ask any personal questions (she had given birth to baby Shiloh a few months earlier). Some reporters get bent out of shape if they're asked to sign such paperwork, but I think they're overreacting. It isn't compromising their journalistic integrity to be asked to stick to the subject at hand (usually whatever project the celebrity is out to promote) and any interviewer worth his salt should be able to come up with enough interesting inquiries to fill a few minutes of chat time, for goodness sake! Personally, I take it as a challenge to figure out how to navigate the conversation into some unique or unexpected territory.

Even if I had been worried about topics, it would have been unnecessary. I was rushed into Angelina's chambers, my head swimming with the scads of accumulated factoids about her from years of following her every move. While I greatly appreciate a person's physical beauty, it doesn't mean I'm swayed by it. But then there's Angelina Jolie! She was the most beautiful woman I had ever seen—prettier in person—and I was gobsmacked. She must be so used to that reaction, especially from men, that she took charge and immediately put me at ease. She extended her hand for a firm shake, introduced herself and made chit-chat while I got miked up for the cameras. I stuck to the subject of her film (*The Good Shepherd*) but she almost at once segued into telling me about her pregnancy and the etiquette classes she'd taken to learn the proper character traits for her period character…personal stuff, hooray! Thinking of her now as a 'yummy mummy', instead of the world's most famous living beauty, we gabbed beyond the allocated three minutes about the gift of good manners which parents can pass on to their children. It was a marvelous conversation. She was gracious and down to earth, laughed easily and possessed the self-confidence of a real star without any pretension.

Would Brad be the same way, I wondered, when I went to the Toronto Film Festival to meet him? No special paperwork had to be signed, but security was massive. He even had an armed plainclothes policeman positioned outside his room. It's true what they say about his friendship with George Clooney, by the way. Danny Ocean was right down the hallway doing an interview for his film *Michael Clayton*. I was happy to be there for Brad, though…the only excitement Clooney was generating that day was the frantic requests from his assistant for somebody to cough up a cigarette for him.

When I came in to see Brad, his eyes widened and he broke into a wide smile. 'Hey! Nice to see you again!' Now, unless he remembered me yelling at him when he blew through that stop sign and almost ran me over in which case I doubt he'd have been smiling, there was no way he knew who I was! I figured it would be a bad foot to start off on if I mentioned the incident, so I just assured him that we hadn't met…although maybe we'd 'run into one another' over our mutual time in Los Angeles. I can't resist a pun, even in the presence of A-listers.

We had a bit of a chat about his movie, *The Assassination of Jesse James by the Coward Robert Ford* (which was pretty to look at, but a slow-moving snooze for me frankly), but then got into the good

HOLLYWOOD INSIDER
EXPOSED!

stuff. I knew that, like his partner, he'd love talking about his kids and that's really when he's at his best. Well, who isn't the most interesting and attractive when they're enjoying the subject matter? Even with the newsboy cap he'd taken to wearing, he somehow never looked better. I asked him about his tattoos and how old the kids would have to be before he'd let them get inked, and he replied that they would probably go out and get them on their own, long before he'd ever give them permission. Perfect papa response. Maybe it's sexist, but I expect mothers to want to chat about their kids and it always is a happy surprise when dads feel the same way (Hugh Jackman, Matt Damon and Mark Wahlberg have all gushed to me about their children). He was warm and charming which made me want to go back and give the film a second viewing. (I'm one of those weirdoes who likes to watch the DVD features about a movie before I see the movie, itself. I think it's more interesting to have the background information ahead of time…)

Whether he's skimming pools or rebuilding New Orleans, Brad's not just a hunk…he's a hunk of talent, too. I'm not one to swoon over celebrity couples, but Brangelina are my hands-down faves. I hope they'll be happy together always!

My Mentor, Mary Stuart

This isn't about the girl from *Fried Green Tomatoes* or the Scottish queen beheaded by Queen Elizabeth I. *My* Mary Stuart may be an actress not known by many people under 40 or international audiences unfamiliar with her work, but I guarantee you that she had a profound effect on anyone who watches daytime television. Dearest to me is the fact that she was my longtime mentor and friend, whose profound influence on so many facets of my life makes her presence felt to me every day.

In 1951, with an extensive but uninspired résumé full of forgettable film roles, Mary was part of a small creative team in New York City who created the very first soap opera to ever air on television. Originally only 15 minutes long, *Search for Tomorrow* debuted with Mary playing the heroine, Joanne Gardner. Televised serial drama was a completely new medium and became an instant pop culture phenomenon…and Mary was its face. They were called soaps because the programs were sponsored by the makers of household products like laundry and dish detergents. Mary was the undisputed Queen of the Soaps and reigned as such for over three decades. Even Sir Laurence Olivier can't lay claim to keeping one character compelling for *that* long!

As America's leading lady of daytime, Jo faced thousands of episodes worth of births, deaths, disasters and dilemmas. She went blind (twice!), was kidnapped (many times!), got stuffed in the

trunk of a car, was swept down a raging river, was tied up and left to die atop an elevator shaft, became trapped in a burning riverboat and even...gasp!...got a divorce from Jennifer Aniston's father. She was the first soap star ever nominated for an Emmy Award (against Shirley Booth and Mary Tyler Moore) which spawned a separate division specifically for Daytime TV. The apron she wore for so many hours of hand-wringing is now prominently displayed at the Smithsonian Institution. When *Search* ended its unprecedented 35-year run as TV's longest-running show, Mary had the distinction of being the only original cast member...she'd been there from Day One. And legions of fans had been there with her as she grew up from the sweet, simple Joanne Gardner to the complex matriarch of the fictional town of Henderson, USA as Jo Gardner Barron Tate Reynolds Vincente Tourneur.

Like every other child of my generation, a visit to my grandmother's house always meant having to watch her 'stories' while we had lunch, so I was introduced to Mary's work early on. Thanks to Mom Mom (my name for my grandmother), I had a working knowledge of the show's characters and storylines when I eventually moved to New York City. (Okay, who am I kidding? I was a fan!) So I was beside myself when one of my first jobs as an adult actor was playing a small part on the very show I'd grown up watching—*SFT*! My first scene was with an actress who went on to win an Oscar for her role in *Moonstruck*: Olympia Dukakis. Funny how *Search* isn't on *her* résumé.

> ✯ ✯ ✯ ✯ ✯ ✯ ✯ ✯ ✯ ✯ ✯ ✯ ✯ ✯ ✯ ✯
>
> Lots of stars got their start on the soaps. Christopher Walken, Kylie Minogue, Catherine Zeta Jones and, on *SFT*, Viggo Mortensen and Jill Clayburgh. Some stars are such soap *fans* that they gladly guest star, and Elizabeth Taylor, Carol Burnett and Phyllis Diller have all appeared on one or other at some time.
>
> ✯ ✯ ✯ ✯ ✯ ✯ ✯ ✯ ✯ ✯ ✯ ✯ ✯ ✯ ✯ ✯

Sunny Adamson, played by sunny Marcia McCabe, was the first friend I made (she and I are still close mates to this day. I adore her!). Mary was the second. She made a point of introducing herself and welcoming me aboard. That night I couldn't wait to call Mom Mom and tell her all about meeting Sunny and Jo. A few weeks later at Christmas time, Mary approached me with an offer too good to resist: if I would give her a hand answering her holiday fan mail, she'd be my acting coach. Needless to say, I was practicing my cursive 'Much love and Merry Christmas, Mary Stuart' that very weekend! And so began our very unique friendship.

★ ★ ★ ★ ★ ★ ★ ★ ★ ★ ★ ★ ★ ★ ★

> Another of the show's longtime stars, who played the ongoing nemesis of Mary's character, was unexpectedly and unceremoniously fired after more than a decade on the show. Someone had overheard her in the makeup room the day before, reading about some natural disaster that had made headlines in the paper. She dryly quipped, 'Over a hundred people killed. Tsk tsk. And not one of them was a writer'. The walls certainly had ears and someone tattled to The Powers That Be. Viewers wound up seeing her start a scene with her TV daughter on a Tuesday and an entirely new actress picking up mid-conversation on a Wednesday. (This is not a business known for its job security.)

★ ★ ★ ★ ★ ★ ★ ★ ★ ★ ★ ★ ★ ★ ★

The first day I walked into Mary's apartment (a fabulous Madison Avenue penthouse…the elevator opened right into the apartment's vestibule!), I discovered her in the kitchen putting together a lunch tray. Her big border collie, Mozart, bounded in to greet me. 'You're just in time to help me with this, presh', she said handing me a bag with plastic utensils, napkins and cans of soda…and Mo's leash. The next thing I knew, we were down the block in Central Park serving lunch to a homeless woman Mary had befriended. There was the Doyenne

EXPOSED!

of Daytime serving lunch to a bag lady who lived under a fortress of discarded umbrellas. She did this every day. Years later, when Mary and I learned how to use a new fangled device called a PC, she wrote a story about her relationship with this woman entitled *My Shadow*. It ran in the prestigious *New York Magazine* and then became a TV movie, *Face of a Stranger,* starring Gena Rowlands and Tyne Daly.

Although I still found plenty of time to hang out with friends my own age, I had more fun at Mary's. The fan mail and acting coaching exchange soon transformed into more of an excuse to simply hang out together. Along with her partner, a charming architect named Wolfgang, we'd spend weekends at her Connecticut country house… watch old movies on TV…write plays…play piano, sing together… and cook meals. She taught me how to mix martinis, serve asparagus and make a perfect omelette (the secret, I learned, was not to cook it all the way in the pan, but rather to slide it onto the plate and fold it over there to finish cooking). I still have the omelette pan she gave me as a gift, advising, 'Every bachelor should know how to make an omelette'. It's true, you can throw almost anything you have in the fridge or pantry into an omelette. You know what I discovered is delicious? Left over Chinese Food! Although I am a very good combination of both my wonderful parents, so much of my knack for entertaining and performing I can trace directly back to my years by Mary's side.

At the studio we'd hang out in her dressing room and secretly work on ways to improve the daily scripts. She was the grande dame of the studio, but away from there we were just mates. She knew she was a great star…she didn't need to have an attitude to go along with it. When I did my first cabaret show in New York City, she and Wolfgang were right there in the front row. I sang one of her original songs, *Tiny Band of Gold,* and she blew me a kiss, so I knew I'd done a good job. Whenever my family came to town, they were always invited up to the penthouse for drinks and dinner. You can imagine how all this thrilled my grandmother! There were a thousand memorable moments with Mary and I was so proud to become a member of her extended network of friends and family. She was fiercely loyal to those she loved.

In 1986, *SFT* was cancelled and it was hard on everybody but no one more so than Mary…who'd been there from its inception and had fought so hard for three and a half decades to maintain the popularity and quality of the series. In the final scene ever broadcast, Jo and her longtime pal, Stu, find themselves looking at the Christmas tree (ironically, the axe fell on our show at Mary's special time of year). 'Jo, what is it you're searching for?' he asked as she looked up at the star atop the tree. 'Tomorrow', she answered with the beautiful simplicity she'd taught me to deliver in every line. 'And I can't wait!' It required two takes because of a technical glitch in the control room and Mary nailed it perfectly both times, with just the right feeling of bittersweet optimism. That scene turned up posted on YouTube recently and it brought forth as many tears for me as the day I heard it live from behind one of the studio cameras. (Her 1980 autobiography, *Both of Me*, is not only a highly entertaining read but one of the best chronicles of the birth of the daytime genre ever written. She gave me a copy when we first met and appropriately inscribed it, 'Nelson…at the beginning!')

★ ★ ★ ★ ★ ★ ★ ★ ★ ★ ★

> Marcia has been drop-dead gorgeous since the day I met her, and one of my funniest memories is of going down to the dingy Manhattan Unemployment Bureau after *SFT* was cancelled. This stunning blonde bombshell cut an unforgettable figure, dripping with diamonds, in her full length fur as we waited in line for hours to file our claims. She was the epitome of class and confidence.

★ ★ ★ ★ ★ ★ ★ ★ ★ ★ ★

The end of the show didn't bring an end to our times together. We'd still get together to hang out; in fact, her home felt as much like my own as when I'd go back to Pennsylvania to visit my Mom and Dad. Holidays at Mary's were always family affairs, and no celebration was more joyous than when she and Wolfgang officially tied the knot, becoming husband and wife.

In 1990 I decided to relocate to Hollywood and I can still hear Mary's voice on my answering machine saying, 'Hollywood? Wow!' She'd been there, done that, but was completely supportive and enthusiastic for my pursuits. A short time after, the National Academy of Television Arts & Sciences honored her with a special Emmy Award and she had to come to Los Angeles for the gala. She asked me to be her date and I remember picking her up in my beat-up old Toyota Corolla to escort her to the event. As my second-hand car sputtered up a steep hill on La Cienega Boulevard, she leaned forward in her seat as if to encourage the engine. 'My car had the same problem on this hill when I lived here.' She may have collected the golden award that night, but I certainly felt honored.

Mary's post *SFT* years were busy with a new project she seized with her characteristic enthusiasm. In partnership with the Screen Actors Guild, she founded Book PALS (Performing Artists for Literacy in Schools), and was often found in inner city New York classrooms getting kids excited about reading. It's a national program that still thrives to this day and I believe she would consider it her greatest legacy.

In 1996, she was asked to join the cast of another classic soap opera, *The Guiding Light*. The writers were planning to reintroduce a character from its early days as a new matriarch for one of the core families and they wanted Mary to play the role of Meta Bauer. She called me and admitted that she knew Meta had a rich history but it was all new territory to her. That's when I set out to come to the rescue for my mentor and I researched all the old show archives and wrote a character 'bible' of all Meta's trials and tribulations so Mary could have that back story with which to infuse her new character. Mary was an immediate hit in her new role, bringing class, sensitivity and a familiarity to every scene.

Sadly, she developed multiple forms of cancer but it didn't keep this trouper from working. She remained on the air until 2002 and passed away a short time later. That was the first year I didn't receive her traditional photographed Christmas card and I've missed them every December since.

I flew back to New York, so Marcia and I could attend her memorial service together. It was a moving tribute to our dear, sweet Mary, full of wonderful testimonials and music. An olio of love, laughter and tears–just like most of Mary's best onscreen moments. Wolfgang had us back to the penthouse for a reception afterward and it was a reunion of familiar faces and friends she would have loved. Mary's daughter-in-law told me how much it had meant to Mary that I wrote about her in my first book, *Let's Dish Up a Dinner Party*, and how often she mentioned me. That made me feel good.

I think of Mary all the time, not just when I make an omelette. When I call someone 'presh', sign a Christmas card or learn a script. Her style and generosity of spirit on screen and off stick with me all the time. How lucky that I get to pay homage to her by being on live television every weekday. I hope my career and reputation will be as enduring and respected as hers. *That's* a showbiz role model worth emulating.

Just something to think about the next time you channel surf past a soap opera. Maybe you'll pause and say, 'Hey…thanks, Mary Stuart!'

How Hugh Grant Hiring a Hooker Helped my Hollywood Career

There are certain moments in one's career that can definitely be considered turning points. Hugh Grant's arrest for soliciting prostitute Divine Brown on June 27, 1995, was one of those for me. It happened on a West Hollywood street not far from where I was living at the time—but that's not why it had an impact on me.

Several months earlier, I'd been hired as a freelance writer to pen an article for *Playgirl* magazine about Hugh Grant's love life. He was being touted as the next Cary Grant back then, after enjoying romantic leading man status in such films as the smash hit *Four Weddings and a Funeral*.

He was, of course, linked to his then-girlfriend Elizabeth Hurley, but everyone was clamoring for whatever information they could find out pertaining to his amorous side. I culled together a lighthearted collection of quotes and anecdotes (he once answered when asked who was the best kisser he'd ever lip-locked with: *Maurice* co-star James Wilby who 'had a tongue like a conger eel!') which gave the editors a good opportunity to run lots of sexy photographs with the piece.

His arrest was the hot topic of Hollywood water cooler conversation the next morning and I was talking to one of my fitness clients who happened to be a producer on the wildly-popular syndicated TV entertainment news program, *Hard Copy*. I mentioned the *Playgirl* article and he offered me an opportunity to come on the show and share the stories myself. I happily accepted and fell easily into the pundit mode and became their resident Hugh Grant expert for the duration.

I made dozens of appearances on *Hard Copy* in the years that followed. They liked having a designated on-air person for certain celebs, so I soon segued back and forth from Hugh stories to ones about Leonardo DiCaprio, Keanu Reeves and several others. It was not only a great entry for me into talk-TV, but the publicity was massive and led to my holding similar positions on other such shows like *American Journal*, *National Enquirer Uncovered* and *Inside Edition*.

Whenever Hugh Grant gets into a scrape nowadays (like pelting a prying paparazzo with baked beans), I am reminded of how lucky I got with that story.

I had two personal encounters with Hugh after that. The first at a BAFTA screening and panel discussion for *Bridget Jones: The Edge of Reason*. He was mercilessly teasing co-star Colin Firth, and Renée Zellweger was doing her best to fade into the curtains, puckering her lips more than usual in terror of what he might direct her way. Can a man be catty? If so, that's the best word I'd use to describe his behavior that night. But when I met him in 2006, he was doing the press tour for *Music and Lyrics* with Drew Barrymore and was very well behaved and downright effusive. I mentioned the James Wilby quote and we had a good laugh about it, with him still contending that James' 'Best Kisser' status remained intact.

I was just relieved that he hadn't been a *Hard Copy* viewer, otherwise I might've had a face full of baked beans!

Facing The Prada-Wearing Devils

People sure seem to love the movie *The Devil Wears Prada*. Personally, I thought it was only Meryl Streep's wonderful screen presence that elevated it above the level of a campy TV movie—or extended episode of *Ugly Betty*. Obviously, I'm in the minority. But that didn't mean I wasn't enthusiastic about flying to New York to interview the cast…especially La Streep. To me, she was worth the exhausting red-eye flight from LA and boarding my beloved springer spaniel at the kennel for a few days.

No sooner did I get to the interview location than I was thrown into a room with costume designer Patricia Field, best known for her creative work styling the ladies of *Sex and the City*. She's as colorful as her wardrobe designs and I tried to get her to chat with me about some of her choices for style icons, but when she couldn't even muster up some raves for chic Cate Blanchett or glam Nicole Kidman, I knew it was pointless. I didn't bother to tell her that her entire row of top front teeth were smeared with bright red lipstick, because I knew it would delay our shooting schedule and possibly cut into my time with Meryl. Besides, shouldn't a fashion 'guru' check that sort of thing or have a minion on hand to give her a once-over before the cameras roll?

Wonderful character actor Stanley Tucci was such a disappointment, only giving me obligatory answers of a few words at a time. I was getting nowhere fast, so I did something I almost never do: wrapped up the interview early!

Emily Blunt was gorgeous and gregarious. She's going to be a massive star, I predict. Unlike Ms Fields, Emily's smile was picture perfect and she immediately complimented me on my teeth…my complexion…my eyes. Wow! Not only was I flattered, but I was stunned because I'd been instantly struck by her own triple crown of terrific traits: smile, skin, sparkly cornflower blue eyes. Separated at birth!? I'd loved her in an obscure British TV movie about Henry VIII in which she'd played wife number five, Catherine Howard, so once we finished talking about skin care, we launched into our mutual love of Tudor history. It was a good thing I didn't have time to get into her relationship with crooner Michael Bublé, or we'd've ended up yackety-yakking about standards and show tunes and never gotten around to her work in the movie!

By the time I finished with Emily, my jet lag had fully kicked in. I was informed that my chat with Meryl would have to wait until the afternoon and I was grateful I'd have a few hours to grab a cat-nap and refresh myself. But I still had one more interview before I could go to my hotel room: fresh-faced Anne Hathaway. I took my seat outside her interview room and waited.

Suddenly, her publicist burst out of the room rudely yelling at no-one in particular. 'We are running so far behind schedule! The next interview is going to have to be really short!' Well…I was the last scheduled reporter, so that meant me, myself and I. Bleary eyed, I looked at her blankly and said, 'Hey, we can skip it altogether as far as I'm concerned. I'm only interested in Meryl Streep, anyway'. That did the trick. 'Oh, no, no, no!' she cooed, suddenly sweet. 'Come right in!' And I'm glad I did…Anne was lovely and had a cute anecdote to tell me about Dame Julie Andrews saying 'shit'. We wrapped up our chat and I went immediately for a nap.

Showered and refreshed for my meeting with the multiple Oscar-winning Ms Streep, I arrived a few minutes ahead of schedule and waited while she wrapped up another interview. I happened to be sitting across from Tape Control, where several different monitors recorded what was going on in Streep's suite. Of course, I was interested in what she had to say to the journalist ahead of me. But all I could see was panic in the eyes of her handlers when her blouse popped open to expose her brassiered breast. 'Stop tape!' echoed through the corridors and a flurry of folks rushed in to tend to her wardrobe malfunction. I chuckled and waited out the repair work.

Thinking of all her great films I've enjoyed over the years (*Silkwood*, *Out of Africa*, *Sophie's Choice* and *Heartburn* my top picks), I shook her hand and said, 'Well, it certainly is nice to finally see you *in person*'. She quipped, 'If you'd been in here five minutes ago, you'd've seen a lot *more* of me!' I sat down across from her, winked and said, 'Oh, I saw it all on the monitor'. She gave a hearty laugh and I knew we were in for a great conversation.

'Since I found out I'd be meeting you,' I started off, 'I've been telling everyone and the reaction is always the same: "I love Meryl Streep!" Is that a burden?'

'No!' she emphatically responded with a wide smile. 'It would be worse if they said "I hate Meryl Streep!"'

'Oh, come on, that's never been uttered in the history of mankind!' I said. 'How do you manage that constant level of adoration?'

She rolled her eyes and thought about how to answer. 'It's mixed with a healthy dose of…(and then pantomimed a gigantic yawn)… from another segment of the population.'

I was feeling playful after our exchange and teased, 'That's no way to speak about your family!' She got the joke and threw her head back with a big belly laugh. I'd tickled Meryl Streep's funny bone! That made my day and the enervating red eye flight was instantly well worthwhile.

We went on to chat about some mutual friends and of course her film work. Since everyone seems to have at least one special Meryl Streep movie, I wondered which one was HERS. *A Cry in the Dark* came to mind, she revealed (she played Australian Lindy Chamberlain, who uttered the now-famous line, 'A dingo took my baby!'). She knew I was reporting for an Australian TV outlet, so it was very clever of her to give me an answer my producers would love.

She may not always make the Best Dressed List at Awards time, but Meryl Streep definitely gets my prize for Greatest Star in Motion Pictures!

Comic Geeks

If there's any truth to the philosophy that if you do what you love, you'll never work a day in your life, then it certainly has paid off that I've always unapologetically embraced my love for all forms of animation…especially cartoons and comic books. Thanks to Hollywood's success with the medium, geeks like me have been enjoying a revenge of the nerds for years.

Growing up in rural Pennsylvania, our family farm was a veritable fantasy land for a kid's imagination. The barn was a combination Fortress of Solitude and Hall of Justice. The fruit cellar became the Batcave. My tree house in the apple orchard replicated the Jetson's flying saucer. One minute I was Robin the Boy Wonder, zipping across the fields on my mini-bike and the next I was Aquaman, diving into the pond. My room was plastered with comic book memorabilia and littered with action figures. When I wasn't reading or play acting their adventures, I was writing and drawing original ones of my own. My sketching skills, especially making buff and buxom superheroes and spot-on perfect renditions of *The Flintstones*, eventually led to one of my more interesting survival jobs as a caricaturist. (Was there ever worse casting than Rosie O'Donnell as wasp-waisted prehistoric cutie, Betty Rubble?) I still see people through the eyes of a fan and will almost immediately let my first impression of someone be comics-related. 'Gee, he sure would make a great Martian Manhunter!' 'Wow, that face lift left her looking more like the Joker's Daughter!'

But it wasn't until I started my adult career in showbiz that all those years of fandom really paid off. In 1999, I was hired to MC and coordinate talent for the second Annual Niagara Falls Film Festival, which was to have a superhero theme. The biggest coup was landing none other than Christopher Reeve to attend as the honoree. I was never more impressed than when I saw what was entailed in getting him from point A to point B for an event such as this. He and his team of medical staff and security were amazing. As exhausting as it must have been for him to travel to Canada, make his way to the venue, address the assembled audiences, meet-and-greet, oblige press requests…he was always smiling, upbeat and warm.

Coordinating the presence of his *Superman* co-stars Marc McClure (Jimmy Olsen) and Jeff East (Superboy) not only gave me the chance to spend lots of quality social time getting to know these gents, but to become lifelong friends. Marc and his gorgeous wife Carol are two of my funniest, closest pals and we all still laugh about finding an item labeled 'Jeff East in a Jock Strap' on ebay. You really *can* find anything on the internet.

Representing the Caped Crusader's camp, we brought up two of Batman's arch-villains from the 1966 film, Frank Gorshin (Riddler) and still-luscious Lee Meriweather (Catwoman). Plus, we had the original Batmobile for them to ride in! Frank's always been a character and, with apologies to Jim Carrey and John Astin, the all-time perfect casting for the role of Edward Nigma, aka Riddler. Lee, who is such a playful and classy lady, may be in the company of other foxy felines who've donned the cat suit over the years (Julie Newmar, Eartha Kitt, Michelle Pfeiffer, Halle Berry) but if you check out her portrayal, you may agree with me that she's purr-fection in the part! One of my most disappointing interviews ever was the old Robin, Burt Ward. I didn't even bother to invite him to the Falls. Just like hosting a dinner party, why risk your good time with a problematic guest? Terrence Stamp (General Zod) couldn't attend, but I chatted with him recently on the set of the new *Get Smart* movie and was as charmed and impressed as I suspected I'd be!

HOLLYWOOD INSIDER
EXPOSED!

A real treat for me was getting the widow of Batman's creator, Elizabeth Sanders Kane, to join us at the Festival and accept an Achievement Award on behalf of her late husband, Bob. I'd actually met the legendary Bob Kane in 1997, a year before his death. Not only did he draw a priceless rendition of the Dark Knight at my request, he confided that his own choice as the best Batman, out of all the incarnations over the years, was none other than George Clooney. Bob believed that Clooney's lantern-jawed, swarthy good looks were the closest to his illustrated version. I'll agree with that!

I mentioned in the introduction about my encounters with Kevin Spacey and Parker Posey while working on my *Superman Returns* story, but now's a good opportunity to talk about the rest of the team. Bryan Singer, who enjoyed such success with the *X-Men*, seemed to have gotten confused between honoring the definitive Reeve version of 1978 and trying to amp up the story for today's youth-driven audience. I think his mistake was not paying more mind to the diehard fans who can make or break movies in this genre. Let's hope he'll get back to basics for the upcoming *Superman: Man of Steel*. He told me of the empathy he felt for Kal-El/Clark Kent, because of his own childhood memories of being an adopted only child. When you're dealing with a character as iconic as Supes, it's probably best to put your vision on the shelf and stick to tradition.

I wish somebody would have told that to Kate Bosworth. She all but sneered at me for admitting I was such a fan that I'd named my rescued springer spaniel pup 'Lois'. Maybe she was just grumpy from hunger…I swear she was so skeletal she'd've been more convincing as The Invisible Woman. She was ideally suited for *Blue Crush*, but may go down in history as the recipient of Worst Casting Ever, for taking on the part of feisty firecracker, Lois Lane.

At least James Marsden gets it…an alumnus of both *Superman Returns* and *X-Men*, he's perfectly cast in fantasy-friendly roles (look at his great work in the colorful cartoon-ish comedies *Enchanted* and *Hairspray*). He maintains a great sense of fun and joie de vivre that only serves to compliment his leading man persona, complete with square-jaw, toothy grin and sparkling eyes. You'll be happy to know he's as likeable and modest a guy as you're likely to find in this town. And he really can sing, too! He and Hugh (from *Wolverine* to *The Boy from Oz*) Jackman are two guys who seem to be able to do anything.

Brandon Routh, while lacking the gravitas-in-blue-tights possessed by his predecessors Reeve, George Reeves or even Dean Cain, gets bonus points for his consistent grace under the pressure of all the scrutiny he endured. I've met and interviewed him a few times and he is consistently a soft-spoken, intelligent gentleman. All too rare… particularly in Tinseltown.

Ironically, it's the Clark Kent who's never worn a red cape, *Smallville*'s Tom Welling, who may ultimately hold the key to success in future Super-casting. There's rampant buzz that he may be persuaded to take on the more grown-up film version of his television role. And it's exciting that the *Justice League of America* and *Flash* movies are in the hands of talents such as George Miller and David Dobkin, who have enough historical background and personal enthusiasm to do the job right. The Flash is my all-time fave superhero (not in small part because I'm an avid runner) and I've even gone so far as to go on the air (multiple times!) wearing my Halloween costume of The Scarlet Speedster to prove it! Boy, the fun we had with simple fast-forward special effects. I was tickled that it did not go unnoticed or unappreciated by the brass at Warner Brothers. I'm not easily impressed by industry swag, but a simple Flash t-shirt sent to me from the Powers That Be simply made my day. Maybe a dream will come true and I'll someday get to play a reporter in one of these big budget action flicks!

EXPOSED!

I'm not the only Flash fanatic, either. Hunky Ryan Reynolds is so besotted with the character that he was, for a long time, considered to be the frontrunner for the movie. He finally withdrew his name from consideration when his career had elevated to the point that he opted out of 'spending the next ten years wearing red tights'. When I knew I was going to interview him, I wore my lightening bolt logo T-shirt and brought him a souvenir gift of the latest Flash action figure. He loved it. Even hunks can be geeks! (Was it over the top to get that same logo permanently tattooed on my arm as part of a TV segment? Probably, but I love my ink! I'm forever the Flash now, even if actor Neil Patrick Harris wasn't impressed when I showed it off to him at the gym. He provides Flash's voice in the cartoon series, so I thought he might appreciate it, but I guess he just considers being a part of the Justice League to be another paying gig. What a waste!)

But I'd give the prize for the biggest comic book geek among Hollywood's A-List to Oscar winner Nicolas Cage. He was trying for ages to develop a *Superman* remake/update before it finally fell into Singer's hands and happily settled on developing *Ghostrider*, instead. Nothing proves his devotion to the lore of The Man of Steel more than when he named his newborn son Kal-El, which is—of course for all you trivia experts—Clark Kent's Kryptonian birth name. (Kal-El Cage had better develop some super-skills of his own, methinks. With a name like that, junior high school could be pretty tough going!) When I met Nic, I couldn't help but ask him 'as a father yourself, are you more of a *Jor-El* or a *Jonathan Kent*?' I was surprised at how stumped he was by the question. It seems like any real fan would be quick to have a definitive answer…and I was even more surprised when he finally decided to respond: 'Pa Kent'. I thought for sure he'd see himself more like the Kryptonian scientist we remember so well from Marlon Brando's portrayal on film.

Meeting industry pros who share a common interest is definitely one of the many great benefits of my work. One memorable assignment was touring the vaults of Disney's animation department, even getting to handle the original pencil sketches of *Steamboat Willie*, the short that introduced the world to a rodent named Mickey Mouse. And you can't help but be impressed by an up-close encounter with the original puppet that modeled as Pinocchio. Still at the top of my interview Wish List, though, is the definitive Wonder Woman: ageless Amazon Lynda Carter. How could you not be a fan of her portrayal of the star-spangled super heroine!? Now *that* was perfect casting!

Ellen, Anne, Portia & a Coupla Dogs

The sex-tacular love life of Ellen DeGeneres is certainly one of the most renowned in Hollywood history...especially since the talented funny lady has never been perceived as particularly sexy. Remember that rotten tomato she made in 1996, *Mr. Wrong*? But her undeniable charm has brought her legions of loyal fans who extend to her the acceptance not always given to other 'out' celebs like Rupert Everett, Rosie O'Donnell or even Sir Elton John. Seeing her long-term commitments with the previously perceived-as-straight Anne Heche and then Portia De Rossi only seems to up her cred as simply too damned irresistible.

My connection with this little triumvirate began in 1987 when I went to work on the now defunct daytime drama, *Another World*. *Search for Tomorrow* had just been axed, so I came on board and quickly became familiar with the new cast, storylines and production process. *Another World*, however, was an hour-long daily show as opposed to *SFT*'s 30-minute format, so everything was doubled: including a shockingly talented teenage actress who'd just been discovered while acting in an Ohio school play. This plump (yes, plump!), long-haired blonde was named Anne Heche, and casting directors had whisked her to New York City to play not one leading role, but TWO: identical twins Vicky and Marley Love. On camera, she so convincingly played these completely different (albeit identical looking) sisters that she got immediate attention and kudos for being 'the Streep of soaps'. Off camera, she was coming of age and managed to leave the workaholic side at the studio and be a wild child at night. I was only a couple of years older than her, so we all reveled in the fun of being young and free in the heavenly Manhattan of the late 1980s. Annie knew how to let her hair down after hours, because during the day she had such a heavy weight with the TV show and a family to support resting on her shoulders.

When Anne and Ellen's love affair went public, lots of us were surprised (probably no one more so than Steve Martin, whom she'd seriously dated for two years). I had to admit I never knew a girl who liked men as much as Annie liked men! After all, in addition to Martin she'd dated a fair share of super hunks. However, she was the first to admit that she was one to fall in love with the inside of a person, not the exterior package. So as such a great personal admirer of her talent, work ethic and elan, combined with knowing how tough she'd had it growing up, I was very happy for her and proud for standing up to so many haters who were against her union with Ellen. Smooching at the White House at a party for President Clinton may have been an unnecessary display of public affection, but then again there was definitely something in the air at the Clinton White House, LOL!

The first time I ran into Anne after her coming out, was at the MTV Movie Awards and she was hanging out with Jeff Goldblum (they were working together at the time on a picture called *Auggie Rose*). When I commended her on how well she was handling it all, she made a point of saying she'd seen some of my TV reports on the 'Ellen and Anne' story and appreciated how I'd handled it, too. That made me feel good. Too many people were bashing them.

Allow me to pause for a moment to tell you that Mr Jeff Goldblum, while certainly one of filmdom's most quirky character actors, is also one of the most charismatic and media savvy. (No need to explain that to his exes, Laura Dern or Geena Davis…they certainly succumbed to his charms.) He always remembers my name, is a gentleman, makes direct, penetrating eye contact and shakes hands with his right hand while placing his left hand over top…a warm, welcoming gesture that speaks volume for his good manners. At 6'5", he's also one of Tinseltown's tallest…so when he looks down into your eyes, he owns you. The first time we'd met in 1997 was for an online chat I'd conducted for the Microsoft Network and he showed up in an immaculate, tailored black suit (no cameras, mind you…this was an online text interview!). My first words to him after, 'Nice to meet you' were 'You don't own any pets, do you?' 'Umm, why, no Nelson, how do you know that?' There wasn't so much as a spec of dust anywhere on those six feet of black wool. Now THAT, my friends, is how a star should look!

And so life went on for Ellen and Anne. The scandal of their romance soon died down and, unfortunately, so did the ratings for Ellen's sitcom and Anne's movie career. They seemed to take it all in their stride and I continued to defend the legitimacy of their relationship, even with saucy Rebecca Loos (remember the British former assistant to David Beckham who alleged an affair between the two of them?) when we teamed up for a documentary about Sapphic Showbiz entitled *Power Lesbians*.

Enter Mr Moon

I got a frantic phone call from a friend of mine who worked with one of LA's top dog trainers. He'd been on his way home to the tiny studio apartment he shared with several cats when he came upon a homeless man being taken away by police. 'Mr Moon…please take care of Mr Moon!' the man called out as he was driven off into the night. There was the now-abandoned dog, Mr Moon, looking up at my friend from the street corner. Could I possibly adopt Mr Moon, my friend asked, or did I know anyone who could? I already had a dog and a cat, but I promised I'd ask around and try to find a new guardian for the cute pooch.

The next day, I was shooting a fund raising program for our local public broadcasting station and got a call from him. 'Not to worry! Ellen DeGeneres adopted Mr Moon!' I was elated. Animal-loving Ellen had saved the day. It was such a happy ending (so I thought) for the down-on-his-luck doggie, that I told the story the next morning on my radio show. A day later, I was told that Mr. Moon was given back to my friend, apparently because Ellen felt like she'd been used as part of a publicity scheme for the dog trainer. I couldn't believe she'd give back a dog she'd just rescued! Of course, after the now-infamous 2007 'Iggy-gate' incident with the pound puppy she adopted, then gave away, before having a public meltdown on her chat show, it makes one wonder if there isn't a pattern there. In fact, some outlets reported several cases of her being too ambitious in pet-rescue and opting out after saving animals in need. Who knows what the real story is, but I'm happy to tell you that Mr Moon went back to my friend and they're still together years later and own their own Bowser Boutique near Beverly Hills. Living well is the best revenge, Woof Woof!

Ellen and Anne's breakup in 2000 fueled more salacious headlines when Annie had her strange detachment as an alien alter ego she called 'Celestia' (Celeste is her middle name, fyi). She moved on to marry a man, become a mother, divorce and have a popular TV show, *Men in Trees*. I've only seen her once since then and she was sweet and polite, but definitely a more subdued version of the girl I remember from (maybe not such a pun, after all) *Another World*.

HOLLYWOOD INSIDER
EXPOSED!

> Here are some Degrees of Separation you'll appreciate: after her relationship ended with Anne, Ellen dated actress/director Alexandra Hedison whose father, David 'Al' Hedison, not only worked on *Another World*, but starred as the original 'Fly' which was ultimately remade years later by Anne's pal, Goldblum. Some speculate that the world was getting too small for Ellen, which is why she was rumored to have ended things abruptly with Alexandra before moving on to Portia. Oh, the tangled and complicated web of celebrity romance! That's another good reason showbiz people shouldn't date each other.

Ellen, of course, has rebounded with her greatest role to date: herself. And in spite of whatever you may read in the scandal sheets about her relationship with Aussie beauty Portia De Rossi, they've been making a go of it since 2004 and—as of this writing—don't show any signs of stopping.

9-11

Everyone has vivid memories of where they were on that terrible Tuesday, 11 September 2001, and my experience is still fresh in my mind…especially when I get a residual payment for the Lifetime TV show, *Any Day Now*. Let me explain…

Any Day Now was a drama that ran on the Lifetime Television Network from 1998 to 2002 and told the ongoing story of childhood friends, one Caucasian and one African-American, growing up in racially-charged Alabama. The star was Annie Potts, best known from her long run as Mary Jo on the sitcom *Designing Women*. I was cast to guest-star in an episode entitled 'Rebel with a Cause', playing a sarcastic Lifestyles reporter (no cracks about typecasting). I occasionally get called in to read for roles like this but, as is the case for most actors, there are always many more auditions than there are bookings! (I remember meeting the producers of *Will and Grace*, who tested me for the role of flamboyant Jack, but they ultimately decided I was too 'Will'…and they already had Eric McCormack for *that* part.)

And the *Ugly Betty* production team called me in so many times to audition for a nemesis of America Ferrara's character that I told my agent they should keep me on retainer just for try-outs! For the record, their official reason for not hiring me was that no matter how nasty I acted, I simply came off as 'too likable'. How can a guy complain about that?

I was supposed to be going to NYC to see friends and family on September 10 when the Lifetime production office called to inform me that my shooting day would be 9-11, so I had to postpone my trip. Fate works in mysterious ways. My call time was 6am at the location in Pasadena, an old graveyard that was being redressed to look like an Alabama Civil War memorial cemetery. Anyone who knows me knows I'm compulsive about being early (a non-negotiable for live television, of course) so I was actually pulling into the parking lot before dawn. The radio had just reported the breaking news that a plane had struck one of the Twin Towers and, like everyone else, I had no inkling of the magnitude of what was unfolding.

During my Manhattan residency, I'd enjoyed many Thanksgiving holiday dinners in the Trade Center's Windows on the World restaurant. The skyscrapers were a familiar sight to me on a daily basis for many years, so this announcement seemed likely to be a small private plane or perhaps news chopper which had a collision with the building. I reported as instructed to my trailer to await Wardrobe, Hair and Make-Up. As the sun began to rise, scores of background actors arrived and began to be outfitted in ante-bellum attire for the scene we were shooting (the plot being that I was a reporter at a Civil War-themed remembrance, hence all the extras in period costume).

For some reason, of all the trailers, mine was the only one that had a television that was working. I flipped it on to watch the morning news while I had my coffee and bagel. That's when I saw what was happening, as Katie Couric and Matt Lauer commentated in shocked disbelief, themselves. Word was spreading around the location and I was soon packed like a sardine in that trailer as dozens of strangers poured in to join me and we all stayed glued to the screen.

The director, producers and Annie Potts had to make the decision to continue with the day's production or cancel shooting. Literally hundreds of cast and crew members were on location in this Los Angeles suburban neighborhood. The freeways had all been shut down in the consequent security scare. We were essentially stranded in the cemetery, so they opted to continue filming as planned. But it was surreal. No one's heart or mind was in the scene…and every spare moment was spent running back to my trailer to check in with the TV news, or dash to a car radio for a live update of the horror going on across the country in New York, Washington and Pennsylvania. I tried to call home, but there was no cellular phone service and the shutdown of air traffic made the atmosphere eerily silent.

I finally made my way home late that night…trying to navigate my way out of Pasadena on unfamiliar surface streets, since the highways all remained closed. Like the rest of the world, I spent the better part of the next 48 hours watching the continuing tragedy on television.

Every few months, when I get a small residual payment for rebroadcasts of that episode in TV syndication, I am reminded of 9-11 and the strange circumstances of where I happened to be, and the strangers I happened to be with when the Towers fell.

Uncle Nelson

Being the youngest of five children, I became an uncle pretty early. My first nephew, Mickey, was born shortly after I turned 5 and no-one in my school believed that I was an uncle, so I had to take a snapshot in for Show and Tell, with the baby on my lap holding a sign that read: 'Nelson is my uncle'. So I've been Uncle Nelson for a looonnng time!

Growing up with a posse of nieces and nephews closer to my age than my own siblings influenced me to really respect and enjoy the company of kids. With that Pied Piper mentality, I went on to act and direct a lot of children's plays in the years that followed—and now I'm a great-uncle so many times over that I've lost count.

Probably because of the proximity (she lives next door), my honorary niece, Merryn, is the one I spend the most time with. We have a tradition at Christmas now that she comes on TV with me and we sing a carol together. Some kids are pushed into performing by star-struck parents while others, like Merryn and I, just have a natural inclination to be hams! She definitely has a presence that people remember; I was at a race event in California one summer morning and another runner knew who I was from having seen me sing *Rudolph the Red Nosed Reindeer* with Merryn months earlier… on Australian television!

Thanks to my broadcast career, I get to make friends with people I never even meet and have become Uncle Nelson to children all around the world. I was flattered to find out some fans had named their household pets after me, but in September 2007 I was left totally *verklempt* when notified that an Australian family had named their beautiful baby boy Nelson because he is 'very happy and smiling all the time'. I really appreciate it so much, which is why I try to give back by choosing children's charities, in particular, to support for my charity work. I always tell folks who admit their admiration for certain celebs to research where that star directs his or her philanthropic efforts and then support it as well. It can be as great a way to get behind your idol as buying a movie ticket at the box office. I think all of us, especially those in the public eye, should have a designated charity…it sure makes gift-giving easier! 'What do I want for Christmas or my birthday? Why don't you make a donation to my charity?' A tax-deductible good deed!

★ ★ ★ ★ ★ ★ ★ ★ ★ ★ ★ ★ ★ ★ ★ ★

> Nelson is an English name literally meaning, 'son of Neil'. In my case, my great-grandmother was Ellen and her nickname was 'Nell'. Hence, she named my grandfather Horace Nelson, who in turn named my dad Nelson Page—and I subsequently am Nelson Page, Jr'. It's a big name to hang on a little boy (admittedly much better than Horace!), so I was always called JR, short for Junior. I went by JR Aspen until the *Dallas* craze of 1980-1, when people around the world were wondering who shot JR. I was getting so tired of every person I met asking me, 'Who shot you?' (Even *Dallas* star Patrick Duffy couldn't resist when we did a play together) that I decided to abandon my lifelong moniker and started using my proper first name. I'm forever JR to everyone I've known prior to that, so if you shout it out you'll still get my attention.

★ ★ ★ ★ ★ ★ ★ ★ ★ ★ ★ ★ ★ ★ ★ ★

When I started running marathons, I trained with a program sponsored by APLA (AIDS Project Los Angeles) which provides vital service to people living with HIV/AIDS. Over the course of training for several

EXPOSED!

races in Honolulu, Los Angeles, New Orleans and Florence, Italy, I was able to raise about twenty thousand dollars.

Keeping a daily journal (my 'Book of Blessings'), I record five things every day for which I'm grateful. It can be something as simple as 'my comfortable bed' and 'laughing at a funny joke' to 'my mother's good health', 'modern medicine' or 'happy memories of my grandmother'. The point is to try and be as constantly aware as possible of good fortune that can too easily be taken for granted. You don't have to be a 'Brangeloonie' and try and save the world, but seemingly simple little choices can make a big difference…it's why I always look out for fun 5k and 10k races that benefit good causes.

★ ★ ★ ★ ★ ★ ★ ★ ★ ★ ★ ★

Did you know that Nike stores in America will accept worn-out old sneakers and athletic shoes to recycle and turn into sports and play surfaces? Their Reuse-a-Shoe program helps make basketball courts and playgrounds for kids who might not otherwise have a place to play and be healthy.

★ ★ ★ ★ ★ ★ ★ ★ ★ ★ ★ ★

Deciding to segue into a children's-specific charity, I discovered the St. Jude Children's Hospital in Memphis, Tennessee. It is a magical place for kids and their families who have to live with debilitating and life-threatening illnesses. The caring spirit of every staffer is evidenced in all aspects of this special place and, having run two marathons on its behalf, I made them my designated charity for 2006. Actress Marlo Thomas is its National Outreach Director and many celebrities such as Jennifer Aniston, Jim Carrey, Robin Williams and Calista Flockhart find themselves drawn to its wonderful work and brave, beautiful patients.

Using both my journalism career and recreational running as positive platforms to spread the word about ways to help children

✶ ✶

Talk show pioneer Steve Allen, who essentially created the TV Talk format with his original *Tonight Show* back in the 1950s, also wrote more than 50 books and 7,400 songs. I had the privilege of interviewing him on several occasions before his death in 2000 and he had some wonderful things to say about the challenges facing contemporary youth. I asked him if he believed they were desensitized and he said, 'To some extent, yes. This is partly because of exposure to so much more reality than any previous generation in history could comprehend. Everyone seems now to acknowledge that we are in a period of moral chaos. This is not just an old man's opinion. It's all too readily confirmed by looking at the relative statistics, divorce, crimes of violence, political fanaticism or almost any other measuring stick. The news is very depressing.' Interestingly, this was pre 9-11, and his reflections now ring truer than ever. 'We must individually, personally determine to play a role in this large campaign. It's true that not every individual can scatter his energies and give proper attention to all the serious problems that perplex our society. But that's no excuse for inertia or apathy. Start with something. Visit children in an orphanage. Visit prisoners in jail. Offer your services at an AIDS hospice, do something. And if millions of people do that, it will be a large step in the right direction'. His brilliant mind, his 46-year love affair with wife Jayne Meadows and his gift of the gab are still sorely missed in Hollywood, but anyone who communicates over the airwaves still owes this gentleman a debt of gratitude.

✶ ✶

in need, I decided to elect a new charity each calendar year. For both 2007-2008, I chose Camp Heartland. I discovered their wonderful work a few years ago when I caught the founder, Neil Willenson, on *The Oprah Winfrey Show*. They provide educational and summer camp opportunities for children living with HIV/AIDS. Fantastic. I also allowed myself to be 'auctioned off' for the Children's Cancer

HOLLYWOOD INSIDER
EXPOSED!

Institute of Australia. I'm proud and privileged to have fetched $10,000 to help those cool kids and I got to have a lovely, long lunch with the generous givers at the swanky Beverly Hills Country Club.

★ ★ ★ ★ ★ ★ ★ ★ ★ ★ ★ ★ ★ ★

My nattily dressed buddy Jeff Goldblum and I chatted about how great it is to be around kids, even without being parents ourselves. I commented that there is an honesty in children that an actor could surely appreciate. 'Yeah, that's true, Nelson', he agreed. 'Acting requires you to be childlike and I love the playfulness in kids. And I love to play with them!' And no wonder he can appreciate the joyful abandon of childhood…he revealed that the first celebrities he ever met were The Three Stooges! Nyuk nyuk nyuk!

★ ★ ★ ★ ★ ★ ★ ★ ★ ★ ★ ★ ★ ★

You don't have to be either rich or famous to help out a child… whether he or she is in your community or somewhere on the other side of the world. Be an aunt/uncle figure to a boy or girl and prepare yourself for some most excellent karma.

Unlike some of my peers, I am not titillated or even very interested in the spoiled rotten misdeeds of Hollywood's 'bad kids' and resist reporting on them whenever possible. I actually heard one so-called journalist say 'a day without Britney Spears [news] is like a day without sunshine'. Barf. I can't giggle with glee when it comes to irresponsibility, rudeness and bad manners. My mates at *Sunrise* started teasing me about being an old fogey whenever I'd wag a reproachful finger when having to deliver the latest on Paris Hilton's antics—and 'Uncle Nelson's Campaign to Clean Up Young Hollywood' was born. I'm especially pleased that so many viewers responded to it and are as fed up with the insanity as I am. Just say no to rotten role models!

★ ★ ★ ★ ★ ★ ★ ★ ★ ★ ★ ★ ★ ★ ★ ★ ★

Some young celebs have the opposite problem of Britney Spears—they listen too much to the advice of their publicists. Real stars know how to find the happy medium. Tasmanian stunner Rachael *(Transformers)* Taylor backed out of our two-minute TV interview to promote G'DAY USA on the advice of her publicist because she 'wasn't supplied with hair and makeup'. Not only did she miss a great opportunity to promote herself, her country and get more Hollywood buzz going, she missed out on some lighthearted fun and the chance for her friends and family back home to see her. Instead, she came off as a spoiled celebutante by ditching the promised appearance at the last minute. For the record, she was already wearing plenty of makeup and looked beautiful. Fortunately, World Champion surf legend Layne Beachley was on hand and filled in—making a splash with her sparkling good humor! She became my instant 'Blue Crush!'

★ ★ ★ ★ ★ ★ ★ ★ ★ ★ ★ ★ ★ ★ ★ ★ ★

Hangin' With Leo

Leonardo DiCaprio is one of my favorite movie actors, interview subjects and all-around A-Lister, but it wasn't always that way. As much as I loved James Cameron's *Titanic*, I never bought Leo as a leading man and even with all the accolades he received for *The Aviator*, I still wanted to wipe that little mustache off his upper lip. Other than his tour de force supporting role in *What's Eating Gilbert Grape* (one of the first films I bought on DVD, I love it!), it was the 2006 double whammy of *The Departed* and *Blood Diamond* that won me over to being such an ardent admirer of his work.

And not just his work on-screen. He's grown into a great man, and I've had the pleasure to spend a bit of time with him and his charming mother, so I feel confident in vouching for their integrity away from the spotlight, too. My association with Leo started much earlier though, long before I actually met him.

In 1998, just in time for the release of his film *The Man in the Iron Mask*, *Playgirl* magazine splashed him on the cover of their October issue with a headline that screamed, 'The Photos Hollywood's Heartthrob Didn't Want You To See!' It was right over the second feature tease, 'Orgasms Forever—The Big "O" in 5 Easy Steps'. In anticipation, the then-23-year-old Leo filed a lawsuit in Los Angeles Superior Court claiming the pictures had not been released by him and resulted in his 'shame, mortification, hurt feelings, emotional

A past life revisited! I channeled first-class passenger Milton Long at the Titanic's last port of call, Queenstown (Cobh) Ireland.

Dame Julie Andrews is the classiest star I've interviewed.

What an honour it always was to interview the late, great pioneer of talk TV, Steve Allen.

Playtime at Venice Beach with GMTV's lovely Lorraine Kelly.

The Man Who Would Be President—John Edwards, not me!

The two Nelsons. Every time I run into Judd, he quips the same line, "If you married me, you'd be Nelson Nelson".

With Carol McClure at my "Gods and Goddesses" party.

In Central Park with my longtime crony, Alexandra, and her niece Rebecca, c. 1990.

Gram & Mom Mom were both sweethearts and complete opposites!

My Gram!

Mom Mom

With my niece, Molly Kate.

Happy Birthday...to me! How many times can a guy turn 29?

Photo courtesy of Disney ABC Cable Networks Group

Dishing up more helpful holiday advice with Lisa and Ty.

Dad and Mom

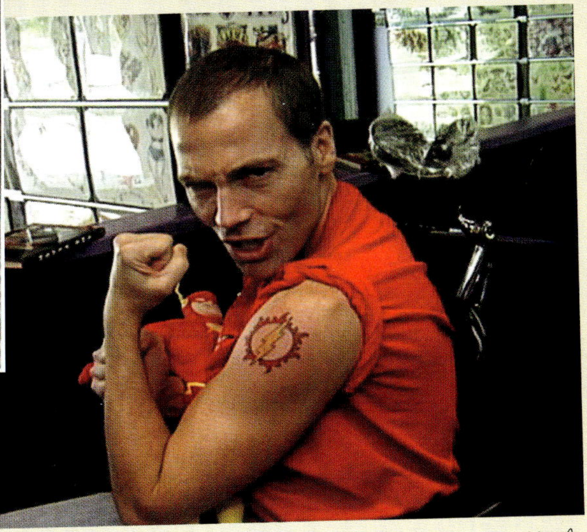

Taking my devotion to comic fan-dom all the way to the tattoo parlour!

Aussie Corner!

Laura Csortan and I had fun bopping around Beverly Hills for "The Great Outdoors".

Melissa Doyle is like a sister to me. Here we are having a pizza party at world-famous Spago of Beverly Hills!

One of my proudest moments: being made an honorary member of The Wiggles.

Covering the nuptials, outside the church where Nic & Keith tied the knot.

I haven't been to Melbourne yet, but I got to hold the cup! (Oops, no gloves!)

You're never too old to play dress up. Here I am as my all-time favorite superhero, The Flash!

distress, embarrassment, humiliation and injury to his privacy and peace of mind'. (Brad Pitt went through something similar with the publication when they got hold of some racy snaps of him on holiday with ex-girlfriend Gwyneth Paltrow...) The suit was settled 'amicably' with the terms never publicly disclosed. When the mag hit newsstands, it flew off the shelves but many were disappointed not by the sight of his anatomy, but rather the grainy and far from erotic still frames from his 1995 flick *Total Eclipse*. I was struggling as a freelance writer and had been hired by *Playgirl*'s editor to write a short bio on Leo's film career to accompany the highly promoted full-frontal shots. Looking back, I highly doubt anyone paid much interest in the text portion of that spread! I also wrote the copy for the issue's 'Soap Stars: Naughty in Nightwear' fashion layout which had been shot in the eerie environs of the dilapidated Ambassador Hotel in mid-city Los Angeles.

One person who had taken note of my by-line on the controversial article was the Executive Producer at *Hard Copy*. He quickly enlisted me to come on the show as their Leo expert whenever the young actor was making headlines...and in those randy days of his youth, he was making plenty of 'em. This led to being booked by a production company who was putting together a direct-to-video documentary about his life. Along with *Star* magazine columnist Janet Charlton, I would be offering up commentary and perspective for the target audience of pre-teen girls.

Entitled *Hangin' with Leo: The Unauthorized Documentary*, this 35-minute biography was comprised primarily of paparazzi footage of him tooling around Tinseltown. There he was going in and out of nightclubs with dates, driving down the boulevard with friends or playing frizbee on the beach. Pubescent girls around the world were lured by the colorful, heart-laden cover art and graphics that said, 'Attention Leo Fans! This is the Real Leo! You Gotta Have It!' And they did...it was a huge seller. Too bad I didn't negotiate a cut of the profits.

HOLLYWOOD INSIDER
EXPOSED!

Then, a couple of years ago, I met a lovely German woman at a Christmas dinner party thrown by my friend, British actress Carolyn Seymour (classically trained stage actress but best known in sci-fi circles for her work in both *Star Trek* series sequels and *Star Wars* video games). This gal was funny, feisty and we got on like gangbusters… being the last guests to leave at the end of the night and playing a Charades-like game, 'Celebrity', with the other hangers-on. Turns out, she is Irmelin DiCaprio, Leo's mother. I'd've loved her to bits, anyway, but it was especially heartening to see what an effervescent, no-frills person she was and we were all excited to propose a new Christmas tradition chez Seymour.

That's just what we did. But in the year that passed in between Yuletides, I'd been invited to interview the cast and crew of Leo's new film, *Blood Diamond*. I enthusiastically accepted and when I attended the screening, in spite of the intense violence and subject matter, I was spellbound by the story and performances. It was absolutely my favorite film of the year (2006) and I thought both leading actors (Leo and Djimon Hounsou) deserved not just their Oscar nominations, but should have won!

I had nice conversations with Djimon and director Edward Zwick. Jennifer Connelly not so much…beautiful, but she struck me as a little uptight (her handsome and self-effacing husband, Paul Bettany, is a much more laidback and chatty interviewee). The whole controversy surrounding the mining of diamonds in Sierra Leone made a fascinating backdrop for this dramatic adventure tale. When I sat down with Leo, he was every inch the impressive professional I'd enjoyed on screen. He radiated intelligence, humility and self-confidence, speaking articulately and with great passion. A bonus was how perfectly groomed and styled he was for our meeting. It was instantly obvious why he's such a power player in this town.

This was not the pudgy little club-hopper from *Hangin' with Leo*, this was a grown-up man to be reckoned with! He's only a few years younger than I am, but I felt like a proud uncle and couldn't help but tell him so. 'Who else is proud of you in your personal life and communicates that to you?' He replied, 'I'd say my Dad. He's been a huge part of my process as an actor and being attached to certain movies and he's always been the one there that's kind of guided me to pay more attention to certain types of films'. That's when I mentioned how crazy I was about his mother! Even though his parents are no longer together, it's great to see how close the family remains and says a lot for their collective character.

★ ★ ★ ★ ★ ★ ★ ★ ★ ★ ★ ★ ★ ★ ★ ★

According to showbiz legend, Leo's namesake is none other than artist Leonardo da Vinci…because while heavily pregnant, Irmelin was admiring a da Vinci painting in Italy's Uffizi Gallery when her unborn son suddenly began kicking furiously.

★ ★ ★ ★ ★ ★ ★ ★ ★ ★ ★ ★ ★ ★ ★ ★

Again at Carolyn's house, I saw Irmelin not too long after that interview and was anxious to share with her how impressed I was with her son's latest work…and his demeanor on the publicity circuit. She told me how very enthusiastic he was about his upcoming project, *The 11th Hour*. What she modestly neglected to tell me was that she would be serving as the film's executive producer as well as being the CEO of his foundation which champions conservation causes. Of course, sentimental softie that I am, the sweetest news she shared with me was that they, along with her 90-something-year-old mother, would be moving into a three-house compound in Malibu.

When you go to Carolyn's, you're always welcome to bring along your dog and you'd definitely better be dog-friendly. She is probably the most tireless champion of canines in all of L.A. So this time,

HOLLYWOOD INSIDER
EXPOSED!

Irmelin brought along Leo's French bulldog, Django (named for jazz great Django Reinhart). I'm glad I had my camera…he was the cutest pooch next to my own Lois. (I made double prints so I could give copies to Leo next time I'd run into him on the red carpet!)

Of course, when Awards season rolled around, Leo was front and center with his double nominations. I made no secret of the fact that he was my pick for the gong, and a Manhattan bakery sent me a tin of their gourmet Nominee Cookies (all iced to depict the competing actors). Proving that dogs and their masters share a special bond, Lois couldn't help herself and immediately devoured Leo's cinnamon-y likeness.

Having the opportunity to interview Leo a second time was even better, now that we'd developed a bit of a rapport. It didn't hurt that I was so impressed with the quality of *The 11th Hour*, his powerful documentary about the eco-state of our planet. It was neither dry nor depressing, and once again I left the screening room feeling like the humanitarian hunk was at the very top of his game. How ironic that, after all the environmental flack hurled his way by activists in 2000 while shooting *The Beach* in Thailand, he has emerged as one of the most important players in the campaign to save our planet.

Trust me, any time hangin' with Leo is indeed time well spent.

★ ★ ★ ★ ★ ★ ★ ★ ★ ★ ★ ★ ★ ★ ★ ★

Irmelin missed our third consecutive Christmas dinner *chez Seymour* in '07. I was told she was in Germany with her boyfriend. Hmmm…stay tuned for more information on that.

★ ★ ★ ★ ★ ★ ★ ★ ★ ★ ★ ★ ★ ★ ★ ★

Mr and Mrs Douglas

Like most people, I was surprised when in 2000, Oscar-winner Michael Douglas married a woman whose father is even younger than he is. But Douglas was no mid-life Lothario trying to rejuvenate his public image with a trophy wife, any more than his bride was a gold-digging girl on the make for a Daddy Warbucks. Mr and Mrs Douglas are every inch equal partners and, while they might (thankfully) lack some of the same scandal-sheet appeal of some of their younger counterparts, they make up one of Hollywood's most well-respected and powerful super couples.

I liked Michael certainly from his work in films such as *Wall Street* and especially *Falling Down*, but I never paid him much attention until the acrimonious split from his first wife, Diandra, just a short time before his wedding to Catherine Zeta Jones. The estranged Mrs D number one claimed that he was compulsively promiscuous, so when the young, stunning Mrs. D number two came along, so did the whispers that he'd had to sign a monogamy agreement that included a huge financial settlement in the event of any infidelities. It's even tougher to imagine a husband straying from CZJ than from the 'perfect wife' image of Anne Archer in *Fatal Attraction*, but the rumor seemed to have credibility if for no other reason than the Welsh beauty is such an obvious force to be reckoned with! I'd done quite a bit of research on her history for a British documentary on her life for which I was a guest commentator, and if there's one thing you can say about her: she's a dame who goes after (and usually gets) what she wants.

Whether that is in taking on the paparazzi (as evidenced by their successful lawsuit against some illegally purloined photographs from their lavish wedding), making bold creative choices (their provocative work in *Traffic*, her jaw-dropping star turn in *Chicago*), or personal decisions (having two children together and raising them in the tiny British island colony of Bermuda), Michael and Catherine are a fearless team. They play sports, are politically active and philanthropic. But they also know how and, wisely, when to eschew the spotlight and maintain their private lives.

I met them separately, a year apart, and had two especially great experiences, which only served to reinforce my instinctive good feelings about them.

In 2006, Michael Douglas had granted me an interview in the lead up to the release of his film, *The Sentinel*. I'd heard mixed reports from some colleagues about his ease around the press. Considering he'd grown up in a showbiz family, I'm sure he could flip on the charm like a light switch, so all I had to worry about was being prepared, and hope I'd catch him on a good day.

I was one of a small number of journalists waiting for our one-on-one time with the actor and a publicity rep came to talk to us beforehand. She wanted to know who among us had interviewed him previously. A few people raised their hands and she made a note of them on her legal pad before disappearing back into the Douglas' suite. When I was called in a few minutes later, he rose from his chair with his hand extended in greeting and said, 'Hello, Nelson, it's very nice to meet you'. Now, I'm sure that had I raised my hand to the publicist outside previously, he would have said, 'Hello, Nelson, it's very nice to see you again', but it speaks volumes about his media-savvy and good manners that he went to a little extra bit of effort to make me feel comfortable and kick-start a positive interview experience. I couldn't help but wonder if it was an old trick he learned at the knee of his legendary father, Kirk Douglas.

We had a really nice conversation, a lot of which revolved around our mutual affection for all-things Bermudian, and I remember in particular how appreciative he was for a copy of my dad's book, *A History of Bermuda and Its Paper Money*. Pretty dry reading unless you're a Bermuda-phile, but I pointed out that I knew he was as proud of his dad as I am of mine. I did surprise him, however, when I asked him why he didn't exercise a little of showbiz clout to arrange for his lovely wife to secure the role of Wonder Woman in a big screen adaptation of everyone's number one comic book super heroine. Think about it: she'd be great! 'Really?' He seemed mystified by the idea. How can you be married to Catherine Zeta Jones and NOT think, 'I'll be damned! My wife IS Wonder Woman!'

In 2007, I was flown to New York to meet with Catherine in the lead up to her film *No Reservations*. As a foodie, I was looking forward to seeing the movie and also to visiting the New York Culinary Institute where she and co-star Aaron Eckhart had trained with Chef Michael White to learn all the techniques their characters would use in the cooking scenes. Remembering all the commentary I'd done over the years about her early career, I always openly admired the fact that she didn't give in to the Hollywood ideals of beauty by being a rail-thin, botoxed blonde. She retained the fierce determination of a hoofer—continuing to hone all the song and dance skills she'd grown up with and employed to such success in the United Kingdom. I saw her as a young woman who had set her sights on being a star of the silver screen, and that's precisely what she did. Was marrying into one of the great motion picture dynasties part of the plan? Who knows, but she certainly possesses all the talent in the world to back it up…

and has the Academy Award to prove it. Incidentally, Chef White assured me that she was a dedicated student in the kitchen, which wasn't at all surprising.

While waiting outside her suite to begin the interview, I saw her walk through the corridor with an associate. She was tall, tan and leggy, wearing a colorful, diaphanous dress I overheard someone mention was designed by Diane von Furstenberg. Va-va-va-VOOM! For me, if I'm a big admirer of the person I'm about to interview, it's best just to acknowledge it and move on. It worked with Matt Damon, I hoped it would with CZJ.

After receiving her impressively firm handshake and giving her the gift of an eco-friendly blouse made by my designer friend Samantha Robinson, I 'fessed up. 'Let's just get this out of the way right at the beginning. I love you, I always have and I can't pretend to be cool, calm and collected.' She accepted my gushing with the perfect combo of modesty and appreciation. Just as she can pirouette across a dance floor, belt out a Broadway show stopper or duel with Zorro, this babe can charm the socks off a reporter! I admit, she had wrapped me around her bejeweled little finger.

We talked primarily about our mutual interests: cooking, Bermuda, musicals…like two school mates catching up. She even said herself that our connection was 'ironic' and wondered out loud: 'Are we related? Maybe psychologically related. We're kindred spirits!' It made for interesting conversation, but the most insightful comments she made were when I got around to asking her about being that 'kid from Wales' with the pluck to find her way to the top of the showbiz elite—dining with world leaders and adored by millions of complete strangers. She candidly told me, 'I think to get anywhere in life you do have to have a drive and I did have big dreams and aspirations, I'm the first one to admit. I saw myself in a different light from the "girl from Wales" and I worked hard and it paid off'. You've got to admire that. And then she added something that makes you unable to ever begrudge her any of her hard-earned success: 'You know what's really funny? People say "You're so lucky, Catherine". I say it's bizarre because the harder I work, the luckier I get.' How is *that* for fantastic advice to young people?

Before I wrapped it up, dazzled now by her charm and brains as much as by her beauty and talent, I pulled a Wonder Woman doll out of my briefcase and held it up. 'Now about this Wonder Woman movie…I asked your husband about this and I want him to start campaigning to get you the part!' She laughed and examined the action figure. Without missing a beat, she observed the star-spangled skimpy costume on the doll and said, 'I think I have this same outfit'. I didn't miss a beat, either, and volleyed back with, 'It's a Diane von Furstenberg'. She looked up at me in amazement with those big doe eyes. Attentive listening in hallways paid off again.

> ★ ★ ★ ★ ★ ★ ★ ★ ★ ★ ★ ★ ★ ★ ★ ★
> It should be noted that my friends at Warner Brothers agree with me when it comes to my enthusiasm for CZJ's resemblance to Wonder Woman. It's just a crying shame that they're obliged to cast relative youngsters to satisfy the mega-picture obligations of the big budget action franchises.
> ★ ★ ★ ★ ★ ★ ★ ★ ★ ★ ★ ★ ★ ★ ★ ★

MR and MRS URBAN

Thanks to my five-year stint on Australia's top morning news program, *Sunrise*, I've had a real education on the talent from Down Under. Not only are Aussies the most agreeable, laid-back culture of all the international outlets I've reported for, but their sense of national pride in their exports to Hollywood is second to none. 'Our' Naomi, the late Heath, Kylie, Cate, Hugh, Eric, Russell, Mel, etcetera. But one star seems to reign above all others, even though she was born in the United States: Nicole Mary Cruise Urban, *née* Kidman.

The elegant Oscar winner went through such obvious turmoil during her high-profile divorce from enigmatic Tom Cruise that when she announced her engagement to country star Keith Urban, it touched off a nuptial frenzy Down Under that would rival Princess Diana's. Details were sketchy at best, but all indications pointed to a weekend wedding on or around June 25, 2006, with many of Hollywood's brightest celebrities jetting in for the event and subsequently on call for the actual exchange of vows. In addition to celebrities, Nicole's two adopted children with her ex-husband, and other family members, the guest list also included voting members from the Hollywood Foreign Press (the small group responsible for handing out the annual Golden Globe Awards). Smart move, Nic!

> ✦ ✦ ✦ ✦ ✦ ✦ ✦ ✦ ✦ ✦ ✦ ✦ ✦ ✦ ✦ ✦ ✦ ✦
> Schmoozing the HFPA (Hollywood Foreign Press Association) is a time-tested Tinseltown tradition. I remember being at a party back in 1998 with Lynn Redgrave who was looking resplendent. She was actively campaigning to the voting contingent for her bravura performance in that year's *Gods and Monsters.* Unabashed, she was handing out picture postcards of herself in the unglamorous role of the stern, European housemaid, 'Hannah'. It did the trick…she not only won the Best Supporting Actress Golden Globe, but the Academy Award, as well!
> ✦ ✦ ✦ ✦ ✦ ✦ ✦ ✦ ✦ ✦ ✦ ✦ ✦ ✦ ✦ ✦ ✦ ✦

I may not have been on the guest list, but I DID get an invitation to attend. Sort of. My producers at *Sunrise* asked me if I'd like to fly in to cover the event. Have tux, will travel! Next thing you know, I was on board the long flight to Sydney for my second visit to the beautiful continent I love so much from long-distance. The great thing about the show's phenomenal success is the family aspect it shares with the viewing public. There's no 'star' attitude within the ranks and it's always great to be acknowledged for my contributions with a friendly 'G'day, mate'. So the 17-hour flight, and journey through Customs, was actually quite pleasant and had the same festive vibe as if I were indeed traveling to attend a fun, family wedding.

I hit the ground running. No sooner had I grabbed a shower and change of clothes at the InterContinental Hotel than I was whisked to the Seven Network's studios to begin a day-long series of TV, radio and print interviews about the hunt to track down every possible wedding detail for our viewers. I'd all but lost my voice by the end of those scores of interviews and was looking forward to kicking back that night with my show colleagues. Fighting the jet lag, I crashed at the house of *Sunrise* co-host Melissa Doyle, and enjoyed a delicious roast lamb dinner with her gorgeous kids and hubby. Fellow 'Sunrisers',

Natalie Barr and Simon Reeve, joined us too, with their partners and Nat even brought a homemade lemon meringue pie that still makes my mouth water when I think about it. On the ride back to the hotel, Simon and I rehearsed a special treat we'd cooked up for the next morning's broadcast.

The 4am wake-up call was a toughie. But at least I had the luxury of the studio's makeup department to help hide the dark circles under my eyes. I joined Mel and her co-host David Koch (Kochie) at the news desk to report on what details I had coming in about the upcoming wedding and we also found ourselves costumed in team colors for some sporting playoff (AFL? soccer? rugby? I don't recall, but there were yellow and green scarves around our necks). During commercial breaks, Simon and I kept working on our wedding present to Keith and Nicole, which we unveiled at the end of the show: a musical duet of *Bewitched* and *Makin' Whoopee*. We didn't hit any sour notes and it's one of my very fondest memories of my entire career in television. Where else but on *Sunrise* could the entertainment correspondent and news/sports presenter team up to put on a live cabaret show for Nicole Kidman?

From there I made an appearance at the network's retail outlet, The 7 Store, adjacent to the Martin Place studios where *Sunrise* is based. That was a fantastic chance for me to meet and greet a few hundred loyal members of the 'Sunrise Family'. Being from the other side of the world, it was a rare and treasured opportunity to interact with everyone. And it seemed like we all shared a case of wedding fever! So as soon as I wrapped things up there, I was off in hot pursuit of the story!

We tooled around Sydney and the Manly Beach area where the breathtaking old church was being readied for the weekend wedding. We got great shots and chatted with some of the security team and local characters…I even coerced my darling friend, Kate, to film a comedy bit. Wearing her own wedding gown, she let me chase her down the beach yelling, 'Nicole! Come back, Nicole! Mrs Urban!' Camp-tastic!

Then it was up to the Kidman home to witness the throngs of assembled media camped outside on the narrow street, with a sweeping view overlooking the harbor. It was indeed madness, but unlike most gatherings of press like that, this one was remarkable in that everyone seemed to be in a good mood. No one was pushing or shoving or impatient or grumpy. Everyone seemed genuinely happy for the bride-to-be and she obviously felt the good will, because at one point she sent out beverages for one and all. I was interviewing some of the people on scene when suddenly the garage door opened and Nicole slowly backed out in her Mercedes sedan…cameras descended upon the vehicle and started to click like a plague of locusts. I found myself swept into the crush and right up against the glass, facing her. I smiled widely and rolled my eyes to acknowledge the craziness of the scene. We made brief eye contact and she smiled sweetly. I hope it was because she liked Simon's and my tune crooning!

Moments after she pulled away, another car appeared and the occupants rolled down their window to say hello to me. They introduced themselves as the parents-in-law of Nicole's sister, Antonia. Lovely people and obviously *Sunrise* fans (I think everyone in Australia is! Even Melbournian superstar Geoffrey Rush admits to knowing me from his morning telly. Pass the Vegemite, Captain Barbosa!) It wasn't enough to get me an invitation into the backseat for a ride over to the rehearsal dinner, but heck…I appreciated their sweetness! From there, I went back to the InterContinental where Keith and his family were also staying. Bodyguards were stationed outside the elevators but all was quiet for the time being. I took advantage of the available moments to go for a recuperative run through the nearby Botanic Gardens and around the Opera House.

**HOLLYWOOD INSIDER
EXPOSED!**

Running in Sydney is by far one of my all-time happiest athletic experiences. If Sydney were a woman, I'd marry her tomorrow!

With Keith's stag party right nearby the hotel, the rehearsal dinner, the preparations around the church and all the fan gatherings, there was a lot to report on and package for my reports. On that chilly Sunday morning, my producer Yoko and I met the satellite truck out at the church as helicopters hovered overhead. We had it covered. We reported from the location and then by telephone from the car as we eventually made our way back into the studio. A much more upbeat live broadcast than covering the Michael Jackson molestation verdict or Anna Nicole Smith's autopsy, for sure! The new Mrs Keith Urban was a gorgeous bride and her pal Hugh Jackman even performed a song at the reception. Too bad Simon and I couldn't have been there to make it a trio, ha ha.

By the end of the day, all that was left to do was record a wrap up of the day's events and then go out to enjoy a dinner with my friends, Mike and Tracy Amor. Social time was at a minimum...I was scheduled to fly out first thing the next morning, directly from my final *Sunrise* segment. I was sorry to leave my mates after such a whirlwind trip and promised to try and make it back for a proper visit sometime soon (and hopefully another homemade dinner at Mel's!).

But the star-spotting wasn't over, yet. I checked in to the Business Class Lounge at the airport and two of the airline employees were such *Sunrise* fans that they generously bumped me up to the First Class Lounge. A very sweet perk I was thrilled to accept! And guess who was there, also waiting to fly back to LA? Naomi Watts and Nicole's kids, Connor and Isabella, who were being escorted by their aunt (Tom Cruise's sister). It was announced that the flight would be delayed approximately 90 minutes, so I had a unique opportunity to observe these famous folks under completely unguarded circumstances.

I'm delighted to tell you that there's really nothing to tell you! The kids were the most polite, unaffected showbiz progeny I can ever recall meeting. We all waited patiently and contentedly before eventually boarding our flight, and I thought it was amusing that one of the movies being shown was Naomi's *King Kong*. (I once sat next to Whoopi Goldberg on a red-eye flight while *Sister Act* was on the screen. Very surreal!) Back home at LAX, they even retrieved and schlepped their own luggage. I was impressed.

Having enjoyed so many of Nicole's films and Keith's music (I really appreciated the coincidence of his wearing a T-shirt that read 'NELSON' when I saw him in concert! If the reports are true that he and Nic are planning a fashion line, I certainly hope this item will be included), I was thrilled to be a part of their wedding weekend. Even if I didn't have a seat in the pews with the rest of the invited guests, I certainly joined the rest of their loved ones and countrymen in celebrating their union and hope theirs will be a long and happy marriage.

Famous Persons' Disease

Famous Persons' Disease or as I more commonly refer to it, FPD, is a highly communicable condition that can strike anyone, at any time. 'Doctor' Andy Warhol believed the duration of this illness is generally limited to 15 minutes, but I can assure you that once it has taken hold of its victim, the grip can remain firm until (but not resulting in) death.

This clever diagnosis was named by my non-medical pal Alexandra after we had witnessed a stack of our friends over the course of many years succumb to its symptoms: self-importance, a sense of entitlement, rudeness, irritability, a disregard for authority, and unreliable behavior to name a few. Ironically, you don't have to be famous to catch FPD. There are plenty of CEOs, politicians, patriarchs and principals who also suffer from this Big Fish Syndrome.

It's particularly disappointing when it infects someone close to you…someone especially normal in your eyes, who can no longer handle the flattering siren's call of constant adoration, only further complicated by excessive privilege and (literal) fortune. Insidious in its ability to spread from its host, FPD can quickly affect the victim's closest friends and relatives as well, as they get inadvertently and happily swept up in the perks of fame.

In all fairness to actors, most of them toil for years in their quest for acceptance into the elite inner circles of show business. You would think that all that rejection would build up an immunity to FPD. However, it is more often just the opposite case. After too many years of financial struggles and/or hearing 'NO' at every turn, they can't help but yield the instant that some completely unrelated third party begins to say 'YES! YES!' YES!' Throw in all those valuable prizes found in Hollywood goody-bags and all the countless special favors happily thrust in the star's direction and it's a toxic recipe for immediate FPD infection.

There is only one cure for FPD: an extreme dosage of self-awareness that is usually accompanied by some sort of unpleasant comeuppance such as a very public embarrassment, scandal or disappointing loss. Why do you think so many celebs 'Do Not Pass Go/Do Not Collect $200'—and run immediately for rehab?'

Jon Heder, a.k.a. Napoleon Dynamite from the movie of the same name, said to me, 'Don't get caught up in the lifestyle. Remember who you are'. Problem is, so many of these actors…especially young ones, have no idea who they are in the first place. And speaking of younger, Julia Roberts' charming niece, Emma explained it to me this way: 'I think when you're a young actor, there are going to be younger kids looking up to you. You *do* have to be a little more careful of where you go, who you're with or what you're wearing. That's just what comes with it'. It also helps when stars can be objective enough to appreciate their good fortune. International superstar Chow Yun-Fat is one of those and he reflected on his experience in *Pirates of the Caribbean: At World's End*. 'Every day when I was on the set I felt like the luckiest man on earth. Every day was Christmas Day.'

As I told Sky News when they interviewed me about the proposed legislative changes to protect celebrities and the general public from overly-aggressive paparazzi media, for better or for worse I think we have only begun to scratch the surface of 'famous frenzy'. Every generation has its super scandals…look at Fatty Arbuckle in the 1920s,

HOLLYWOOD INSIDER
EXPOSED!

Lana Turner in the 1950s, OJ Simpson in the 1990s, and so forth. As technology advances, so will the pandemic of Famous Persons' Disease! On one level or the other in the stratosphere of Hollywood, almost everyone is a carrier of the FPD virus. But some big names are worth mentioning precisely because they are so obviously immune to its obnoxious grip. There are only a small number completely free of its insidious spell, which is why I find them noteworthy. I discuss most of them in this book, but here are some others, in no particular order, I have to point out.

★ *Jodie Foster.* She told me: 'I am not a person who gets cappuccinos given to me a thousand times a day and lives in fancy hotel rooms or whatever. That's just my job. It's my job to be on TV. It's my job to put makeup on and fancy clothes. That's not who I am. 'Cause when I come home, I'm this other person and it's always been important to me to separate those things'. THAT, ladies and gentleman, is what makes her a STAR and keeps her, more or less, from being of interest to tabloids. She's wisely demonstrating by example with her kids, too. When her young son Charles asked her to use her influence to get him a TV gig, she refused and told him he could do theater after school if acting was something he felt really compelled to pursue. She's seen all too well the impact broadcast fame has on young people in Hollywood and good on her for trying to shield him from it as long as she can.

★ *Eric Bana.* A gentleman and a wit. I wish he'd 'fess up more often to his early roots in comedy and let it show, but I suspect he might be afraid of endangering his serious actor/leading man status.

★ *Cate Blanchett.* Is there something in the Aussie water that keeps so many of their stars grounded? Come to think of it, Rachel

Griffiths is another one. Cate may be the darling of directors and designers around the globe, but just because she can strut down a red carpet and deliver pitch-perfect performances doesn't mean she's ever lost the human touch she acquired being a nice Melbourne girl.

★*Hugh Jackman.* This talented guy just wants to work, play and be with his family. Sounds like a good recipe to me. Notice how the scandal sheets don't pick on him, either.

★*Wentworth Miller.* He manages to keep a private life and doesn't seem too bothered when the media infringes on it. He's a cool dude and admits that he enjoys the perks and accolades of fame, but that's not what he's in it for…

★*Sally Field.* Ever since she gushed, 'You like me, you really like me', she's been the butt of jokes for representing the ultimate insecure actress. But it might just be that very insecurity which keeps this adorable powerhouse such a grounded and ever-working force in Hollywood. Strong women are often considered bitches, while powerful men are commended for their strength and leadership. Sally is one of the most complex, talented and durable professionals in our biz and deserves all our respect.

★*Jude Law.* Jude started out as an immensely talented and physically stunning young actor. I first met him and his very lovely family at their London home when he was still a teenager, before the Fame Train hit. He valiantly fended off FPD for many years until shortly after his first Academy Award nomination. A lot of madness followed, but to his credit, his brush with the illness seems to have been relatively short-lived (and part of me thinks his close friendship with the ultimate anti-FPD actor, Sir Michael Caine, may have more than a little to do with it).

★ *Daniel Day-Lewis.* He's neither an agoraphobic hermit nor a fussy drama dilettante. Rather, he's a committed father, husband and (obviously!) actor. If he's not working on perfecting a breathtaking new performance, he's home with the family.

★ *Woody Harrelson.* Right in between his genre-defying roles in *No Country for Old Men* and *Semi-Pro*, I was invited to interview Woody. I really had no idea what to expect. On screen, he's never the same twice and his off-screen persona vacillates between hippie 'granola-dude' and reluctant star. So I just waited. And waited. Ten minutes turned into twenty, then thirty and finally at forty minutes after our scheduled interviewed time, one of the PR reps told me it was because he had to brush his teeth. I know it's important not to rush your brushing, but…40 minutes? Well, vegan environmentalist Woody apparently only uses all-natural toothbrushes and paste, and there were none available, so everything came to a grinding halt while someone rushed out to a health foods store to stock up. But I have to say, even though I live my life regimented by the clock, I had no issues whatsoever waiting for Woody. Not only am I a huge fan of good dental habits, I really am glad to know that he's a principled guy who walks the walk when it comes to his beliefs. We ended up having a great interview, as it turned out, and he was one of the more accessible, sweet-natured and chatty celebrities I've ever spoken to. (It's worth pointing out that he was bare-footed too, and those tootsies appeared to be as clean and polished as his teeth.)

Too Hot to Handle

When it comes to the most sordid stories in showbiz, the media tends to put them into one of two categories: Urban Legends or Blind Items. Urban Legends are usually fantastical rumors that have no basis in fact whatsoever, but take on a strangely legitimate life of their own with incessant telling, re-telling and all the elaboration in the process. Stories like a certain peace-loving leading actor who wound up in a medical mishap with a gerbil. Or the macho man with a particular implant that required pumping to activate. Or the teen-scream queen who was alleged to have been born gender-nonspecific and surgically modified as a female. Probably no one has been more of a victim of Hollywood's Urban Legends than Michael Jackson. It seems like everyone in Los Angeles can claim some connection to one or more of his imagined idiosyncrasies. Blind Items are bits of gossip with more credence, but still too litigious to name names. Lots of Tinseltown tattletales have a field day recklessly printing these, delighting fodder fans with the ultimate gossip guessing game.

I had to tangle with one powerful publicist when she denied me access to a certain star from her stable of clients, based on the fact that I'd been quoted in the *New York Post*'s widely read Page Six column. I was quick to point out that I was quoted because the writers had read some of my columns and blogs on the internet…and that it is

HOLLYWOOD INSIDER
EXPOSED!

highly flattering to be found quotable as a reliable showbiz source. My comments, insights and news items are often cited in other publications, regardless of any highbrow or lowbrow perceptions. One man's *People* magazine is another man's *Wall Street Journal*. I'm happy to tell you, I eventually was granted the interview I was chasing. No-one respects a star's boundaries more than I do, and she eventually understood that. I have no control over who quotes my statements in the public domain and I certainly don't want to be a sensational, scandal-mongering Geraldo Rivera type! It's that mutual respect that winds up gaining me the access to exclusive information. Obviously with the degrees of separation provided by the internet, Freud can be found on Fark.com, as easily as Run DMC can be on Reuters!

After all my years in the biz, I've become a bit of an expert on deciphering Truth from Trash. I say 'True' to CNN's Anderson Cooper wearing his undies in the gymnasium showers, because my trusted friend told me he'd seen it with his own eyes. Does Andy have an embarrassing rash? More likely he's smart enough to know which of his fellow gym-goers could be lurking about the locker rooms with a camera phone! I say 'Real' to the fact that Kathy Najimy created a SoCal (Southern California) snowstorm in her own backyard for her daughter's birthday fete. Bales of hay blasted with a machine-generated blizzard made it possible for pampered party-goers to enjoy warm-weather sledding! Here are a few of my own Blind Items that are way too hot to handle. Maybe you can figure out who these mystery men and women are, but I'll never tell.

★ This grande dame of the silver screen is a frequent patient at a local LA hospital. In addition to being able to have private nursing staff and her Maltese dog in her well-appointed room, she doesn't settle for the cafeteria food: she orders in pizza and fried chicken.

★ Once considered to be among the most beautiful and talented leading ladies in cinema, this train wreck has been running riot in Tinseltown off-camera for decades. But her nastiest penchant may be a fetish for…yuck…urinating!

★ Digital retouching isn't just for still photographs. One of the world's most beloved supermodels and an ageless rock icon get more than a little help in the editing room to slim down their thighs. And a style icon of the small screen may be known for her great looks, complexion and figure…but it takes a small army of post-production magicians to make her look that way!

★ Long-time celeb and family man, Mr X, secretly shared a European villa with his male companion of many years: a foreign film star.

★ One of television's longest-running leading ladies has had many on-screen romances with handsome fellows over the years. But in real life, her heart belongs to only one *woman*.

★ This TV beauty dated a much older A-lister and was so determined to keep her man happy, she agreed to his request to have a certain part of her lower anatomy bleached for him. It didn't keep them together, so I wonder if she regrets it now.

★ Which gorgeous new mommy and superstar relied on the magic of micro-dermabrasion and Restalyn to fill an unsightly scar she acquired in a driving mishap?

HOLLYWOOD INSIDER
EXPOSED!

★ This talented, androgynous chanteuse prefers to perform in bare feet, so demands brand new Persian rugs beneath her tootsies from any venue that invites her.

★ An English sex symbol learned the skills of lovemaking when only a teenager: from one of his parents' married friends!

★ This movie legend actually suffered facial paralysis while undergoing a cosmetic procedure.

★ A famous, Emmy-winning TV comedy star seduced his child's under-age babysitter and launched into a long, illegal affair.

★ This funny lady is famous for her sweet disposition, but the kids from her husband's first marriage would be much more likely to deem her a 'Wicked Stepmother'.

★ This married hunk had a male personal assistant who assists him with much more than household and office chores, if you catch my drift.

★ A longtime columnist in his declining years couldn't keep up with the pace and demands of his job and asked me if I would anonymously author his popular syndicated columns. I graciously declined, happy to be this charming old guy's GUEST writer, but I'm no one's GHOST writer! He found someone else and, as far as I know, his secret is still safe.

★ The iconic pop-culture star of situation comedy went on to reality TV competition and eventually game shows, but his least funny moment was breaking the heart of his devoted fiancée shortly before their high-profile wedding, when she discovered he'd strayed with a certain past-her-prime siren. He wound up marrying a similar gal to the first femme fatale, but managed to botch that one, too, in less than two years' time.

★ One of daytime soap opera's super-couples, on screen and off, these two finally called it quits after his boozy misbehavior with members of the opposite sex made them both industry gossip fodder. In a case of quick-acting karma, he's all but disappeared and she's a hit show hottie.

★ This child star grew up and turned sex symbol. She launched into a torrid affair with a married co-star and when they finally parted ways, she left him with an unfortunate case of STD…which he passed on to his wife! Oops! Needless to say, that marriage ended badly and the frisky femme fatale has since discovered religion and settled down in suburbia.

★ This sci-fi/action leading man is a Hollywood icon, but he got his start in the biz peddling pot and supplying a famous movie producer.

★ A pretty TV blonde found herself pregnant by her boss: one of the most prolific producers in showbiz history. He 'took care of it' and his famous family was none the wiser.

★ This oft-married musical ingénue had a long love affair with another woman, who was herself a well known TV actress.

HOLLYWOOD INSIDER
EXPOSED!

★ This sexy 80's primetime soap star is a single gay man who twice donated his sperm to help some lesbian gal pals start a family of their own.

★ One of the most talented and famous stars in the world has been helping care for her ailing son from a former marriage.

★ A European singing superstar who never 'made it' in Hollywood might have 'made it' instead with a Brit-born TV actor who often leaves his wife and kids at home while off cavorting with Mr. X.

★ Which Oscar-winning actor has a look-alike brother who enjoys passing himself off as the star, himself?

★ This obese veteran broadcaster may have a lot of experience in TV and radio, but he still doesn't understand the concept of an open microphone. He repeatedly made disparaging remarks about his colleagues, until one of his victims finally complained to management. Isn't that the first lesson in Communications Class 101? Duh!

★ Guess which veteran talk show host has a chronic flatulence problem that is well known to his staff and repeat guests?!

★ This self-absorbed TV sexpot has a serious hair problem on her famous upper lip, arms and legs (and Lord knows where else!) that requires constant attention. The facial hair on her cheeks and jaw line has gotten so bad, it's actually more like whiskers!

★ This recently-deceased multi-award winning stage and TV character actor was known more for his talent and battles with substance abuse than for his life as a gay man with a penchant for *much* younger men...which he felt compelled to cover by dating an attractive, live-in lady friend.

★ Guess which handsome daytime TV talker, known as a bright and well-mannered family man, got so wasted ringing in 2008 on New Year's Eve with friends and colleagues that he stripped down to his undies and ran wildly into the Pacific Ocean.

Ships Ahoy!

I have never really understood my lifelong fascination with ocean liners and classic twentieth century passenger steamships. As geeky as I was with all my interests in monster movies and comic books, it was admittedly out of character that I spent such an inordinate amount of time in the swimming pool playing out shipboard emergency and rescue operations with toy boats and rafts. When *The Poseidon Adventure* opened in 1972, I pleaded with my parents until I got to go see it. Not just once, but several times. I've probably seen that film more times than any other motion picture, far out-pacing other multiple viewers like *The Sound of Music*, *Gone with the Wind*, *The Wizard of Oz* or *Mommie Dearest*. And I know I'm not alone… over the years, I've met a lot of folks who are actively involved in the cult of *Poseidon* (see the 'My Favorite Movie Star' chapter).

As a child, I cruised with my parents on several vacations to Bermuda and took my first-ever solo trip at 15, on an American Film Institute voyage to the Virgin Islands. I got to spend eight days learning about the Art of Film and meet other aficionados. One of the real highlights of that trip was making friends with Gisele Galante, the beautiful daughter of silver screen star Olivia de Havilland. It was a very fortuitous friendship, because it afforded me a place at the table with Ms. de Havilland and two other late, great film legends, Glenn Ford and King Vidor. I was—and am—fascinated by liners, their design and even the aspect of shipboard life. In spite of numerous offers over the years to work as a performer on cruise ships, it's the mystique of the great vessels themselves that piques my interest. I'm lucky that the RMS *Queen Mary* resides in permanent dry dock at the port of Long Beach, so I'm only a short drive away from visiting her whenever I have the urge!

In addition to *Poseidon*, I couldn't get enough of maritime disaster films, books and stories. *The Last Voyage, The Perfect Storm, A Night to Remember, Voyage of the Damned, Speed 2: Cruise Control, Ship of Fools, Lifeboat, Raise the Titanic* and of course, both versions of *Titanic* still grip me, and whenever I run across them on television (even though I own the DVDs), I am compelled to watch them through to the closing credits. Whether it's the *Andrea Doria, Lusitania* or even December 7th at Pearl Harbor, something about tragedy at sea strikes a chord with me. No happy episodes of *The Love Boat* for me.

It wasn't until I was almost an adult that I started to get an inkling of what was behind the irresistible attraction. In fact, I still continue to uncover more clues all the time and suspect I will for the rest of my life. The key came in an unlikely recurring dream I'd had in my childhood: that outwardly seems to have nothing whatsoever to do with sinking ships!

Did I scare you off yet? I hope not!

In this dream, I was sliding down a long banister but instead of falling off or dismounting when I reached the bottom, I would continue to descend into the vast blackness. Nothing nautical or particularly creepy about that especially since our house had a long banister on the front stairs. I frequently slid down it every time Mom called us for dinner. It wasn't until I moved away from home, a few weeks after I turned 17, that this benign little dream stopped. I hadn't even noticed at first that it had.

One day, I was in a New York City book store at the South Street Seaport, where I'd gone to admire the boats docked. Remember, this was way back in the olden days before the internet so books were the source for information! I came across a new book called *The Titanic:*

End of a Dream by Wyn Craig Wade and flipped through it. I came across a passage that immediately struck me:

'Jack Thayer and his companion straddled the starboard rail abreast of Number 2 funnel. Thayer's friend put both legs over and, facing the ship, clung to the rail by his hands. 'You're coming, boy, aren't you?' he asked Jack. 'Go ahead', Thayer replied, 'I'll be with you in a minute'. Jack's companion let go of the rail, slid down into the water, and was swallowed up in the pounding torrent that was pouring into A Deck.'

★ ★ ★ ★ ★ ★ ★ ★ ★ ★ ★ ★ ★ ★ ★

> My devoted father was so supportive of my obsession that he actually tried to purchase an authentic *Titanic* life preserver in a Philadelphia auction. Not only is Philly our hometown, but that of Jack Thayer! Dad learned the hard way that you cannot out-bid the Titanic Historical Society when it comes to those rare artifacts! But it goes to show you the kind of man he is!

★ ★ ★ ★ ★ ★ ★ ★ ★ ★ ★ ★ ★ ★ ★

A chill ran through me. I could *see* it happening, as if it were me sliding down the banister before plunging into the blackness! Who was this companion? Jack Thayer was 17 at the time of the disaster… was his friend the same age? Is that why the dreams had stopped for me at 17? Was I a reincarnation of this mysterious person…picking up a life to live where his had run out!? My overactive imagination was going wild and, in those pre-internet days, I knew the person who could provide me with answers would be the author of the book, himself! Three dollars fifty later, I owned the book and was planning to compose a letter to send him, care of the publisher. I had to find out the identity of Jack Thayer's companion!

Mr Wade wrote me back quickly with a wonderful letter on his personal stationery that, unfortunately (and uncharacteristically!),

I have since lost. But he provided me with the next puzzle piece: the name, Milton C. Long, Jr.

From reading my 'Uncle Nelson' chapter, you know that I, too, am a 'Junior' and went by the nickname of 'JR' until I was 18 years old. Flash forward a year when I began using my first name, Nelson, both professionally and personally. I was still getting used to my new name and careful to always pronounce it distinctly when introducing myself. So why did so many people, then as now, address me as Milton? I can't tell you how many dozens and dozens of times people will accidentally call me Milton. I'll even get mail or food deliveries to Milton Aspen! Coincidence?

I began to blithely accept the fact that, whoever Milton C Long Jr was (again, little information was available to me), I was his second chance at life. It was a fun and fanciful story that helped to explain why I was such a maritime enthusiast. I remember going to a psychic once and, without prompting, she told me that she felt I had drowned in a former lifetime. Cue *The Twilight Zone* theme music!

A couple more years went by and then came September 9, 1985: Headlines around the world announced, 'Explorer Robert Ballard Discovers the Wreck of the Titanic!'

I *had* to contact him. I had to somehow connect to/with the one person who was closest to the actual place where Milton had been pulled into the abyss. I didn't know where to begin. In my tiny studio apartment, I sat down on the bed and picked up the telephone. I asked the operator to connect me with the United States Navy. A few voices later, I was directed to the Woods Hole Oceanographic Institute in Woods Hole, Massachusetts. It rang a few times and I asked the lady who answered, 'This is Nelson Aspen in New York calling. May I please speak with Dr Robert Ballard?' She put me on hold. Now, let's have some perspective here: I am a young, unknown actor living in a metropolis. He is suddenly the most famous and sought after explorer in the *world*! Why would he ever take an unsolicited call from *me*?!

I heard a click and then his voice say, 'Hello, Milton?' You cannot make this stuff up!

I decided it was best not to get into the metaphysics of past lives with this man of science, so I simply congratulated him on his amazing discovery and asked if there was any way an enthusiastic and dedicated young *Titanic*-phile could possibly be a part of the expedition to dive to the wreck. As inundated as I'm sure he was, Dr Ballard took the time to have a conversation with me and explained how far off such an adventure would be, but that he would arrange to have paperwork sent to me if I wanted to make a formal submission. I was elated when I hung up the phone, ready to drop whatever career strides I was making in show business to run off to sea and swab decks, peel potatoes or whatever drudgeries were part of the package. True to his word, a few days later a package arrived from Woods Hole with a long application form to enroll in the Oceanographic Institute. Common sense prevailed and I decided that I would have to be content with waiting for the scientists and other professionals to do their thing. That would *not* have been the life for me. I did, however, correspond with Dr Ballard a few times over the years that followed and will always admire and appreciate the time and kindness he extended to a zealous stranger. These are the courtesies in my role models I most try to emulate in my own life. Making time to acknowledge and encourage others is, to me, the greatest way to live The Golden Rule.

The *Titanic* connection to my life pretty much died down after that (no pun intended) until years later when my close friend, Alexandra, came to me in need of some help. James Cameron was preparing to cast his epic movie version of *Titanic* and, stickler for period authenticity that he was, auditioning just about every Brit in Hollywood for even the smallest of parts. An interesting hook was that actors were being asked to research and write their own monologues based on the lives of actual passengers or crew from the ill-fated 1912 voyage. Knowing what a nut I was for the ship's legacy, Alexandra asked if I'd help her prepare. Getting my genuine lump of *Titanic* coal (which I'd purchased after the excavation of artifacts from the debris field) for inspiration and luck, I told her to hurry over and we'd get to work! Together, we came up with a dramatic account from the point of view of the Countess of Rothes, a First Class passenger who handled the tiller of a lifeboat. (While Milton C Long and Jack Thayer don't appear in the movie, there are two young men who playfully kick around chunks of ice after the collision with the 'berg, and I believe Cameron intended them to represent our boys.)

> ★ ★ ★ ★ ★ ★ ★ ★ ★ ★ ★ ★ ★ ★
>
> In spite of all this time in the water, I'm still insecure about being seen in a bathing suit. Backstage at a friend's play, I met Olympian diver Greg Louganis, who invited me over to his house for a late-night swim. Super nice guy, but come on… no way I was going to slide on a pair of Speedos around a specimen with such a renowned physique. What's next: skinny dipping with the Thunder from Down Under?
>
> ★ ★ ★ ★ ★ ★ ★ ★ ★ ★ ★ ★ ★ ★

While our friend Rochelle Rose won the role of the Countess ('I felt a shudder!'), Alexandra was cast as an unnamed First Class Passenger and had a lucrative and memorable three-month shooting experience. Look for her boarding the ship with her little dog, descending the Grand Staircase to be seated at the Captain's Table for dinner and a close-up giving Leonardo DiCaprio a sly grin and arched eyebrow as he enters the Dining Salon. It was a thrill to hear all her stories from the

set and be a part of the great excitement that surrounded this record-setting motion picture. For example, before handsome Ioan Gruffud was Mr. Fantastic or Horatio Hornblower, he was Titanic's Officer Harold Lowe and Alexandra rightfully gushed about how he'd regale cast mates between takes with traditional Welsh songs.

When director Cameron and his team came out with their 3-D documentary follow up, *Ghosts of the Abyss* in 2003, it was with great happiness that I accepted an offer to MC a promotional Q&A appearance for Mr Cameron and his two colleagues, Ken Marshall and Don Lynch (both well known and respected *Titanic* historians). The real trick for me was going to be allowing anyone *else* to ask any questions! They were all great gentlemen and I was able to confess my Milton-connection to Don and Ken, who didn't even blink. Don told me how many people had admitted to similar experiences about souls lost on that terrible night and Ken even signed a book for me, 'May your voyages be free of icebergs'.

So that is my own personal little ghost story and, aside from the usual mistaken introductions as 'Milton', there have been no further developments to report. Yet! I'm always on the alert for a new morsel of information about Milton that will provide further clues into the mystery behind that eternal trip down the banister.

★ ★ ★ ★ ★ ★ ★ ★ ★ ★ ★

> Milton Clyde Long, Jr's body was recovered and returned to his surviving parents, Judge and Mrs Charles Long. He was interred at the Springfield Cemetery. Interestingly, the only known memento of the man is his vest pocket watch with his initials engraved on the sterling silver case. The *Titanic* sunk at 2:20am and the watch is frozen in time, stopped presumably when he entered the water: 2:14.

★ ★ ★ ★ ★ ★ ★ ★ ★ ★ ★

Quirks, Foibles & Foul-ups

Everyone has their own little habits, characteristics and superstitions. If I don't knock seven times on my headboard before getting out of bed on the first day of every month, it doesn't bode well for the next four weeks. I think it's safe to assume that we all possess some quirks that others might find offbeat, and certainly stars are no exception. In fact, we've come to expect weird behavior *especially* from them. The richer and more famous they are, the more outlandish the stories of their demands, rituals and compulsions seem to be. A temperature-controlled dressing room filled with only white gardenias, special brands of soft drinks and bowls of M&M candies (green ones removed) are not unusual requests.

Some stars, like Rhianna, don't even bat a mink false eyelash when their entourage leaves behind a room like that completely trashed. It's true that pop star Mariah Carey demands to get her required minimum eight hours of sleep in a blackened out, humidified room. And Robert De Niro's notorious lack of eye contact results in adjusted camera angles so an audience won't suspect he's just looking off into space. Some stories take on a life of their own. Harrison Ford and Tommy Lee Jones, for example, are famous for being grumps but when I asked the latter why he is quoted as saying he has no sense of humor, he wittily replied, 'That was a joke'. Streisand is said to demand rose petals in the toilet bowls, while Madonna requires

brand new, never-before-used toilet seats altogether!

I paid a set visit to a so-called comedy called *Over Her Dead Body* (formerly titled *How I Met My Boyfriend's Dead Fiancee*) starring Eva Longoria, Paul Rudd and Jason Biggs. In spite of the fact that the location was outside in midday, sweltering SoCal summer heat, everyone was in good spirits…on ONE condition. No one was permitted to stand in the sight line of the Desperate Diva while she was acting, otherwise filming came to a grinding halt and there would be hell to pay. Imagine a lavish outdoor wedding scene with scores of actors, extras, cameramen and crew. How do you stay out of a single person's sightline!? My solution was to hide out in a nearby shady tented area and wait for a break in shooting to chat with Eva (I should point out that this is a great example of a star's foible, because she is generally one of the most low-maintenance and cheerful, chatty celebrities…especially when there are cameras in the vicinity).

When out to promote his drama *We Are Marshall*, Matthew McConaughey wouldn't begin our interview until he'd psyched himself up with a set of push ups. I was kind of embarrassed for him that he felt he needed to stop everything and do this ritual in front of me and the assembled camera crew, but I guess I can't fully understand the pressure of having to show off beautiful biceps to maintain a hunk factor. All I could think was, 'how many girls would be drooling to have this guy *literally* at their feet doing push ups', while I was just sitting there feeling weird. For the record, I didn't notice his rumored hygiene problem. Believe me: I was close enough that if there *had* been any unpleasant smell, my sensitive nose would have picked up on it!

It is rumored that the real reason mega-mogul Donald Trump could never make a serious bid for a US political seat was because of his Howard Hughes-esque refusal to shake hands with strangers: a necessary evil when hitting the campaign trail. Heart-throb Orlando

Bloom suffers from the same reticence (I should declare that I keep a bottle of hand-disinfectant on my desk) and is known to excuse himself from a handshake by saying he's fighting off a cold and doesn't want to spread his germs.

The Donald figures into one of my earliest performance mishaps. But it wasn't my fault, I swear! It was 1989 and in honor of the centennial for the venerable *Wall Street Journal*, I was employed as the off-stage announcer for their elegant all-star celebration. Big stars were everywhere, but all I got to see was the microphone booth backstage in the dark. I had a script of pre-written announcements to make when cued over the course of the evening, which consisted of dinner, musical performances and speeches. The most important one was announcing the President and Mrs George W Bush. That went off without a hitch. I was more nervous about twisting the words relating to the pyrotechnic dessert being served by a force of effeminate servers. 'And now, ladies and gentlemen, your waiters present a flaming fruit extravaganza!' Whew! I made it through that one, too. But I was mistakenly given the wrong script to announce Mr Trump. Since I couldn't see the dais from where I was positioned, I had no clue he was walking on stage to my booming announcement, 'Ladies and gentlemen, please welcome the Ambassador of Jazz, Mister Lionel Hampton!' Trump handled it well and ad libbed a jovial reply that won him laughter and applause. Later on, I made an ad lib of my own when I said, 'And with apologies to Donald Trump, you may *now* welcome the Ambassador of Jazz, Mister Lionel Hampton!' *You're fired!*

My height (or the lack thereof) seems to frequently be a talking point when viewers meet me in person. 'I thought you'd be taller!' is a phrase I've learned to react to with a smile, albeit with clenched teeth. I guess it's better to be *shorter* in person than balder, older, uglier or something else. Ninety per cent of the time I'm only seen from the waist up, so it's understandable. But it doesn't help that so many of my on-air mates (like Australia's *Sunrise* crew) are so tall. Put heels on Melissa and Natalie and I look like a ventriloquist's dummy! I never think of myself as being particularly short (I am, after all, exactly 5'7"—the same height as Tom Cruise, Robert Redford and Paul Newman and I wear the same suit size as Brad Pitt—in fact, I've purchased some of his movie wardrobe at the fabulous *It's a Wrap* boutique) until someone makes a remark. We have a cameraman at our news bureau who feels compelled to have to refer to me as 'Short Ass' every time he has to adjust the camera angle, but I've come to accept it as a term of endearment. After all, he's in control of the focus and lighting, so why make waves?

One time, I was shooting a segment for *LK Today* with Lorraine Kelly at the scenic pool deck of the Shutters Hotel on the beach in Santa Monica. We were having a roundtable discussion with the Fridge Doctors, a married couple of fitness trainers, famous for giving nutritious makeovers to the refrigerators of the rich and famous such as Julia Roberts, Benicio del Toro, Jennifer Lopez and Britney Spears (back when she actually looked healthy). On a commercial break, I walked off the set to grab a bottle of water and was approached by an enormous middle-aged tourist in a bikini practically obliterated by layers and layers of sagging flesh. 'I've seen you on the telly', she said. I turned and smiled, extending a hand in greeting. 'You are so much littler in real life', she went on. Well, I have to admit I was a bit taken aback by her effrontery, but I considered that she may have just been one of those people who lack any kind of editing switch between her brain and her mouth. Fortunately, I do possess such a switch so I opted against a saucy retort and silently hoped she had plenty of sunscreen for all that skin.

✫ ✫ ✫ ✫ ✫ ✫ ✫ ✫ ✫ ✫ ✫ ✫ ✫ ✫ ✫ ✫ ✫ ✫ ✫ ✫

I asked the Fridge Doctors who has the best refrigerator in Hollywood and was told, 'Nobody has a great fridge until we've fixed it, quite honestly'. The worst? 'Kevin Costner's was *bad*, because of his kids. I just cleared out a shelf for him to have to himself.'

✫ ✫ ✫ ✫ ✫ ✫ ✫ ✫ ✫ ✫ ✫ ✫ ✫ ✫ ✫ ✫ ✫ ✫ ✫ ✫

For an Irish television audience, I was sharing a story about Michael Jackson's alleged jitters over meeting Queen Elizabeth II. Like most of us, the Irish love hearing reports about the Royal Family. I was enthusiastically regaling the show hosts with this silly story and referred to QEII as 'your queen'. (As I recall, my exact line was, 'Imagine Jacko being nervous to meet your Queen, let alone any queen!') We finished the segment full of laughs and it wasn't until I got off the air that my producer informed me that, of course, unlike England, the south of Ireland is a republic and does not have a Queen. And you can bet I was reminded the next time I checked my email and received several strongly worded letters from Republican viewers! Hey, it's never too late to get a brush up in political science. God Save the Queen…whoever she belongs to!

When I joined the morning team at our local Los Angeles ABC news affiliate as their weekly Party Patrolman, reporting on the weekend's goings-on at area hotspots, I was welcomed warmly by the anchors and crew. I love local news, so I was excited to be there… especially with the newsreaders, David Ono and Ellen Leyva, whom I'd been watching for years. During the commercial break, as I got seated in my chair and put on my microphone, handsome triathlete David asked me, 'Would you like a phone book to sit on?' My mouth fell open! I didn't have a Napoleonic complex, and what kind of nerve does it take to ask a newcomer such a question? Before I could

summon up some words in response, I glanced up at the monitor and saw the wide shot of the three of us. Sure enough, I was at least a head lower than them. I glanced down at David's seat and, to my surprise, **he** was sitting on a phone book. He was trying to help me out! 'Yes, please!' I quickly called out as we were less than thirty seconds to coming out of the commercial break. By the time I delivered my report, we were all seeing eye to eye.

While we're on the subject of height, I should mention that one of the most gracious stars I've interviewed is *Las Vegas* heartthrob Josh Duhamel. When I paid him a set visit, this 6'4" gentleman generously suggested we do the interview seated so he wouldn't dwarf me. I'm sure his beloved Fergie doesn't mind. As my mother once quipped, 'It's all the same *horizontally*'.

> Here's an interesting Fergie footnote: back when she was just little ole Stacy Ferguson, she provided the voices for the characters Sally Brown and Lucy in the animated *Peanuts* movies and cartoons. I asked her once about her greatest musical influences and she told me, 'The first person I used to copy off the radio was Donna Summer. Madonna and Whitney Houston really influenced me as a young girl to want to be like them'. When she joined the girl group Wild Orchid though, she said, 'As a group, we all aspired to be like En Vogue, The Jackson Five. We adore Chaka Khan'. I've always liked Fergie… she has way more intelligence and talent than most people give her credit for. Some other Fergie factoids she revealed to me: Her favorite Disney movie is *Cinderella*, her first pet was 'Sneaky' the cat and she likes to wear men's boxer shorts to bed. She confessed to being over-analytical since, 'Whenever I give my honest opinion about something, and it's not what everyone wants to hear, I always feel guilty afterwards because I feel like I was rude. My friends all laugh at me because of it'.

My dog seems to be especially popular with UK viewers (she was even spotted by a British tourist one day when we went hiking in the canyons—what a star!) so I often took her into the studio with me for *GMTV* and she'd sit right on my lap and look directly into the camera. It was so late for us (11:30pm–1:45am) that she was pretty placid, unlike her usual rambunctious self. But one night, a local entertainment reporter, Mindy Burbano, was at the satellite facility to do a report to some international outlet, so Lois and I had to wait until she finished before we got into the studio chair. I'd roll in at that hour usually wearing my sweat pants and sneakers…after all, no-one sees you from the waist down, but Mindy was all glammed up like she'd just stepped off the runway of the Miss Universe pageant. She was all set in the chair, ear piece in and microphone attached. I gave her a friendly wave and she started cooing about how cute my dog was and trying to call Lois over to her. I cautioned her against it so close to going on the air…but Mindy insisted. So Lois bounded over and in the glee of Mindy's warm greeting proceeded to urinate all over her Ferragamo pumps just seconds before she was live for her report. When she came off the air, let's just say she was not a happy woman, and after warning her against it, I frankly felt no compulsion to offer more than an apology. Lois Aspen is still known around Hollywood as 'the bitch who peed on Mindy Burbano'. I wonder whatever happened to Mindy…she married well and then soon after quit her reporting job to make what she presumed would be a huge career leap: appearing in the reality-TV version of Gilligan's Island in 2004. I don't think she's been seen or heard from since.

HOLLYWOOD INSIDER
EXPOSED!

★ ★ ★ ★ ★ ★ ★ ★ ★ ★ ★ ★ ★ ★ ★

Some foul-ups are beyond anyone's control. When I was working on the ill-fated sitcom *The Dictator*, back in the mid-1980s, we had shot only two episodes when the writers' strike put us on an unplanned hiatus. It dragged on so long that it killed the show altogether and nothing ever made it to the air. It was supposed to be zany character actor Christopher Lloyd's big post-*Taxi* comedy triumph, but fortunately the *Back to the Future* series came along for him! It took a little longer for young David Alan Grier to rebound with *In Living Color*.

★ ★ ★ ★ ★ ★ ★ ★ ★ ★ ★ ★ ★ ★ ★

One gut-wrenching foul-up stands out in my mind as the absolute worst. I'd been doing a standout series of exclusives at the Toronto International Film Festival and had rushed to the airport in time to make my flight back to LA after a grueling 36-hour whirlwind of screenings and interviews. I had more than a dozen tapes, way too many to stow in my carry-on luggage and there had been no time to arrange for international shipping before my departure, so I had to keep them in my checked bag. It was very nerve-wracking to place that valuable cargo onto the conveyor belt and watch it disappear. Everyone assured me I was being overly concerned, but seven hours later when I was standing all alone at the Air Canada baggage claim of Los Angeles International Airport staring at an empty carousel I was feeling justified by having those anxieties. The airline rep claimed to have checked the bar code on my claim ticket and informed me that it would be arriving, safe and sound, on the *next* flight from Toronto. So I sat there for another ninety minutes and went through the ordeal of watching the bags come down the chute from the second flight. Mine was not among them. All I could do was file a report and wait. And wait. I couldn't eat or sleep for the next 36 hours, I was so berserk about the possibility of losing all that hard-earned footage.

It was bloody awful! No matter how many times I repeated Mark Twain's words, 'Never love something that can't love you back', I could find no comfort. Time, money and effort had all been spent and the expectation for these was a potential career make-or-break. I nearly kissed the deliveryman when the bag eventually turned up on my doorstep, with all the tapes intact. I made a firm vow to never again travel without my tapes *in hand*, unless guaranteed shipping is arranged beforehand…even if it means taking a later flight! It all worked out in the end, but if anything aged me in the last decade it was *that* experience. What was it the *South Park* kids sang? 'Blame Canada.' Well, Air Canada, at least!

Pranks are something altogether different. I remember in one of our college plays, an arrogant upper classman was playing the romantic lead in a production of *The Prime of Miss Jean Brodie* and he had a particularly annoying habit of upstaging other actors by constantly plunging his right hand into his trouser pocket. One of the best practical jokes (and unintended acting lesson!) I'd ever seen was when one of my buddies on the costume crew filled that pocket with shaving cream. He could only put his hand in *once* during that performance!

I confess to pulling one on my über-talented friend, Melanie, way back in my early days when she and I were touring around New England doing a musical revue, *Mabel's Emporium*, for senior citizens. We ate rubber chicken for lunch every day for a year and sang our hearts out for those appreciative oldsters. But it was the same routine day after day after day after day and one afternoon, I just had the itch to mix it up a bit. In a musical intro to the ballad, *What'll I Do*, Melanie and I are sitting on a steamer trunk, pretending to read the newspaper story about the broken engagement of composer Irving Berlin. But, unseen by the rapt audience who sat only a few feet from the stage, I had written inside the prop newspaper a very naughty X-rated headline she wouldn't be able to miss. Poor Mel couldn't keep a straight face and then neither could I. We both got such an acute attack of the giggles that we laughed until we cried. Even though the little old ladies didn't know the reason behind the hysterics, they laughed along too and we eventually made our way to finishing the number.

In another show with Melanie, she was to stroll through the audience in her flesh-toned leotard with a white towel wrapped around her waist. My stage direction was to come up behind her and give her a pinch, then with mock anger she would launch into her *I'm Gonna Wash That Man Right Out of My Hair* number. But when I gave her the pinch, the towel came off into my hand and she was left in a sea of old fellas who hadn't been that close to a hot-looking 20-something blonde in a leotard in…maybe decades! I couldn't resist dashing backstage with the towel and Melanie proved herself to be a fearless songstress, belting out the best, bawdiest rendition of the *South Pacific* standard I'd ever heard…much to the delight of the ogling octogenarians! Remember, this was back before Viagra! She and I *still* chuckle about that one.

This wasn't Melanie's only inadvertent striptease-for-seniors, as she recently reminded me. There was another time in the snow-covered hamlet of Lenox, Massachusetts, when the teensy backstage area—cunningly held up by a single curtain rod—collapsed on her head during a costume change. This left a special challenge for me to maintain audience focus as I sang *Old Devil Moon* while, directly behind me, she contended with trying to put something on over the leotard. This is what's called paying your dues, folks. We *earned* those memberships in Actors Equity.

Another time onstage, this for the 1994 Los Angeles production of the wonderful Lanford Wilson play, *Burn This* (I played Larry), I was midway through a very dramatic passage with my co-stars Jane

Clark and another actor whom shall remain anonymous. Suffice it to say that working with him on stage was a challenge. Said actor forgot to carry on his prop gun which I was supposed to discover in his coat—the pivotal moment of the scene. Trying not to panic, Jane and I exchanged concerned glances. The audience was in the dark figuratively and literally, so when the moment came I just shrugged and ad libbed a line: indicating the coat label, I quipped, 'Look. Off the rack.' It wasn't a comedy, but I got a laugh while Mr X walked offstage and located his prop.

During another performance (thank heaven it was a limited run), he managed to *drop* the gun. That could be dangerous with a real gun, but because it was a rubber prop it just bounced across the stage like a basketball while the big guy chased after it. Again, unintentional laughter. All that was missing were dancing girls or a monkey on a bicycle.

One of the best things I find about working every day in live television is that there are no second chances. Absolutely anything can happen. Over-rehearsed actors hate spontaneously flying by the seat of their pants, but I love it. The unpredictable nature of being LIVE challenges and excites me, appealing to my love of improvisation and breaking news. I've gone on air for pulse-pounding reports on arrests, trial verdicts, triumphs and tragedies—but once in a while it can seem like it's just another ordinary day then suddenly something unexpected and memorable happens. On the afternoon of August 16, 2006, when John Mark Carr was arrested on suspicion of murder in the JonBenet Ramsey case, I was the only reporter in the news bureau at the time, so it was up to me to break the story and keep viewers up to date in the hours that followed. I thrive on being ready to jump into action (and I keep a suit jacket at the studio, just in case).

I was an unwitting accomplice to one of the most oft-repeated bloopers in modern TV history. After Tom Cruise's now infamous couch-hopping on *The Oprah Winfrey Show*, there was a story going around that Hollywood funsters had initiated a parody dance-craze called 'Doin' the Cruise'. It involved jumping up and down on a couch, waving your arms in the air and shouting things like 'I love Katie!' and 'I can't be cool!' I reported this bit of wacky pop culture live to *GMTV*'s morning team of Ben Shephard and Kate Garraway, complete with a demonstration on my rickety little chair. I encouraged Ben to try it out, after all…he had an entire, proper sofa on which to 'Do the Cruise'. 'Come on', Kate encouraged. Indicating his ear piece communiqué with the director, he hesitated: 'They're saying to me "health and safety!"' A little more prodding from Kate and I and Ben was on his feet, wildly Doin' the Cruise. Seconds later, he flew backwards over the furniture and crashed onto the floor behind. Luckily, he wasn't injured, just red-faced, so we can look back on it as a hilarious happenstance. Ben even joked to me recently that the residual payments from its frequent re-use have helped finance his kid's education.

Sometimes those 'oops' moments occur during taped interviews and still manage to creep into the final edit. I scored the first televised post-pregnancy interview with Naomi Watts and as we were chatting about her new motherhood, she said 'I still can't believe that little thing came out of me'. I immediately chimed in with, 'You can't believe that little thing came out of *that* little thing!' and gestured right to her…um, er…well…anatomical zone of child-bearing. I was *mortified*! (Boy, did her eyes get wide!) Fortunately, I didn't let my foot remain in my mouth for more than a nanosecond and managed to cover with, '…Cause you are so tiny! You got your figure right back!' From there, we segued the conversation into post-partum weight loss, but I shall always remember that as the day I pointed at Naomi Watts' crotch and referred to it as 'that little thing'. Ohhh, I'm blushing again…Sorry, Naomi.

I chatted again with Naomi a few months later after seeing her violent flick *Happy Games*…the first film where I witnessed journalists literally *running* out of the screening room, shaken from enduring two hours of graphic torture and terror. Maybe it was the content of the film, the shock that she was an executive producer and starred in it, or the extra caution after my previous foot-in-mouth, but this time around I kept my line of vision firmly transfixed on Naomi's pretty blue eyes!

Aspiring Actor

Children's theater, cabaret singing for bus loads of senior citizens, bunny costumes in shopping malls, entertaining kids at birthday parties by drawing caricatures: I wouldn't list these performances among my career highlights, but I've never been averse to earning an honest living. I was quite content with my part-time job at Macy's world-famous flagship Manhattan store until I caught a purse-snatcher and Management insisted on promoting me to the position of Assistant Buyer for…*ladies shoes!* Buh-bye, said I and 'Remember me to Herald Square'. The only really horrendous gig I'd never want to repeat was spraying perfume…*shpritz, shpritz!* Maybe if I'd been in a high-end department store offering scented samples of a designer fragrance, but I was in the world-famous FAO Schwarz toy store across from the Plaza Hotel in NYC, spraying *children's cologne!* 'Would you care to sample a fragrance for children?' I asked those spoiled brats and their even-more spoiled mothers and nannies, eliciting either total snobbish attitudes or (more understandably!) disapproving scowls for a toy store marketing beauty products to kids. I tried to tell myself that the ten bucks an hour made the endless loop of musical 'Welcome to My World of Toys', and sore feet worthwhile, but it didn't work.

There were definitely indications that would foreshadow my presenting career, even while I was actively pursuing an acting path. I always enjoyed being in the audience of the local NYC talk-fest, *The Morning Show*, which later went on to become the nationally syndicated *Live! With Regis & Kathie Lee*. They were the original perky morning gab duo, but what set Regis Philbin apart, and made him a hero to me, was his consummate ability to master so many simultaneous aspects of the live broadcast experience. Not only could he carry on a lucid, researched and entertaining conversation with his co-host and their segment guests, but also keep the studio and TV audiences feeling as if they, too, were included in it all. Meanwhile, he was always acutely aware of all the technical details: which camera was on him, how much time there remained in the tightly constricted segments, important details to mention, what graphics or video would be displayed throughout…all the while watching for cues from his on-set producer and stage manager, and listening to cues in his ear piece from the control room. He was like a master puppeteer! I knew that was the kind of multi-tasking challenge I'd enjoy, which is why I still get such a thrill being on live TV every day…and special goose bumps when I'm called upon to test my media-mettle by reporting breaking/developing news items.

> ✯ ✯ ✯ ✯ ✯ ✯ ✯ ✯ ✯ ✯ ✯ ✯ ✯ ✯
>
> While I was lucky enough to have parents who supported my childhood acting aspirations—especially a mom who was happy to hang out with me at auditions and rehearsals—there were no advantages to being related to the famed movie producers Daryl F Zanuck and his son, Richard. Cousin Daryl founded Twentieth Century Fox studios and Richard made a name for himself with blockbusters like *Jaws*, *Cocoon* and *Sweeney Todd*, but neither were much impressed with blood ties when it came to giving me a leg up in the industry.
>
> ✯ ✯ ✯ ✯ ✯ ✯ ✯ ✯ ✯ ✯ ✯ ✯ ✯ ✯

My own inglorious film career helped to pay a few bills during the '80s and only a few clips, I'm relieved to say, survive…so save yourself from running out to rent the DVDs! I did manage to escape the embarrassment of playing a department store clerk in 1987's so-bad-

it's-almost-good comedy *Mannequin*, because I opted to be in Los Angeles for the sitcom pilot season rather than accept the bit part I was offered. Oh, well it didn't seem to damage the long-term careers of Andrew McCarthy, Kim Cattrall or James Spader.

★ *Off-Beat* (1986). Poor Judge Reinhold was supposed to transition from being a *Beverly Hills Cop* sidekick to a fully-fledged star with this wacky police caper co-starring Meg Tilly. It didn't work and this is one of the most forgettable films in history. My two scenes (both with Judge in a set representing a seedy Times Square lavatory, where I was playing a male prostitute) were excised altogether. At the time, I assumed it was because Judge had been uncomfortable playing the gay aspect of the scenes but when I finally saw the final version in the (very empty) cinema, I noticed that entire characters and storylines had been removed in what was obviously a desperate attempt to hastily rewrite a patently bad premise and script. Something tells me John Turturro, Harvey Keitel and Joe Mantegna have all erased this one from their résumés, too!

★ *Seize the Day* (1986). A decade before Robin Williams told students to '*carpe diem* (seize the day)' in *Dead Poets Society*, he was clowning around on the set of this hard-to-find but well-reviewed movie based on Saul Bellow's book. I've actually never seen it and if it ever did make it into the cinemas, it came and went when I was busy doing something else! I played a runner on the floor of the New York Stock Exchange—essentially a featured extra. I remember meeting Robin and thinking of him only as the goofy guy from the TV show *Mork & Mindy*. He was a real card on the set and I remember what an energetic, obsessive compulsive comedian he was, even in the midst of making this very heavy drama. I've interviewed him twice in recent years and always mention this film to him and he obviously has fond memories and deep affection for it. Maybe I should rent it?

★*Ragazzo di New York* (*The Boy from New York*) (1987). An Italian film and an unintelligible mess about a young pop star trying to make it in the Big Apple. An easier feat than making it through this movie! Never saw it and I hope no one else did, either!

★*84 Charing Cross Road* (1987). This is a sweet movie based on a play of the same name. Sir Anthony Hopkins, Dame Judi Dench and the sublime Anne Bancroft starred in this classy, romantic drama that spanned the decades-long correspondence between two very different people. In one scene, Bancroft's character finds herself swept up in a 1960s university demonstration and I was cast as the leader of a student union. How cool, I thought, to be in a scene with the brilliant Oscar winner and wear a groovy period orange turtleneck. All that was required of me was to shout protest chants while some smoke bombs went off around us in the melee. Then I helped another person carry an injured body (played by a dummy) down the university steps. Upon reaching the bottom, we'd put down the stretcher and be pushed into a paddy wagon with Anne and several other protestors. Sounds easy enough—until you're asked to do it a dozen times. That stretcher got heavy fast, the air thick with smoke and Ms Bancroft soon lost her patience after about the sixth time she and I were shoved into the police vehicle. Well, it was an interesting day, a good workout and decent pay. All you can see of me now is some flashes of my orange sweater through the smoke, struggling with the stretcher.

★*Ishtar* (1987). Hailed by many critics as the worst movie in the history of motion pictures, the title itself has become Hollywood slang for 'big budget bomb!' Warren Beatty and Dustin Hoffman teamed up with director Elaine May for what was touted to be one of the biggest comedies ever made. It was received as a disaster on every level, although every time I happen across it on TV, I can't help but think that it was the high expectations that did the most damage in the end. As far as I was concerned, I was just thrilled to be working on a film set with these heavy-hitters and—bonus—I even got a free crew-cut, since I was playing Private Skotch, one of several military personnel stationed in the Middle East. I had three whole lines in the big finale scene and three whole days of gainful employment (keeping the shpritz bottle at bay for a while). By the time I saw the edited version at the movies, all that existed were three shots of me reacting. I'd fallen victim to the famous cutting room floor syndrome. Well, there's a reason we say, 'That's showbiz'. And better to leave 'em wanting more than have 'em be sick of me, right!? At least I have the deliciously dubious distinction of being in the World's Worst Movie.

★ *Martial Arts Hospital Drama* (199-something). I have absolutely no clue what this movie was titled or even the plot of it. I think 'martial arts hospital drama' says it all. I was struggling to get started in Los Angeles, and living in a little studio apartment in a building that was sort of a low-rent version of *Melrose Place*. During the riots, I'd had a plumbing problem late at night, but it wasn't safe to go out to the 24-hour supermarket and buy a plunger, so I went knocking on the door of my downstairs neighbor, JD Disalvatore. She not only let me borrow her plunger (a very personal household accoutrement to be lending out), but a lifelong friendship was born and she called on me for this flick when she was hired to be the assistant director. I played a snarky insurance agent who launches an investigation into some stolen diamonds. One of my lines was something about 'finding diamonds in his bowels', which could explain why we were shooting in a very creepy old abandoned medical centre, but I never did understand why all that kung-fu fighting was going on in a hospital. Maybe it was financed out of Asia? All I know is I'm glad it's never turned up anywhere…I'm sure there was no way I could rise above the material. Talk about needing a plunger.

Once I became known around Hollywood as an entertainment reporter, that is exactly what I got hired to play, as an actor.

★*Puzzled* (1997). Bryce Johnson, Susan Sullivan, and Dana Ashbrook starred in this romantic comedy, which I've never seen. All I know is that I appeared in a scene toward the end, commentating on some star-studded event as if it were as relevant as the Academy Awards. If you ever catch it, let me know how I did!

★*Easy* (2003). A well-reviewed film starring Emily Deschanel and *Lost*'s Naveen Andrews, I had only one day of shooting in front of an industrial building that was standing in for a hospital. Playing a TV news reporter doing a story on someone's suicide attempt, I was the only actor in the scene so, surrounded by the whole production crew, I felt rather important. The writer/director, a nice lady named Jane Weinstock, knew that I was a professional journalist so she was very amenable to my tweaking the dialogue to sound more accurately newsy. A lot of the tech guys who didn't know my *real* job couldn't believe that I could come off as such a convincing newsman. I think on-air news folks should always be cast in parts like this if the director wants true authenticity. Clips of my 'report' were then going to be playing on televisions in other scenes with the rest of the cast. Unfortunately, Jane later informed me that a post-production edit cut my part out entirely. Alas. At least when I run into Naveen at press events, I get to remind him that we share a motion picture credit…

My first Los Angeles TV gig was in 1991 on the sitcom *Anything But Love*, starring Jamie Lee Curtis and Richard Lewis. It was a flashback episode called 'A Tale of Two Kiddies' and I played a teenage version of Lewis' character, Marty Gold. I knew that my height, big eyes and long, mullet hairstyle were behind them casting me as young Richard, but nonetheless I was excited to arrive on the famous Fox studios lot and find my way to my very own trailer. I wish I could say that the stars had been kind and fun to work with, but they actually made it a very uncomfortable and jittery day for me. I was happy to take the money and run. It was definitely *not* an upbeat work environment, even though the show itself enjoyed three and a half seasons. Jamie Lee and Richard seem to have grown up a lot since then and are both pretty cool players on the current showbiz scene…she as a sort of an 'elder stateswoman', children's advocate and author and he on the stand up circuit and recurring on the hysterical, quirky cable hit *Curb Your Enthusiasm*. Whenever I bump into him he very kindly concedes that I should never have gotten the part as Teen Marty because I was 'way too pretty to be him'.

I'm frequently asked for advice from young hopefuls. As I mentioned in my opening chapter, there are no hard and fast do's and don'ts, but I'll try to address these for you in broad strokes…just in case you or a loved one decides to give a career in showbiz a try.

Do I need to be in the Screen Actors Guild? No. There is plenty of non-union work out there (in fact, it's often easier to book) while you build up your résumé and acting chops. Sooner or later, you may be offered a role in a professional, union production that will require your membership. Whichever one you join first will then be known as your 'parent union'.

How do I find a good agent? When starting out, it's tempting to sign with the first agent who expresses an interest. However, I have always found great success in freelancing, and there is no reason to commit yourself to one particular representative unless you like and trust that person completely. Remember: your agent works for *you*! No reputable agent or manager will ever ask you for money up front. Often, the only way to be seen by casting directors is through an agent's submission, so seek out opportunities such as performance showcases that will allow you to meet agents and show off your skills.

How long will it take me to land my first job? There's no sure-fire answer to this. Some actors get lucky right away, but that's not the norm. This is a business full of rejection…especially the younger you are (the odds get better as you get older and the field of competition dwindles). Consider every 'Don't call us, we'll call you' as another layer of steel in your shield. After all, the princess had to kiss a lot of frogs before finding her prince. If you can't stick with it and remain confident that your break will eventually come, you should save yourself the anxiety and opt for a different career path.

Is it all about who you know? It certainly helps to know people in all ends of the industry. Today's catering waiter is tomorrow's executive producer. So be friendly, reliable and ever-conscientious about establishing a good reputation. Contacts you make from day one almost always pay off in the long run. Don't nag or ask for special treatment/favors from friends in high places. Let them come to you.

I don't have any professional experience on my résumé, should I make stuff up? I never condone lying, but don't let a skimpy curriculum vitae stop you from making an interesting presentation about your talents. Keep it simple, clean, easy to read and honest. If you've only performed in school plays and/or community plays, just list the production titles and your roles. If someone in a position to hire you wants to know more, you'll then have the opportunity to go into more detail.

What kind of headshots get you noticed? This is subjective, but don't be afraid to ask your peers to see their portfolios and also to recommend photographers. There are definite trends in headshots, so look through trade publications for what's current. Don't strike a pose. Always be yourself—at the end of the day, that's all you can sustain and any career longevity is going to be based on your own unique self. Agents and other professionals like to be made to feel important and knowledgeable, so why not ask them for advice, too?

Do I have to take acting classes? It is always a good idea to hone your craft, so the answer is definitely yes. It's also a great way to meet other people in your industry and network. If you're musically inclined, keep up with voice, speech and movement/dance classes, too. The more skills you possess, the more you increase your odds of booking jobs.

Do I have to wait on tables until my big break? Well, you have to do *something* to pay the bills until you sign that first contract, and honest work never hurt anybody. And who knows, you might just serve Steven Spielberg one day and he'll see some spark in you that could land you your big break. It's always prudent to cultivate all your skills and continue your education so you not only have career options to fall back on, but you will be a more well-rounded and interesting person and performer. Even Keira Knightley, with all her fame and fortune, understands that she should have something more to her life than simply being a movie star. She is planning to go to university for an entirely different course of study. Jodie Foster famously left her red-hot career as a teen actress to pursue her studies at Yale University…where she even graduated Magna Cum Laude with a degree in Literature, I might add.

★ ★ ★ ★ ★ ★ ★ ★ ★ ★ ★ ★ ★ ★ ★ ★ ★

One of my happiest assignments was to interview 53 teenage grads of the New York Film Academy. They weren't only excited about coming to the big city and getting to see themselves on the big screen, but their intensive course of study instilled in them not only an excited fervor for a career path, but the confidence about beginning relationships they would be able to cultivate and rely on for a lifetime.

★ ★ ★ ★ ★ ★ ★ ★ ★ ★ ★ ★ ★ ★ ★ ★ ★

Is it okay to be nervous? Of course. After all these years, and thousands and thousands of live broadcasts and performances, I *still* get butterflies in my stomach right before they switch me on the air, or I walk out onto a set. You might think that's silly, but one of my first acting coaches, Susan Slavin, taught me to think of those jitters as an indication about how much you truly **care** about doing a good job. So whenever I feel perspiration forming or knees shaking, I try to remember it's all because I'm excited about doing something I love.

That's *my* advice, but I've also had a chat about this with my longtime friend, author and casting director Bonnie Gillespie. She and I started a social mixer for industry folks called 'The Hollywood

Happy Hour', and created a great network of people-helping-people within all walks of the business. Here's what she has to contribute to this conversation about tackling Tinseltown:

What's the most important thing to remember when auditioning for a casting director?

Bonnie: That we want you to be there. We want you to do a great job. We wouldn't have invited you into the room in the first place if we didn't think you had a shot at getting cast in this role. So the whole antagonistic vibe that many actors worry about (that the CD [casting director] is the obstacle between the actor and the role) is ridiculous. We want to see your take on the role, your interpretation, your spin shining through. Never worry about what we're looking for, as you could never know all of the many other factors that are going into our decision-making process for casting your role. Just come in prepared, ready to rock, and then show us what you've got. When you're finished with the read, thank us and leave. You don't score bonus points by being in the room longer than someone else. There are too many variables to consider. You stay on top of your process and let us take care of the rest. If you do good work, you'll get invited back in on the next project. That's how you know you're doing a good job.

Is there such a thing as the casting couch and, if so, how do I avoid it?

Bonnie: I'm sure there is, and I've heard some doozies from the most attractive actors out there about sleazy producers or directors they've encountered. The good news is, most CDs are professionals with many relationships in the industry and we're not looking to score or to manipulate actors with some sexual power trip. We have too many roles to cast on too many projects to risk that sort of behavior. It really is usually at the level above the CD where actors may encounter a casting couch. And the best way to avoid it is to always stay professional, remember that while flirtation is a part of the charm that helps you win the role it's not ever a good idea to let that become a series of mixed signals you're sending. If you are propositioned, simply state that you are not interested in anything other than a professional relationship. Don't ever think that if you just go on a date you'll have a better shot at the role. If they want you to go out with them, it's not about the role anymore. And nothing you do would change that.

What are the essential materials an actor needs to have in his repertoire before making the audition rounds?

Bonnie: Before even submitting on professional projects, actors need the basics: professional headshots, properly formatted résumés, training, and hopefully a good demo reel featuring some of their best work.

Do casting directors like when you follow up on your audition?

Bonnie: Your best feedback is a callback. If I invite you back in for an audition on another project after you've read for me the first time, that's an indication that you're doing a good job and I want to cast you (and eventually we'll find the right role). Ideally, you'll be so busy auditioning that you'll never even have time to think about doing follow-up on your auditions. And really, you shouldn't need to follow up. If we want you to advance further in the process, we'll call you. Otherwise, it's not your role this time. Move on. The best advice is to do your audition and then leave it in the room when you exit. Let it all go. You can't possibly know what is going on in our decision-making process after you audition. And calling us to follow

up isn't going to make it more likely that you get cast. It's simply going to make us think you're not busy enough to be considered a working actor. Instead, you're so desperate to book every single job that you're hounding the CD to try and make sure you get your shot. You got your shot. It was your audition.

I don't have an agent. How do I get a casting director to notice me?

Bonnie: Do good work. We scout plays and showcases. We watch the top videos at websites like FunnyOrDie.com, YouTube.com, and VirtualChannelNetwork.com. We are aware of who is out there making it happen for themselves, without waiting for an agent or manager to represent them and open doors for them. It's a new era, with the internet as the great equalizer for actors. You don't have to even have a SAG (Screen Actors Guild) card in order to produce a hit on a website that turns the heads of every CD and agent in town. Get out there and get to work. We will notice you. And the buzz you'll generate from doing it for yourself will be all the momentum you need. We'll even pick up the phone and help you get meetings with agents, if we're so inspired.

It's your career. Take control of it.

My Favorite Movie Star

I'm constantly asked who is my all-time fave movie star and which is my all-time fave movie. Those are impossible questions to answer...who could possibly narrow the choices down to only one in either category? That is why I find it easiest to just give two simple answers and explain when necessary. That's what this chapter is all about.

★Carol Lynley

The Poseidon Adventure

I could write an entire volume just on those two subjects. In fact, at one point I went so far as to pen a script treatment for a semi-autobiographical film entitled *My Favorite Movie Star*. And I've been imploring Ms Lynley for years to write her memoirs, to no avail. After all, she's known or worked with anyone who's anyone in the twentieth century entertainment industry and it is primarily thanks to my relationship with her that I can almost always win at 'Two Degrees of Nelson Aspen'.

It's a love story that shoots off in a lot of different directions, so I'll endeavor to tell it chronologically. With a few interjections from Carol, herself!

If you're a youngster, you might very well be asking, 'Carol, who?' So let me start off with a sinfully abbreviated biography.

Born in New York City in 1942, fair-haired Carole Ann Jones changed her name to Carol Lynley and began her professional career at the age of ten. She appeared on Broadway, in early television plays and was among the most successful teenage models of her generation, even becoming known world-wide as 'the Coca Cola girl'. After winning a Theater World Award, Hollywood came calling and the studios vied to see who could make her their own important young star. Walt Disney put her in *The Light in the Forest*, Twentieth Century Fox introduced her in the controversial teen-pregnancy drama *Blue Denim* almost simultaneously with the light-hearted family fare, *Holiday for Lovers*. Teen Carol was working alongside film greats such as Kirk Douglas, Rock Hudson, Jane Wyman and Clifton Webb.

Married at 18, a mother at 19 and divorced at 20, Carol's bombshell looks, box office appeal and obvious acting chops landed her a diverse roster of roles in the early 1960s. These ranged from romantic comedy (*Under the Yum Yum Tree* with Jack Lemmon) to drama (*Return to Peyton Place* with Tuesday Weld and Mary Astor) to suspense (*Bunny Lake is Missing* opposite none other than Sir Laurence Olivier). But it was her ensemble work with Irwin 'Master of Disaster' Allen in his unexpected 1972 mega-hit *The Poseidon Adventure*, for which she is best remembered. As Nonnie, the willowy rock singer who crooned *The Morning After* right before the luxury liner was capsized by a massive tidal wave, Carol donned the hottest hot pants in movie history and secured her place among the great action films of all time…starring alongside Shelley Winters, Gene Hackman, Leslie Nielsen and Stella Stevens. Stella may have gotten the best lines, but it was Carol who won the hearts of every male in the audience.

> ★ ★ ★ ★ ★ ★ ★ ★ ★ ★ ★ ★ ★ ★ ★ ★ ★ ★
>
> On the cult of Poseidon, Carol says, 'I can't quite explain it, but it just works. They call it campy, which is true, but there wasn't a bad actor there and it's very human…the action is great. It's about survival which everybody understands and you get drawn to the characters. Even though I played the sappiest one!'
>
> ★ ★ ★ ★ ★ ★ ★ ★ ★ ★ ★ ★ ★ ★ ★ ★ ★ ★

She segued into becoming the most sought-after guest star in 1970s television, with hundreds of appearances on hit shows like *Magnum P.I.*, *The Love Boat*, *Police Woman*, *Charlie's Angels*, *Hart to Hart*, *Kojak* and *Night Gallery*. She also had the distinction of being the most frequent visitor to Ricardo Montalban's *Fantasy Island*. I asked her how she came to do so many episodes of that particular show and she revealed, 'I had to put my daughter through college, so I got lucky—and whenever someone slipped on a banana peel, Aaron Spelling would call me and I'd run right over. Roddy (McDowall, another frequent guest star and lifelong friend of Carol's) would see me in the makeup department and say, "Oh, God, not you again!" I did every fantasy at least five times!'

As is often the case in Hollywood for women over fifty, good parts became more scarce although Carol continues to appear in movies and plays occasionally and is a sought-after panelist and commentator for film retrospectives and festivals. What would be her dream job? 'One where I can lie down and talk endlessly', she laughs. 'What I've always wanted to do is a remake of *Whatever Happened to Baby Jane?* with Tuesday (Weld) but she wouldn't touch it with a ten foot pole. Then I tried with Faye Dunaway, then Carroll Baker. I wanted Roman Polanski to do it.' Who knows, maybe someday.

Okay, so now you know who Carol Lynley is. Hold on to you seats…here we go.

HOLLYWOOD INSIDER
EXPOSED!

You know from my 'Ships Ahoy' chapter that I've always had a thing for maritime disaster stories, so it was only logical that I *begged* my mom to let me see the PG-rated *The Poseidon Adventure* as soon as it hit cinemas. Eight times. As a young actor, I was a quick study at learning dialogue, so before long I could recite every line from the movie (screenplay by Sterling Silliphant) with perfect inflection for each character.

'I saw a young officer on deck the other day. And he looked pretty damned familiar. Even with his clothes on!'

When I'd be splashing around in the pool with my best pal Erik, we were constantly play-acting scenes…swimming through inverted passageways in search of an escape from the sinking ship. And when I'd come up for air, I'd invariably be singing *The Morning After*. Since it was songstress Maureen McGovern who recorded the album version of the Academy Award-winning pop song, I briefly operated under the mistaken assumption that **she** had played Nonnie and was the object of my affection. It wasn't until *MAD* magazine came out with their cartoon spoof 'The Upside-Down Adventure' that I was alerted to the fact that my idol was in fact Carol Lynley.

Carol was already thirty at this point, so there was a lot to catch up on from her two decades-long career. Long before e-bay, I combed through every library, TV guide and memorabilia shop I could find to get my hands on all Carol-related clippings, posters and photos. I was so obsessed I'd even tape record reruns of her movies off the television and transcribe them into script form. My scrapbooks were filling up and my bedroom was rapidly becoming a shared shrine to Carol and The Justice League. A nerd, sure, but a passionately devoted one.

In 1976, my mother got wind of the fact that Carol was starring on Broadway in the romantic comedy *Absurd Person Singular*. It would be my first time seeing a Broadway play…and with CL right on stage before me, no less. This would be the first of many dreams come true in my special kinship with Carol. I remember very little about the show other than the fact that her character was named Eva and she was as gorgeous as I thought she'd be. After the show, Mom and I waited outside for Carol to emerge. It was a gloomy, cold Saturday afternoon but at that moment, the Music Box Theater Stage Door was hallowed ground! (In one of my life's many great ironies that no longer surprise but rather delight me, I'd go on to not only have my first NYC apartment a half-block away from that spot, but have my first Broadway audition on the same stage on which I'd first seen Carol in person. It was to replace Matthew Broderick in *Torch Song Trilogy*, but I didn't get the job…oh, well.)

Mom was poised with her Insta-matic camera and gave me an encouraging shove toward Carol when she finally came outside. I managed to get her to sign two playbills for me before Mom called out for us to 'Smile!' Mom snapped a picture but that flash cube not only didn't turn, but failed to spark any light! It was one of those terrible moments that played out in humiliating slow motion. If I close my eyes now, I can still see that blasted little square bulb locked in eternal, unlit dimness. Then, My Favorite Movie Star sashayed down 45th Street in her suede blazer and mod, purple boots. The snapshot came out from developing as a big, black square with the barely discernible silhouettes of two heads. Nonetheless, it went into my scrapbook with all the other clippings and the newly autographed programmes.

Time passed and my fandom never waned. One night, a year or so later at the dinner table, my father and I were playing our usual post-meal game of multiple choice trivia quizzes. He won that particular night's round and teasingly boasted, 'I can do anything', to which I responded, 'No, you can't. You can't get me a date with Carol Lynley'. Well, if you know my dad, you know that was all the challenge he needed.

The next morning, this country doctor ventured out of his comfort zone and got on the horn to the Screen Actors Guild in an effort to track down Ms Lynley. Before long, he was on the phone with her agents and explained that his young son was an actor who wanted to meet her for lunch at the world-famous, members-only Metropolitan Club in Manhattan (Dad was a member of the Philadelphia Union League Club and was able to finagle some kind of reciprocal access). The agents understandably wanted to meet us first, in case Dad was some nutcase calling in as a prank. So, Mom took me shopping for my first suit—black and white pin stripe—and I played hookey from school to drive into the city with Dad. I was hopeful Carol might be with the agents and I'd get to meet her that day. No such luck. Their official excuse was 'She's hanging out in Australia with David Frost' (the English talk show host whom she was dating at the time), so Dad and I had a very pricey lunch with them in the lavish setting of the dining salon.

★ ★ ★ ★ ★ ★ ★ ★ ★ ★ ★ ★ ★ ★

My usual residence in NYC, the Loew's Regency, is only a block away from the Metropolitan Club. I walk by it often and always think of that special time in my life. The only thing Dad ever asked in return for his loving gift was, 'If you ever have a son, you have to do something like this for him'. What a guy.

★ ★ ★ ★ ★ ★ ★ ★ ★ ★ ★ ★ ★ ★

While I was very sorry not to have had the lunch of my dreams, I was encouraged when they told us that Carol would be happy to oblige our request when she got back to town.

October 12, 1977. Another day off from school and back into the pin stripe suit. Here is exactly how I described the events in an article I wrote for my school newspaper:

At precisely 1pm, three agents entered, all fashionably dressed and business like. My father and I looked at each other in dismay, both thinking that Carol Lynley was merely a fictitious myth whom we would never meet.

Suddenly there was music to my young ears.

'Why, here is Carol now!'

I raised my head and saw a lovely, young-looking beauty bounce into the room. She caught the eyes of all who gazed upon her.

Carol greeted her agents and was then introduced to my father and me. I remained dumbfounded and looked at the stunning creature before me, while she talked casually about Hollywood business with her agents.

Dad, for the sake of time, suggested we adjourn to lunch. Inside the huge dining room, Dad talked business with the agents while I sat at another table, informally chatting with my idol.

Surprisingly, I was very comfortable and at ease. We were both real people with common interests and human problems. For over two hours we discussed our lives and all manner of topics. It was unbelievable.

★ ★ ★ ★ ★ ★ ★ ★ ★ ★ ★ ★ ★ ★ ★

Carol says, 'I remember it very vividly. I had never been to the Metropolitan Club. My agent said, "You really gotta see this!" I lived nearby and it was just great. I saw this bushy-haired little boy, very well versed on film and the entertainment world even at that age and I thought, Wow, the kid's on fire! And it was fun. I was impressed with Nelson's knowledge of show business, 'cause I'd been doing it since I was 10, so I was pretty savvy myself'.

★ ★ ★ ★ ★ ★ ★ ★ ★ ★ ★ ★ ★ ★ ★

Who could have known this would have kicked off a lifelong relationship with so many long, chatty lunches!? I showed her my scrapbooks and

she remarked, 'You've got more on me than my own mother!'

Of course, I wasn't going to risk another encounter with an uncooperative flash bulb, so I handed Dad the Polaroid camera and we had a brief photo session.

I really expected that to be the end of the story. Wish fulfilled. But Fate was far from finished with Carol and me.

Since everyone in my life was well aware of my fanaticism for CL, I'd often get calls from friends who'd spot her out and about during the years we both lived in the same city. I ran into her once on the street and said, 'I'm the kid from the Metropolitan Club', and she said, 'Wow, you grew up!' Another time I saw her jogging in Central Park with her dog, but I didn't bother her. (I know how I hate to have my runs interrupted.)

Our paths wouldn't cross again until the mid 1990s when I was living in LA and, not surprisingly, it was good ole *The Poseidon Adventure* that reunited us. Carol, Stella and costume designer Paul Zastupnevich were appearing at a screening party at a revival house in Santa Monica. I got a group of friends together armed with items from my Carol collection to be autographed and away we went. Not only was it fun to see the movie again on the big screen, it was a great chance to reconnect with CL, albeit briefly. I also got to have my first encounter with the cult of Poseidon—a cadre of devoted fans who made my own interest pale in comparison! I challenge any Trekkies, *Star Wars* geeks or Rocky Horror lip-synchers to match the Poseidon Posse!

Flash forward to 1997. Now the fun really begins.

I was hosting a live, daily celebrity chat show, *Nelson's World*, for the Microsoft Network. It was a groundbreaking concept, if not a little ahead of its time: a one-hour nightly cyber-chat broadcast to an online audience who could contribute questions and comments from their own computers. I was like the Larry King of the internet. Thanks to the coffers of MSN, talent bookers provided me with great guests and it was an invaluable training experience for me as a live, in-depth interviewer. Every night I'd get to have a very intimate hour of chat with greats like Rod Steiger, Edward James Olmos, John Woo, Esai Morales, Carroll Baker, Jill Hennessey, Julia Sweeney, John Schneider, Mink Stole, Pat Boone and many, many others.

> ✫ ✫ ✫ ✫ ✫ ✫ ✫ ✫ ✫ ✫ ✫ ✫ ✫ ✫ ✫ ✫ ✫
>
> It was on *Nelson's World* that gregarious Erik Estrada, forever known as Ponch from the popular *CHiPs* series, told me about the contents inside the locket he always wears around his neck: his son's post-circumcision foreskin. Umm, after my stomach settled I decided maybe it wasn't all that weird…my mom still keeps my baby teeth in a jewelry box. Maybe it was just a case of TMI (too much information) for public consumption. Henry 'The Fonz' Winkler spontaneously confessed he doesn't know how to ride a motorcycle and that the one time he tried it on *Happy Days*, 'I nearly killed the sound man'. Lucie Arnaz was leggy and lovely with beautiful green eyes, and I just couldn't figure out why she looks like neither of her parents…maybe she's more Mertz than Ricardo, if you know what I mean.
>
> ✫ ✫ ✫ ✫ ✫ ✫ ✫ ✫ ✫ ✫ ✫ ✫ ✫ ✫ ✫ ✫ ✫

My only request was that they book My Favorite Movie Star. Boy, was I ever excited and nervous when they told me it was all arranged. No-frills Carol refused the Microsoft car service and drove herself to the studio. She was still beautiful and even more friendly and playful than I remembered. We had a great *Nelson's World* interview. At the end of the show, she asked me (on the air) to accompany her to a *Poseidon* screening at the prestigious American Film Institute, where its director, the esteemed Ronald Neame, was being honored. Naturally, I accepted, and will forever be indebted to Microsoft for letting us have a limousine for the night. I was driving a ridiculously large, open-air Jeep at the time…it would not have been the appropriate coach for this fairytale outing.

I not only got to escort Carol, but I started cherished relationships with director Neame and cast members Stella Stevens, Roddy McDowall, Ernest Borgnine, Pamela Sue Martin, Red Buttons and Irwin Allen's widow, Sheila. I was especially bemused when many people assumed I was Eric Shea, an actor from the film who's about my age. He hadn't shown up for the reunion, so it was only natural to be mistaken for him. More than once Carol played along and joked, 'Come on, little Eric'.

I remember sitting between Roddy and Carol during the film…and when his character perished onscreen, plunging down an exploding shaft, he waved vigorously and called out 'Bye bye', which elicited a lot of chuckles. He also managed to squeeze my thigh a few times, but I'm sure he didn't think I was little Eric.

Riding in the elevator with the cast afterwards, I couldn't believe my ears when Roddy asked Carol, 'What was the name of that awful movie we did with Myrna Loy?' 'I don't remember', she answered. I couldn't hold my tongue, especially considering the setting. '*The Elevator*', I prompted. That got a good laugh.

After 186 episodes, *Nelson's World* was cancelled. For the series finale, I requested Carol to be my last guest. She brought me a bottle of wine with a card that read, 'Here's to Nelson's UNIVERSE!' Yes, it's in my scrapbook.

Three months later, Carol called and asked me if I'd like to be her date to The Night of 100 Stars, a celeb-studded Oscar night party at the Beverly Hills Hotel. I immediately accepted and then ran out to rent a tuxedo. I was still driving that crazy Jeep, so I arranged to rent a Mercedes sedan, so I could drive her in style, but when I showed up to retrieve the car…they'd already given it to another customer. The only thing they had left was an enormous gold Cadillac. I was worried I'd look like a pimp, but Carol, always easy going, thought it was great. 'It looks like a giant Oscar', she observed.

We went to that party two years in a row and coincidentally on the third year, I couldn't accept because I had to report from their red carpet. When Carol arrived and had to pass by me on the way in to the hotel, she said on camera, 'This isn't right. You should be on *this* side of the ropes'. Loved her for that.

So by now, I was pals with My Favorite Movie Star. We still enjoy lingering lunches at Spago, dinner parties at my house whenever my folks come to town and sipping wine on her beach house balcony. One memorable Thanksgiving holiday Carol got to carve the turkey… her grandfather was a butcher and taught her how to wield a knife (although if you have any doubts, check out her performance as a deranged killer in 1969's *Once You Kiss A Stranger*).

We've gone to Canada for a film festival and ridden the Maid of the Mist under Niagara Falls (resisting the urge to sing *The Morning After*). I visited her on the set of her movie, *Vic*, and met her young director, Sage Stallone (Sylvester's son), who impressed us both.

When I staged a reading for a screenplay I'd written, *The Closest of Strangers*, Carol played the leading role and blew everyone away. Being on stage with her was another one of those unreal dream moments for me. Interesting: Joan Van Ark was in the audience, considering developing the script as a TV movie for herself. She once told me that her most famous role, Val Ewing on *Knot's Landing*, had originally been offered to CL by her pal, Larry Hagman. But Carol had been unavailable at the time, so Joan stepped in. Another big break for an actress was Catherine Deneuve's starring in Roman Polanski's 1965 masterpiece, *Repulsion*, when Carol couldn't do it. In tribute, Polanski named the character Deneuve played, 'Carole'.

When Wolfgang Petersen's 2006 remake, *Poseidon*, hit theaters, I interviewed not only him and the cast, but also Carol to get some

reflections on the original. 'It's the ship that refuses to sink. It just does not go away', she observed. She was also glad they had created all new characters to imperil rather than recast the ones from the first picture. 'I don't think I'd want to see myself thirty years younger', she laughed. For the record, Stacy 'Fergie' Ferguson was cast as the requisite blonde shipboard songstress. Mercifully, she only had to sing, sway her hips and was washed away early on.

> I asked CL which of today's crop of stars compared to those of yesteryear. She said, 'There are a lot of good ones out there and a lot of them who have *faces*. Daniel Day-Lewis, Keira Knightley, Reese Witherspoon. For a while, it was all cookie-cutter, but Keira has a face and talent behind it. Johnny Depp? Please, be still my heart!'

Here's a funny story that happened not too long ago. The Hollywood Wax Museum was going out of business and they were holding an online auction of their vast collection of dummies. From their *Poseidon* display were figures of Ernest Borgnine, Stella Stevens, Red Buttons and CL. She'd told me before how creeped out she'd been by a lifelike replica and recalled being measured for it, back in 1972 (I suppose it would be a bit like having a Dorian Gray portrait in the attic?). But I simply couldn't stand the thought of her wax figure falling into the hands of someone from the Poseidon Posse who'd most likely hang it upside-down from their bedroom ceiling in some sort of tribute.

So I bid on it. And I bid high. I was determined I'd get it…even though I couldn't conceive of how I'd ever get it home, let alone what I'd do with it once I got it there. In the final nail-biting seconds of the auction, I mouse-clicked one more giant bid and an auto-generated response burst on the screen to inform me, 'Congratulations! You won!' I was euphoric. For a second. Then up popped my invoice…for the Red Buttons wax figure! I panicked. Had I just bid more than a mortgage payment on a ratty old Red Button life-sized wax statue?

I immediately telephoned the museum. The good news was, they'd been having glitches with their server and would not hold me liable for the purchase of Mr Buttons. The bad news was, someone else would get their hands on Nonnie.

CL and I are both unapologetic morning persons, so we often phone each other in the wee hours. 'You're the only other person I know who'll be up now', we start out saying. She always has insightful comments, an amusing tale or helpful advice…whether it's personal or professional. We have a lot more in common, too. She can be a bit of a loner, an avid reader…she makes a mean pesto sauce, flirts effortlessly and is a dog lover.

So now we're like family, me and My Favorite Movie Star. But every once in a while, when she tells an offhand anecdote about her friendships with Fred Astaire or Judy Garland…or some romantic story involving Oliver Reed, Glenn Ford or Frank Sinatra, I can't help but get a little star struck.

✯ ✯ ✯ ✯ ✯ ✯ ✯ ✯ ✯ ✯ ✯ ✯ ✯ ✯ ✯

> On the subject of dating some of the world's most famous men, I once asked Carol if there was any she'd classify as 'the love of her life'. She responded: 'All of them! I've always hung out with intelligent, interesting guys. Seventeen years with David Frost…hey, I have a tendency to stick around a while. I don't go into things lightly. They are not 'easy' fellows, but very charismatic and talented'.

✯ ✯ ✯ ✯ ✯ ✯ ✯ ✯ ✯ ✯ ✯ ✯ ✯ ✯ ✯

Marathon Mania

Dateline: Honolulu. Pearl Harbor Day, December 7, 2001. 'A day that will live in infamy.' Well, certainly for me.

That was the where/when I ran my first marathon. An event 26.2 miles (42.6 kilometers) in length that has so consumed my life that it earns its own chapter here. In fact, my identity as a 'marathon freak' could easily fill as many books as it has filled my annual sports journals, so I'll try to be concise by limiting this to an event-by-event recounting and omit the 10 kilometers and half-marathons.

Oprah, Will Ferrell, Katie Holmes, Sean Combs, Alexandra Paul, David James Elliott, Billy Baldwin and even George W. Bush may be more famous racers, but no-one is more passionate than I! In fact, I'm vigorously trying to draft Sherry Stringfield and Seann William Scott to train with me.

In 2006, I was invited to join the inaugural, elite Snickers Marathon Team and was one of their 215 sponsored runners and triathletes for the 2-year program. If you'd told me when I was a roly-poly adolescent that I'd grow up to be a runner, I wouldn't have believed you. 'The journey of a thousand miles begins with a single step', and my first step was in the direction of the beautiful Hawaiian islands...

✯ ✯

The third time I interviewed Will Ferrell was the best, because by then we were old buddies (it pays to do goofy things to make an impression: I wore all my marathon medals at our first meeting!). It really was as if we picked up our conversation where we'd left off a few months earlier and we started gabbing about our own memories of the 1970s. I told him, 'For me it was all *Partridge Family* and *Poseidon Adventure*, *Brady Bunch* and Billy Joel'. His eyes lit up at the mention of the *Partridge Family* and he especially remembered Susan Dey's Laurie Partridge character fondly. In fact, he said that one time he came home late and got into trouble with his mom who proceeded to give him his choice of punishment: a spanking or missing that sitcom. He opted for the spanking, and I suggested he might want to consider what it might have been like for Laurie to administer the spanking. That raised his eyebrows and got him thinking!)

✯ ✯

#1. Honolulu Marathon. 2001. 4:51:31.

I was picking up headshots from a photo duplication shop in Hollywood and, while waiting for the clerk, leafed through a brochure on the counter display. 'Train for and Run a Marathon in 6 Months!' How is that possible, I wondered? I was fit from aerobics, but knew little about the sport of distance running. 'Notice you never see anyone running and smiling at the same time', my mom once observed. But I couldn't help but be intrigued by the idea of learning how to accomplish such a feat. Plus, what a great way to stay fit…culminating in a trip to Hawaii? Count me in. I registered immediately, figuring the commitment alone would keep me motivated. The training program was in tandem with fundraising for AIDS Project Los Angeles (APLA), which provides services for people living with HIV/AIDS, so it certainly seemed like a win/win deal.

HOLLYWOOD INSIDER EXPOSED!

✫ ✫ ✫ ✫ ✫ ✫ ✫ ✫ ✫ ✫ ✫ ✫

I believe in karma, so it's great to choose racing events that benefit causes I support. Because of my work in the public eye, I also think it's important for me to have a designated charity so when people want to support something that has a personal meaning to *me*, I can direct them appropriately.

✫ ✫ ✫ ✫ ✫ ✫ ✫ ✫ ✫ ✫ ✫ ✫

I gravitated immediately to the rigors of training. I loved the discipline it required, and charting my progress certainly appealed to my obsessive-compulsive tendencies. Having worked in the gym biz with so many fit friends, this structured agenda provided me with an entirely new community of health-fanatical peers. Six months later, I'd not only raised thousands of dollars for people who benefited from APLA, I'd conditioned myself to run up and down the Diamond Head volcano and be awarded my first Finisher's Medal. I may have been over-zealous in my carbo-loading and gained twelve pounds (almost a full stone) in the process…but I was a Marathoner, and I was hooked. From here on in, I proudly identified myself as A Runner.

#2. Los Angeles Marathon. 2002. 5:08:11.

Not quite recovered from my first one, but enthusiastic enough to make a stab at a second, I ran my local LA marathon less than three months later. I wish I could say the route showed off the best my adopted homeland has to offer, but in an attempt to attract maximum entrants/commerce, the Race Director's choice of courses snaked primarily through some of our flattest and most unattractive areas of town. Combined with a late start-time and the subsequent overhead sun, it was a less than perfect race. Still, it was very exciting and fun to pass on foot what would ordinarily be seen from behind the windshield of my car. Bonus: Another race to benefit APLA.

#3. Honolulu Marathon. 2002. 4:32:52.

A personal best. Back in Hawaii…more dough raised for APLA and another medal to hang on my office curtain rod. Aloha, baby.

#4. Los Angeles Marathon. 2003. 4:28:35.

A new personal best. Okay, I know I complained about the course last year, but how could I resist an event right in my own back yard?

#5. Honolulu Marathon. 2003. 4:47:55.

Back again. I'd established a little pattern. Overconfident, I landed in Waikiki a couple of days early and over-indulged in Mai-Tais and learned a big lesson when I paid for it on race day. At least I had a long weekend of sun, surf and sand…and helped out my charity with more money raised.

In 2004, I ran a half-marathon and plenty of 10 kilometers, but a busy work schedule and some personal challenges kept me off the road. It was amazing how much I missed it. So when I welcomed in the New Year 2005, I also renewed my commitment and resolve to the sport of distance running.

#6. Los Angeles Marathon. 2005. 4:14:01.

Back on the road…and with another personal best, to boot. Just the incentive I needed. That got me to launch into a new series of 5 kilometer, 10 kilometer and half-marathons that saw a burst of PRs (personal records) and a closet full of commemorative T-shirts that would eventually be turned into a quilt.

#7. St. Jude Memphis Marathon. 2005. 4:11:39.

I shaved off enough time for another personal best, but this race experience was my best yet and would have been worth a million dollars regardless of my finish time. Not only did I meet some lovely new friends from Tennessee and get to see their beautiful city up close on foot, I got to raise money for and learn about the amazing St. Jude Children's Hospital, which I'm proud to promote for its breakthrough science, loving care and inspiring patients and staff. It's easy to understand why so many stars like Jennifer Aniston and Robin Williams support this fine hospital's great work.

#8. Los Angeles Marathon. 2006. 4:13:37.

Eight is my lucky number, so I figured 'What the heck?' and tried LA once more. However, the crazy and overcrowded event (26,000+) and brutal heat combined to make me vow 'Never again!'

#9. Florence Marathon. 2006. 4:22:11.

After my great joy of discovering the wonders of Memphis through racing and some memorable running tours of Sydney and Dublin, I decided that 'destination racing' was how I wanted to approach my future marathon'ing. I revisited my old mates at APLA and registered for their Firenze, Italia, program. (I'd trained for and fundraised for their involvement in the New Orleans Mardi Gras Marathon but unfortunately it wound up conflicting with my biggest work day of the year: The Academy Awards.) Florence was a great decision…I reunited with old friends and made many new ones, with the special bonus of spending time in the beautiful medieval city and its outskirts at Villa Bertini. Running on cobblestones among hundreds of pushy

European runners and all the diesel exhaust fumes might not have been ideal, but the vacation was *molto bene*!

#10. D.C. National Marathon. 2007. 4:03:46.

Not bad for an old fart: another personal best and an admittedly sweet victory in besting the athletic mayor of the city, Adrian Fenty, who was running with an entourage of bodyguards and news cameras. What made this wet, chilly morning extra special is that my niece, Page Ann, ran the first half with me. No-one else among the Aspens seems to understand my passion for distance running (in fact, the words 'you must be nuts' are often heard at clan gatherings) and we don't spend nearly enough time together, so this was a real treat. Not only did I get a tour of our nation's beautiful, scenic capital, it was an excuse for a family reunion with my own cheering section waiting for me at the finish line that reduced me to tears.

#11. San Francisco Marathon. 2007. 4:15:55.

This one was kind of an impulse. I decided I had the itch for a mid-year event and it was a commutable travel distance from LA. In spite of several previous visits, I'd never really understood the passionate enthusiasm for 'The City by the Bay', so I figured checking it out first-hand from a runner's POV would solve the mystery for me. I had a ball. I even bumped into my buddy Marlin while crossing the famous Golden Gate Bridge and we ran together for a while. I also found it happily remarkable that my new running-specific trainer, Charlayne Barger, with whom I'd been diligently working bi-weekly for several months, had proven herself worth every ounce of effort…

I had virtually no stiffness, soreness or recovery down-time. You know what that means…

★ ★ ★ ★ ★ ★ ★ ★ ★ ★ ★

> My last long-term relationship ended when my partner had a midlife meltdown, so when I entered into my forties, I was determined not to follow suit. That's when I opted for midlife *makeover* and got into the best shape of my life. Sure beats making an ass of yourself with a bad dye job, an age-inappropriate date and a cherry-red convertible!

★ ★ ★ ★ ★ ★ ★ ★ ★ ★ ★

#12. Catalina Eco-Marathon. 2007. 4:41:30.

Coming out of San Fran feeling fit enough to increase my pattern of twice-yearly to thrice, I impulsively signed up for this inaugural racing event. Only in hindsight can I say that I'm glad I did. 26+ miles on trails is an entirely different experience from a traditional, paved course! My decision to register coincided with seeing so many of my peers fall victim to mid-life crises that I decided to train rigorously for this off-road challenge which was being touted as one of the most difficult in the world. That claim turned out not to be an exaggeration. The seemingly sadistic route of tough terrain felled 66 entrants before they could finish! The natural beauty of Catalina Island was almost as awe inspiring to me as was the unexpected opportunity to run about 12 kilometers with my sports guru, Dean Karnazes (The Ultra Marathon Man). It was grueling, for sure, but where else could you go trotting past a herd of buffalo in their natural habitat? (I admit to being nervous about wearing red shorts in front of those burly beasts, even if I'd been assured they wouldn't charge.) Crossing the finish line was one of my proudest marathon accomplishments, albeit not one I'm feeling compelled to repeat…at least not yet.

☆ ☆ ☆ ☆ ☆ ☆ ☆ ☆ ☆ ☆ ☆ ☆ ☆ ☆ ☆ ☆ ☆

Running with Dean was such a great experience for me, just as it was to host a post-screening Q&A panel with him, when his documentary premiered. I love that I get so many of those up-close-and-personal moments with people who inspire me. I once asked him: 'If you could run through Hollywood with a celebrity from the showbiz or sporting world, who would it be?' He replied, 'Lance Armstrong, as he's someone I very much admire and I know that he's a gifted runner. Governor Schwarzenegger, too, as he has the power to allocate more funding for health and fitness programs in California'. Actor Jake Gyllenhaal also counts Lance among his most motivating celebrity pals. He loved it when I asked him about their 'bromance', as a welcome distraction from more movie biz chatter. He also appreciated the gift of some of my preferred energy bars for his next tour-de-Lance cycling expedition. I couldn't get him to admit he was planning to play Lance in a biopic, but I still think it could happen.

☆ ☆ ☆ ☆ ☆ ☆ ☆ ☆ ☆ ☆ ☆ ☆ ☆ ☆ ☆ ☆ ☆

#13. Bermuda International Marathon. 2008. 4:17:51.

Maybe my finishing time wasn't spectacular, but the memories made over this January weekend certainly were. After a lifetime of family visits to this magical island colony, I hadn't counted on ever being back there again until I discovered that the race coincided with my Dad's 83rd birthday. In spite of their infirmities, I convinced my parents to make the trip for a combo-celebration. My best friend, Glenn, decided to join us (even pulling some strings to have us all upgraded to suites. SWEET is right). Gale-force winds, heat, 80-plus per cent humidity and relentless, undulating hills made it a grueling feat. Glenn ran the half-marathon portion, while I toughed out the full 26.2 miles. I enjoy smaller events and that was one consolation:

there were only 79 entrants (I finished 33rd). Seeing Mother, Dad and Glenn cheering me on at the finish line is now one of my most cherished life memories. Another unexpected highlight was getting to meet sports legend Kathrine Switzer, who was in attendance for the Race Weekend. Thanks to our mutual Kiwi and running connections, we became fast friends. Her autobiography, *Marathon Woman*, is as charming as she is and chronicles her rise to becoming one of the most revolutionary figures in the world of athletics. What a plus that she also happens to be an energetic and fun gal as well as a role model.

On a sad note, just as I was preparing to settle into some long overdue post-race R&R, the news broke of Heath Ledger's shocking death and I had to depart paradise early to report the story from New York City. News doesn't take a holiday. I spent two solid days shivering on the curb of 421 Broome Street in some hideous winter wear I'd picked up at the airport. How fragile and unpredictable life is, eh? It was certainly a week of extremes for me, and a reminder to carpe diem.

I'm most fortunate that many of my media outlets like *Sunrise*, *GMTV*, *The Afternoon Show* and *Running Times* have welcomed and supported my runner's addiction, so that I can share my excitement and inspiration with comrades all over the world. It's gratifying to receive mail from people who have taken up the healthy pastime or tackled new athletic challenges as a result of learning more about my passion for it all. As a 'dawn patroller', I'm often out there logging my training mileage long before the sun comes up, dodging sprinklers in the last vestiges of moonlight. So if you're ever driving along Rodeo Drive or Sunset Boulevard in the wee hours, please be careful and keep an eye open for the sweaty entertainment reporter chugging along the side of the road.

✯ ✯ ✯ ✯ ✯ ✯ ✯ ✯ ✯ ✯ ✯ ✯ ✯ ✯

I continue to add to my vast collection of racing medals and, while they might not be of much value on the open market, to me they are *priceless*. I have them all dangling from the curtain rods in my office and on breezy days, they become great wind chimes to musically remind me of my time on the tracks and trails.

✯ ✯ ✯ ✯ ✯ ✯ ✯ ✯ ✯ ✯ ✯ ✯ ✯ ✯

I aspire to continue increasing and improving my number of events and racing performances, becoming one of those goofy old geezers you see hoofing along the roadsides. So, stay tuned. My marathon-mania may not be easily explained or understood except by other runners, but I've long said that 'bodies in motion stay in motion', and I intend to keep moving.

✯ ✯ ✯ ✯ ✯ ✯ ✯ ✯ ✯ ✯ ✯ ✯ ✯ ✯

Nelson's Personal Bests in non-marathon events:
2005 Run for the Bay 10k: 45:38
2006 Achievable Foundation 5k: 21:58
2006 Palos Verdes Half-Marathon: 1:47:47
2007 Santa Monica Mountains Trail 9k: 52:14 (1st Place Men 40-44, 9th Overall)

✯ ✯ ✯ ✯ ✯ ✯ ✯ ✯ ✯ ✯ ✯ ✯ ✯ ✯

On The Campaign Trail

A great bonus to the showbiz niche I've carved out over the years is getting to offer up my opinion on a variety of subjects as opposed to having to solely remain silently objective when reporting. As an experienced journalist, I have excellent access to information and a critical eye to report it thoroughly and fairly. But with the extent of the Blog-osphere and the chat dynamic of my TV and radio affiliations, I am regularly called upon to offer up my own take on a variety of subjects, rather than strictly give 'just the facts, ma'am…only the facts'. Not everyone may agree all the time, but we always enjoy the dialogue of good conversation.

With the litany of Hollywood's 'bad kids' antics and misdeeds, I could never hold my tongue. Britney Spears, Lindsay Lohan, Paris Hilton, Tara Reid, Lane Garrison, Keifer Sutherland…I can't just repeatedly state the latest details of their arrests, failed rehabs and other assorted dirty business illustrated with the mug shots du jour. After wagging a disapproving finger for the umpteenth time, 'Uncle Nelson's Campaign to Clean Up Young Hollywood' was born. It was inspiring to see how many people responded. While gossip reporters may revel in the bad behavior of stars, I discovered that it was much healthier all the way around to try and *explain* it or offer up suggestions on how to *fix* it. I'm proud to say I started a bit of a trend and you're seeing more and more positive spin on showbiz news stories every day.

When it came to politics, I generally always steered clear of opining. Even within my own family there are so many differing views on the subject that I found it best to remain neutral…and silent! That's one of the reasons I earned the nickname, 'Switzerland'. But with the deteriorating state of world affairs in modern government (particularly in the USA), by 2007 I was sufficiently frustrated that I wanted to get involved in making a change…not just privately with my vote and contributions, but publicly.

I found that opportunity when my longtime friend, Erin O'Brien, emailed me about a party she was hosting with her husband, James Denton (aka Mike Delfino, the hunky plumber on *Desperate Housewives*). It would be a fundraiser for Democratic Presidential candidate, Senator John Edwards. Rather than being held in a hotel ballroom and serving rubber chicken dinners, this would be an intimate, catered house party. I'd supported the Senator in his 2004 bid for the White House as the Vice President on John Kerry's ticket, so I was excited to RSVP 'yes' and brought along my friend and news colleague, Louise Pennell. She's a brainiac who's also lovely to look at and we always find something to laugh about wherever we go. I had a feeling this event would be interesting on many levels. Jamie was apparently a diehard Republican before supporting JE, so I thought there must be something special about his message and wanted to hear it for myself.

Lou and I rolled up to the Denton's gorgeous hillside home to join them and about 100 others for this unique, casual opportunity to interact with Edwards and his team. He spoke extemporaneously about his plans and ideas on topics ranging from the Middle East to health care to global warming. He was sunburned and casually dressed in a blazer and jeans, having come directly from a farm event in nearby Bakersfield. No hulking Secret Service men or bodyguards lurked around. No metal detectors or strip searches. From impoverished

roots, this self-effacing, self-made multi-millionaire seemed to typify the persona of 'public servant'. He sure didn't *need* to get involved in the dirty business of politicking…he was drawn to it as a way to help improve the state of the country and the world.

> I was once interviewed by a finance reporter from *The Daily Telegraph* in Australia and asked what I considered to be my 'most indulgent purchase'. My response: '…donating to Senator John Edwards' Presidential campaign, which some say is an indulgence. But if I'm not prepared to put my money where my mouth is, politically, then what right do I have to complain about the problems in Government? I'm proud to stand behind my candidate with my voice, my vote, and with my contributions'.

Aside from our host, there was a fair bit of celebrity presence in attendance. *Dharma and Greg* star Mimi Kennedy, very politically active liberal Madeleine Stowe, Jean Smart, Deidre Hall, Marg Helgenberger, William Petersen, Shaun Cassidy, Gary Cole, Ron Rifkin and *Housewives* co-stars Brenda Strong, Nathan Fillion and Teri Hatcher.

At one point when the Senator was addressing the assembled guests, I noticed Teri kicked off her heels and downed the last of her chardonnay while playing relentlessly with her dyed black extensions. She either has a very short attention span or she was backing a different candidate. I have to tell you, she's a lot prettier in person than some of those harsh paparazzi pictures would indicate…but she's also even skinnier. At one point, I thought she'd disappeared, but it turned out someone had just been standing in front of her. She was completely obscured from view by an average-sized fellow.

⋆ ⋆ ⋆ ⋆ ⋆ ⋆ ⋆ ⋆ ⋆ ⋆ ⋆ ⋆ ⋆ ⋆ ⋆ ⋆ ⋆ ⋆ ⋆

Louise Pennell, incidentally, is the daughter of Heather Horwood aka 'The Doris Day of Australia', who was a popular variety artist in the 50s and 60s. Three of my most fond memories of fun times in Tinseltown all involve Heather when she was in town visiting from Melbourne. 1) Box seats at the Hollywood Bowl to hear Etta James in concert, 2) An after-dinner singalong chez moi with the most talented singers I could assemble on the guest list. 3) She joined me onstage when I performed my cabaret show 'Wake Up with Nelson!' and we did an impromptu duet of *Makin' Whoopee*. Attention, Australia: Heather is one of your great National Treasures.

⋆ ⋆ ⋆ ⋆ ⋆ ⋆ ⋆ ⋆ ⋆ ⋆ ⋆ ⋆ ⋆ ⋆ ⋆ ⋆ ⋆ ⋆ ⋆

So back to Edwards. While most showbiz notables were rallying around Democratic contenders Hillary Clinton and Barack Obama, there were still a few pulling for my guy. I got involved in co-hosting the next LA house party fundraiser and, since my Hollywood hacienda could not accommodate the requisite hordes, I teamed up with Ben Stiller and Christine Taylor, Norman Lear, Seth Green and (again) the Dentons to do this at the swanky Beverly Hills manse of A-list *X-Men* director/*Prison Break* producer Brett Ratner. This time, the lovely Mrs Edwards would be in attendance, too. (Which is more than I can say for Ratner, who was an absentee host at his own party.)

Coincidentally, the very next morning I saw Senator Obama at my gym, Equinox. He's a charismatic, likable fellow (Oprah Winfrey is certainly mad about him), but just observing him in the safe haven of a health club made me acutely aware of the basic differences between him and John Edwards. Obama had four burly Secret Service guys posted in the adjacent corridor (protecting him from the private membership or the spinning instructors?) and meandered from machine to machine, never doing anything more grueling than some deltoid reps. Maybe he figures he should be ready to carry the weight of the world on his shoulders. I was intrigued by what he was listening to on his iPod. He was bopping his head around like it was something pretty rhythmic. He might have spent five minutes walking on the treadmill lackadaisically, but I believe you can tell a lot about a person's character by how they work out. Edwards admits to a lifelong running addiction and has completed five marathons. Like me, he also prefers to go solo when he's working out. One of his aides is quoted as saying, 'He's very private about his running. Asking to run with him is like asking to take a shower with him'.

I've noticed that most Australian media (especially *Sunrise*, but I might be biased) has a magnificent ability of presenting their politicians in a very human light without tearing them down in the process. Through them I've tried to look at our contenders in the same context. It's not easy in the US political media circus, but John and Elizabeth Edwards always seemed to rise above the fray.

That's why we were all sent reeling a bit on January 30, 2008 when he announced that he would be ending his presidential bid, after consistently placing third behind the showier competition of (the first viable female candidate) Hillary Clinton and (the first viable African American candidate) Barack Obama. I was actually wearing my 'Edwards 08' sweatshirt when the news was first reported on CNN. By the time these words are published, America still will not have sworn in their next President. So count on me being out there continuing to sing the praises of Senator John Edwards in the meantime. I just hope and trust that he'll remain actively involved in the fight to restore some of the best things Americans have always fought for and believed in.

It's been an interesting and enlightening experience to be a part of a campaign. I've come to believe that it's as important as voting, to be involved, informed and enthusiastic about the candidate of your choice.

The Guy of 100 Lists

Are you old enough to recall the old Go-Go's song, *The Girl of a 100 Lists*? It was about an obsessive-compulsive female who kept track of everything including 'What should I wear?' and 'Who have I kissed?' I know how she felt. I am constantly called upon to make up 'Top Ten' lists of the Most Sexy, Best Dressed, Worst Dressed, Top Earners, Best Actors, Most Overrated, Biggest Tippers, Worst Drivers, Worst Boob Jobs, etcetera. Now that I've explained the caveat to this in the 'My Favorite Movie Star' chapter, I thought I'd go out on a limb and record a few lists here for posterity. Of course I reserve the right to change my mind at any time. Not only is personal opinion highly subjective and subject to revision, it generally has a rapid expiration date given the climate of pop culture.

After *People* magazine named Matt Damon their Sexiest Man Alive for 2007, I scratched my head as I do every year and simply shrugged at the wondrous work of the Hollywood publicists who campaigned for their guys to get the accolades. Joining Matt for top honors were Patrick Dempsey, Ryan Reynolds, Brad Pitt, James McAvoy, Johnny Depp, Dave Annable, Will Smith, Javier Bardem, Shemar Moore, Ben Affleck, Adrian Grenier, and Justin Timberlake. Ho Hum, how convenient that they all had movies, TV shows or albums about to debut. I think my list was much more interesting!

Since the editors were obviously impressed by 'DILFs' why didn't they consider Hugh Jackman, Eric Bana or James Marsden? Among TV types, why not the boffo brothers of *Prison Break*, Dominic Purcell and Wentworth Miller? McDreamy, no. McSteamy (Eric Dane), yes. Ben Affleck? A better pick would have been his kid brother, Casey. They completely omitted sports stars or politicians, so I flipped through my personal Rolodex and tossed in my mate Sydney Swans star Jared Crouch and Senator John Edwards (the guy's in his mid-50s and could give Madonna stiff competition for discovering the Fountain of Youth). But the top title went to Viggo Mortensen. Actor, poet, linguist, photographer, artist, musician and gifted actor…the dude is also approaching the half century mark and is in awesome condition. Did you see the fight scene in *Eastern Promises*?

On the ladies' side of the aisle, America OnLine did an '07 poll on 'TV's Sexiest Women Ever'. What sleazy chat room got its users together to stack the vote Pamela Anderson's way? Speaking of stacked, her runners up were Farrah Fawcett (*Charlie's Angels*), Lynda Carter (*Wonder Woman*), Heather Locklear (*Dynasty*, *Melrose Place*, *TJ Hooker*), Eva Longoria (*Desperate Housewives*), Diana Rigg (*The Avengers*), Barbara Eden (*I Dream of Jeannie*), Katherine Heigl (*Grey's Anatomy*), Catherine Bach (*The Dukes of Hazzard*) and Tina Louise (*Gilligan's Island*), proving the answer to the age-old question of which castaway most guys prefer, Ginger or Mary Ann.

Being a total junkie for nostalgic TV, I reworked that list in the following order. Lynda Carter (*Wonder Woman*) was such perfect casting for the sultry super heroine that Hollywood may never be able to properly fill those red and white boots. Elizabeth Montgomery (*Bewitched*) was spell-binding as both Samantha and her twin cousin minx, Serena. Jaclyn Smith (*Charlie's Angels*) has always been the most stunning of Angels. Who needs Lucy Liu? Betty Rubble (*The Flintstones*) may be a cartoon but come on…she's the most under-appreciated babe in Toon Land! Barbara Eden (*I Dream of Jeannie*) makes me feel like Major Nelson! Susan Dey (*The Partridge Family*) was the teen dream for a lot of guys in the 70s…even when she suffered through braces. In a parallel TV universe, there was her counterpart Maureen McCormick (*The Brady Bunch*), everyone's favorite cheerleader. Beverley Owen (*The Munsters*) only appeared in a few episodes before being replaced by Pat Priest, but she was a stunner. Julie Newmar (*Batman*) was the first Catwoman and a slinky sexpot. Meowww. Rounding it out is my gorgeous gal pal, Mary Kay Adams, who's known in sci-fi circles for her roles on *Babylon 5* and *Star Trek: The Next Generation*, but will always be *Guiding Light*'s 'India Spaulding' in my eyes. As talented and breathtaking as a young Faye Dunaway, MK is also one of the world's most beautiful people where it really counts: on the *inside*.

I chuckled when a gay website unveiled their readership's choices for the celebrities most gays and lesbians would want to date (Daniel Craig and Keira Knightley were the top vote-getters). Isn't that pretty much proof that there's not much difference between gay and straight tastes!

For Best Actor/Actresses, I tried to look objectively at the bodies of work these stars represent. Diversity of roles, consistency of quality and that elusive trait: presence. Here (in no particular order) are the fine folks, past and present, who I think best represent those attributes.

Actors:
- Robert DeNiro
- Russell Crowe
- Matt Damon

HOLLYWOOD INSIDER
EXPOSED!

- Anthony Hopkins
- Leonardo DiCaprio
- Spencer Tracy
- Johnny Depp
- Montgomery Clift
- Cary Grant
- Dustin Hoffman

Actresses:

- Cate Blanchett
- Meryl Streep
- Shirley MacLaine
- Glenn Close
- Judy Garland
- Doris Day
- Julie Andrews
- Jane Fonda
- Joan Crawford
- Natalie Wood

Style Icons:

Jude Law and Beyoncé both spring to mind as being the hottest celebs who constantly misstep when it comes to red carpet attire. I don't ascribe to the belief that stars need to be picture-perfect every time they set foot outdoors, but since nowhere on earth seems to be paparazzi-proof, here are my ten guys and gals who seem to have consistently displayed a clean, confident sense of style during their careers. There's not a Depp or Bonham Carter anywhere nearby! And I adore Sally Kirkland much too much to mention her, either.

- Katharine Hepburn
- Cate Blanchett
- Audrey Hepburn
- Charlize Theron
- Nicole Kidman
- Elizabeth Taylor
- Jamie Foxx
- George Clooney
- Warren Beatty
- David Beckham

✯ ✯ ✯ ✯ ✯ ✯ ✯ ✯ ✯ ✯ ✯ ✯ ✯ ✯ ✯

Just as I am frequently called upon to offer up my Best/Worst Dressed lists, I'm also constantly consulted about an area in which I confess I have almost NO expertise: Fashion! Fortunately I have many designer friends who can help guide me beyond the basic common sense approach I take to good grooming. My talented designer mate Charlie Lapson told me, 'A man should think about building his own image. Rod Stewart is a trendsetter. Will Smith always looks great and Alec Baldwin dresses to suit his size, perfectly. Brad Pitt is a risk-taker. Who else could make dime store accessories with Dolce Gabana work?' Of course, Brad could probably get away with wearing a potato sack…but if he doesn't stop constantly dying his hair, I'm worried it may soon fall out. Oh, who cares…he'll look great bald, too.

✯ ✯ ✯ ✯ ✯ ✯ ✯ ✯ ✯ ✯ ✯ ✯ ✯ ✯ ✯

I remember when Jessica Alba announced her pregnancy, there was a palpable panic among men who had two fears over the news. One, that Alba would lose her 'hot factor'. (If pregnancy did that, how do you explain Heidi Klum, Madonna or Catherine Zeta Jones?) and two, that on some level it meant she was even therefore completely unattainable (as if any average Joe ever had a shot of getting next to Jessica Alba, LOL). Age and change are tough for Hollywood's beautiful people to survive, so here are my Top Ten lists of who's done it with the most style and grace, and who might want to consider an immediate age-appropriate makeover. These unisex rosters also disprove the commonly held notion that men automatically age better than women.

Who Went From Hot to Not!

- Sylvester Stallone
- George Michael
- Ethan Hawke (there's still plenty of time, Ethan. Take a bath and call David Beckham for a tutorial!)
- Mel Gibson
- Tom Cruise
- Mickey Rourke
- Alec Baldwin
- Melanie Griffith
- Faye Dunaway (yikes!)
- Robert Redford (more like the 'Sun-damaged Kid'!)

Who Looks 'Fine with Time!'

- Rob Lowe
- Demi Moore
- George Clooney
- Brad Pitt
- Kim Basinger
- Sophia Loren
- Jon Bon Jovi
- Elle Macpherson

- Tippi Hedren (Melanie's mom; maybe it skips a generation)
- Paul Newman (who knew Butch Cassidy was the lucky one?)

Top Ten Stars Who Are (Even) Better Looking in Person:

- Mandy Moore
- Alicia Keys
- Steve Carell
- Christian Bale
- Cameron Diaz
- Kristin Davis
- Kate Winslet
- Queen Latifah
- Mark Wahlberg
- Anthony Field (the Blue Wiggle)

It seems like everybody in LA has multiple tattoos, a trend I think should be attributed to Cher. Here are my Top Ten Inked Stars:

- Brangelina (too numerous to mention…dozens. Including Angie's arm full of the geographical coordinates of their children's birthplaces; I asked Brad how old his kids would have to be before he'd approve of *their* getting some ink. He was paternally charming in his response: 'I think the ink will come *before* our approval!')
- David Beckham (a vast array, including the names of his wife and kids and a crucifix. At the rate he's going, he'll have full sleeves by the time he's forty).

HOLLYWOOD INSIDER EXPOSED!

- Jessica Alba (a ladybug on neck, lotus flower on wrist and a bow on the small of her back)
- Eva Longoria (star on left wrist, cross on lower back… and something mysterious on her butt cheek)
- Justin Timberlake (cross on shoulder, angel on back, initials on ankles)
- Rhianna (treble cleft and musical note on foot and ankle, Pisces symbol behind ear)
- Jude Law (Beatles lyrics)
- Mark Wahlberg (assorted images on shoulders and neck and cartoon characters Sylvester the cat and Tweety Pie on his ankle)
- Ryan Phillippe (cross on left calf, ladybug on right foot)
- Sir Sean Connery ('Scotland Forever' and 'Mum and Dad' on right arm)

★ ★ ★ ★ ★ ★ ★ ★ ★ ★ ★ ★ ★ ★ ★ ★

In addition to my 'Flash' logo on my right shoulder, there's a Griffin and Roman Numerals on my left, an Aspen leaf on my back and the Sea God Poseidon on my leg. John Mayer may think your body's a wonderland, but mine is a canvas!

★ ★ ★ ★ ★ ★ ★ ★ ★ ★ ★ ★ ★ ★ ★ ★

When it comes to movies, I explained my devotion to *The Poseidon Adventure* and other stories of ships-at-sea, but I think the best way to give you a sampling of my Fave Flicks is to just browse through my DVD collection and tell you which ones I've watched and enjoyed the most. Film scholar Bernard Dick once astutely pointed out, 'There is the film projected *on* the screen and the film projected *from* the screen. The first is the text…the second is the subtext'. These are films that for one reason or another strike me on both levels.

- *The Godfather I* and *II* (I can't think of them as two separate films…they're meant to be seen together)
- *All About Eve*
- *Bonnie & Clyde*
- *Chocolat*
- *The Women* (it's so brilliantly written, directed and performed that you have to keep your remote control handy so you can go back and catch every witticism in between fits of laughter; I'm holding my breath in fear of the new Hollywood remake and hoping it won't happen)
- *East of Eden*
- *Deliverance*
- *Downfall* (German historical interpretation of Hitler's last hours in the bunker, magnificently executed artwork)
- *Fight Club*
- *Frankenstein* (as scary and strangely moving as it was nearly 80 years ago)
- *Gods and Monsters* (why doesn't Brendan Fraser do more drama? He's great)
- *The Manchurian Candidate* (you'll never think of Angela Lansbury the same way again!)
- *Mildred Pierce* (Joan Crawford's greatest working-class melodrama)
- *The Bounty*
- *The Lion in Winter*
- *Saturday Night Fever* (If he'd never done another film, Travolta deserves his star status for this one)
- *Parenthood* (you'll laugh, cry, and want to have a baby!)
- *What's Up Doc?* (I laugh just thinking about this movie. She can sing like an angel, but I love Streisand best when she's funny)

**HOLLYWOOD INSIDER
EXPOSED!**

- *Henry VIII* (Ray Winstone, Helena Bonham Carter and Emily Blunt in this lusty, lavish period piece that is as guilty a pleasure as a juicy romance novel)
- *The Wonderful Horrible Life of Leni Riefenstahl* (fascinating biography of the controversial late filmmaker)
- *Gone with the Wind* and *The Wizard of Oz*, of course, get Honorable Mention. Who doesn't love them!? I'm tempted to keep going…*Orphans of the Storm*, *The Right Stuff*, *Sudden Fear* and *Freaks* are also up there.

★ ★ ★ ★ ★ ★ ★ ★ ★ ★ ★ ★ ★ ★ ★ ★

For the record, there's a three-way tie for Best Handshakes in Hollywood: the firm-gripped Dennis Quaid, kd lang and Matthew Fox.

★ ★ ★ ★ ★ ★ ★ ★ ★ ★ ★ ★ ★ ★ ★ ★

Dishing Up Homemade Fun

In 2004, my first book *Let's Dish Up a Dinner Party! The Ultimate Guide to Entertaining With Style* was released. It may not have been a big bestseller, but it was very exciting to get to share my thoughts and advice on something I enjoy so much…entertaining in my home. *ELLE* magazine named me as one of their 'Good Time Gurus' for the year, alongside the distinguished company of Serena Bass and Martha Stewart, and my subsequent reputation got me a recurring gig on the TV show *Soap Talk* hosted by the lovely Mrs Harry Hamlin aka Lisa 'Lips' Rinna of *Melrose Place* fame.

The downside of suddenly being known as a party planner extraordinaire is that no-one wanted to invite me to their parties, for fear I'd judge them. How silly! And frankly, after the year-plus of research that writing my book entailed, I was burned out on cooking and trying to throw gatherings that would live up to my newly acquired reputation. I had a good year of pizza and Chinese take-away before I started puttering around in the kitchen again.

As I always say, it's less about the menu and more about the atmosphere a good host creates that is key to a successful party. Hosting a social gathering is really not much different from hosting a television show: with careful and thorough preparation, you can skillfully steer the conversation and make all your guests feel comfortable enough to enjoy the experience.

After a decade in my Hollywood hacienda, I've fallen into a nice little routine of seasonal festivities. Here are some of my most cherished rituals you are welcome to adapt for your own enjoyment….

East Coast New Year's Eve

I don't want to stay awake until midnight just because it's December 31…and there are plenty of other folks like me, so that's how this annual event was born. Since the East Coast of the USA is 3 hours ahead of Los Angeles, I invite the gang over at 7pm and at 8:59pm we count down to the other coast's midnight. After a champagne toast and a chorus of *Auld Lang Syne* or *The Morning After*, everybody can hit the road and go on to the next party or call it a night. It's also a good idea to get to your destination before the drunk drivers take over the highways. I always make a giant cauldron of my yummy turkey chili, and bake loaves and loaves of homemade bread. It's a fun way to usher out the old year. Sometimes, we write down our bad habits on a scrap of paper and toss them into the fireplace with the resolution to leave them behind before going into the New Year. If I have a special someone in my life, there's always the option of ringing in the 'real' midnight afterwards…one on one.

Tree Un-Trimming Party

Oh, sure, anyone can have a decorating party, but where is all the help when you have to take the darned things DOWN? That's why the weekend after New Year's, I'll ask a few close friends over for a super-casual late afternoon gathering. Sports on the TV, board games on the coffee table, a big vat of split pea soup on the stove and everyone welcome to wear sweats and drink spicy Bloody Marys. Even if I only have a few extra helping hands to assist with getting the lights and ornaments off the tree, it's much more fun than handling it all alone. Dismantling the tree from its stand and getting it outside for disposal is also easier with help.

Oscar-Night Viewing Party

I'm always working on Oscar night, but I've given plenty of guidance to movie-lovers on how to throw the ultimate soiree for the big night of nights. A strip of red carpet leads to the front door where your formally clad hosts hand you a homemade Oscar ballot for the betting pool (movie DVDs or soundtrack CDs are the prize). If you have some kids willing to play along, have them act as paparazzi and take pics for posterity. Don't forget to have your guests 'autograph' the Guest Book. Plenty of gold stars and movie memorabilia make decorating easy and elegant. And when planning the bar fare, try and come up with some clever spin from the nominee list. I've served 'Leonardo DiCappucinos', 'Hilary's Swanky Sangria' and 'Blood Diamond Bloody Marys'.

Gods and Goddesses

Since I was off to Italy for the marathon, I decided to celebrate the Roman gods…and all the other deities with a springtime costume party. Everyone was instructed to come representing their choice of God or Goddess, be it Roman, Greek, Egyptian—whatever. Of course, I was Poseidon, complete with fish and shells sewn onto my diaphanous robes and a prop Trident to carry but I was overwhelmed by my clever friends and how creative they were. There were plenty of togas, but the most memorable costumes included my friend Louan Gideon as the Hindi 'Ganesh', and she was stunning in her sari…even with a faux trunk and elephant ears! Carol McClure was a cunning

Cleopatra, but no-one could figure out why her hysterical husband Marc was in drag as a teenage girl until someone asked him, 'What are you supposed to be?' and in his best Valley-Girl dialect whined in response, 'Ohhh Goddd!' The hands-down winner, though, was my pal Gena who wore a dress made out of maps and called herself 'Atlas'. Funny! I served Olympian-style decadent foods and found a fabulous harpist to supply the music. Don't let people fool you into thinking they don't like to play dress-up just because they're adults. Give them no alternative and they'll get into the spirit.

Art for Art's Sake

I don't know much about art, but I know what I like and have collected a few special pieces over the years. I am also very lucky to have been given a few excellent oil and photographic works by audience members which hang proudly in my home. My mother is a talented and well-reviewed painter and sculptor and I have several of her original works, as well. So when she decided to pay me one of her all-too-rare visits, I decided to have an Art Party and display all my different treasures. It was a fun and novel way to have friends over to greet my mom and enjoy art-related conversation. Reaffirming that you really can find anything on craigslist.org, I hired a classical guitarist to play and had a contest among my guests to name the untitled mid-century modern oil painting I'd recently bought at auction. Alison Arngrim (better known as 'Nasty Nellie Oleson' from *Little House on the Prairie*), was the winner and took home one of the guitarist's signed CDs as a prize.

Easter Eggs-travaganza

Who doesn't love an Easter Egg Hunt? My guests arrived for Easter dinner, but first were each handed a basket and turned loose in the backyard until they could find the three dozen (plastic) eggs I'd hidden. I always get a kick out of seeing grown-ups getting in touch with their inner-children. Inside each egg I'd placed either a piece of candy or a number which would then correlate to a designated gift, some silly gag gifts from the dollar store and some more special, like candles, potpourri or books.

Tinseltown Trick-or-Treat

When I moved into my house, the last thing I wanted to do on 31 October was leave it! While many folks like to go to the annual freak-fest of the West Hollywood Halloween Parade, I prefer to hang out at home and hand out candy to all the little neighborhood ghosts and goblins. Since that is also the time of year when the weather turns autumnally crisp, I traditionally light the first fire of the year in the fireplace. I invite friends over, new and old, to enjoy the spectacle of all the kids in their costumes and it seems like they grow in numbers every year. To make sure we don't run out of treats, all my guests are instructed not to BYOB, but instead to bring plenty of candy. Costumes are optional for the invitees, but they ARE required to have one seasonal accessory, be it a funny hat, mask or glasses. I usually order in Thai or Indian food and have a spooky old movie playing on TV while we eat, drink and make merry.

Election Eve

My parents used to throw this patriotic cocktail party and it made a huge impression on me, growing up. Now I copy it when there's a Presidential election, every four years. Nothing out of the ordinary, except I decorate with current and vintage campaign posters, banners and flags and guests have to fill out a ballot upon entering…casting

a vote for their candidate of choice. We kids would count the votes every hour and update the tote board. Nearly every room in the house had a TV or radio on to keep guests up to speed on the results. I can vividly remember chanting 'Nixon Now' over the banister in 1972. You'll be relieved to know I've grown up POLITICALLY, too!

Gussied-Up for the Guest of Honor

If I'm throwing a dinner party in honor of a particular guest's birthday, anniversary, visit to town or other special occasion, I try to make it extra honorific by asking everyone to dress up more than normal. In our contemporary casual culture, the fun of getting all spiffy just to be in the company of a small group of pals is almost a lost art. I also concoct a pre-dinner trivia contest with all the attendees. The subject of the questions is always about that night's special guest…some interesting tidbits of information that will not only stimulate topics for easygoing dinner conversation, but show your friend that you cared enough to remember and share some happy memories from the past. Try it, you'll see how it works magic. ('What costume was the stripper wearing when he showed up for Pam's 30th birthday party?')

As for recipes, I haven't come up with too many new ones since my first book—I got a bit burned out on playing inventor in the kitchen. But here are a few recent faves you might like to try. I've written out US measurements, but if you use the metric system a pound is a little more than 450 grams (so ½ pound is about 225 grams) and an ounce is 28 grams. And remember, if you burn the roast or drop the soufflé on the floor: anything can be forgiven if you're a cheerful, welcoming host with the right mix of guests at your table. When all fails, order a pizza and uncork another bottle of vino!

★Tinseltown Tian

This is a recipe I shared with my *Sunrise* colleague, Barbara Northwood, and she's the expert in the kitchen so her approval means it's fool proof. She even published it in *New Idea* magazine, which was most flattering. Healthy carbs, low fat and delish, Feel free to experiment with different vegetables, spices and cheeses…I do. Like my chili or shepherd's pie, this is one of those recipes that is never the same twice.

Olive oil
2 medium brown onions, sliced
1–2 cloves of garlic, minced
½ lb yellow squash
½ lb Italian squash
1 lb tomatoes
1 lb medium white potatoes (unpeeled)
2½ ounces grated cheese (I usually go for gruyère or sharp cheddar)
Fresh thyme, sage
Kosher salt
Fresh ground black pepper or red pepper flakes.

Preheat oven to 375° Farenheit.

Spray a 2-inch baking dish with non-stick cooking spray. Sauté olive oil and cook onions over medium heat until translucent. Add garlic and continue to sauté for a minute or two. Put onion/garlic mixture into baking dish.

Slice vegetables into quarters and begin layering them around the dish, atop the onions. Keep a consistent pattern: yellow/green/red/white, etc. Try to fit them as tightly as possible, ring within ring of

veggies until the circle is filled in. Drizzle on a little more oil on top and liberally season with salt and pepper. Lay herb sprigs on top and cover with aluminum foil. Bake 35 minutes. Uncover and take off the herbs and sprinkle the cheese on top of the vegetables. Bake, uncovered, for 30–35 minutes.

This recipe is a great side-dish for 4, or main dish if you have a little side of angel hair pasta, adorned with the same oil/herbs/cheese.

★Root Vegetable Soup

Here's one I like to serve on cold winter nights. You can even be showy and hollow out some mini-pumpkins to use as bowls. Serves 6-8.

> 1 large onion, diced
> 2 tbsp chopped garlic
> 4 tbsp butter
> 1½ lbs carrots, peeled and chopped
> 1 medium white potato, peeled and chopped
> 1 large parsnip, peeled and chopped
> 1 large rib of celery, chopped
> Fresh rosemary, thyme, parsley, peppercorns bundled in cheesecloth
> 6 cups chicken or vegetable stock
> ½ cup milk (optional. I use low fat, you may prefer cream)
> Grated nutmeg
> Sea salt and black pepper to taste

Sauté the onion and garlic in the butter. Add carrots, potato, parsnip and celery. Slowly stir in stock. Simmer for 15–20 minutes over medium heat. Add the herb bundle, continue to simmer for 20–25 minutes. Remove bundle and let mixture cool. Stir in milk, then blend in batches (in the blender) to smooth consistency.

Reheat mixture on low heat, add nutmeg, salt, pepper to taste. Serve garnished with a sprig of fresh herbs.

★ Mom's Macaroni and Cheese

This is the exact recipe my mother uses to make the most delish homemade mac n' cheese I've ever had. I followed it precisely and was able to duplicate it perfectly for my ecstatic guests. This is the real deal when it comes to comfort food.

> *1 lb box elbow macaroni*
> *¼ stick of butter, cut into pieces*
> *3 cups shredded cheddar cheese*
> *1 tsp grated onion*
> *1 tsp Worcestershire sauce*
> *1 tsp mustard*
> *Garlic salt, pepper, parmesan cheese, parsley flakes, paprika to taste.*
>
> *Approx. 1 cup whole milk*
> *Approx. ½ cup breadcrumbs*

Preheat oven to 300° Farenheit.

Mix cooked macaroni into a large bowl with butter, cheddar, onion, Worcestershire and mustard. Lightly sprinkle on garlic salt, parsley flakes and pepper. Put contents into a large casserole dish and cover entire contents to surface with milk. Lightly sprinkle on parmesan, paprika and (sparingly) breadcrumbs. Do not cover.

Bake for 30 minutes at 300° F. Turn up to 350° F for an additional 90 minutes, until brown.

★Give Peas a Chance

A plethora of preferred Ps—peas, prosciutto, parmesan, pepper and pasta. This is comforting and delicious, and I like to serve it in small bowls with plenty of crusty bread and a green salad on the side. Serves 4.

> 1 lb small pasta shells
> 4 garlic cloves, chopped
> 2 tbsp olive oil
> 10 oz package frozen peas
> ¼ lb prosciutto, roughly chopped
> 1¼ cups cream
> 1 cup chicken stock
> ⅓ cup parmesan, grated
> ⅓ cup dill, chopped
> Kosher salt and red pepper flakes

Cook the pasta shells in salted water until al dente and set aside.

In a large skillet, cook garlic in heated olive oil for 3–4 minutes before adding peas and ham. In approximately 5 minutes, the ham should be browned. Add the cream and chicken stock. Simmer over medium heat until thickened, approximately 5 minutes.

Stir sauce into the shells. Sprinkle parmesan and dill on top, seasoning to taste with salt and pepper flakes.

★Zsa Zsa Gabor's Dracula Ghoulash

Long before anybody ever heard of Paris Hilton, there was exotic beauty, Zsa Zsa Gabor. Now frail and in her nineties, she's still a force to be reckoned with in Beverly Hills. By marrying husband number eight in 1986, she became Princess Zsa Zsa, and still manages to make headlines with her outrageous behavior and saucy quips like, 'I am a marvelous housekeeper, dahling. Every time I leave a man, I keep his house'.

She sent me this ghoulish goulash recipe I've never had the nerve to try making, but it's fun to share. And the former Miss Hungary 1936 should know all about goulash. She said, 'This is the dish I use to catch a man. And if I want to get rid of him, I stop making it. Even when you serve it with caviar, your guests will rave about the goulash. It's my favorite.'

2 red onions, sliced
3 lbs (stewing) pork
3 lbs (stewing) beef
Hungarian red paprika
½ container caraway seeds
4 lbs pre-washed sauerkraut
2 smoked polish sausages
Light sour cream
Salt and pepper to taste

Finely chop the red onion and sauté with olive oil until translucent. Add the pork and beef. Season with salt, pepper and three tablespoons of paprika (you must use Hungarian paprika and it is available in stores). Turn the meat mixture and cook for ten minutes. Add more paprika and ½ a small container of caraway seeds.

Wash and drain sauerkraut then mix into meat. Cover and stew for 2 hours. Cut sausages into ¼-inch pieces and add to mixture. Add enough paprika to make the stew blood red. Cover and cook an additional 15 minutes. Add a container of light sour cream.

Serve in bowls garnished with sour cream and a little parsley. Serves 10 hungry Americans or eight dieting Hungarians.

★ Mr Pitt's Shepherd Pie

Don't worry if you don't know the name Ian Abercrombie. It is his face and indomitable sense of humor as one of TV and film's busiest character actors that you surely know. Of all the hundreds of parts he's played, usually as a stuffy English gentleman, the one he is most identified with is certainly *Seinfeld*'s beloved, befuddled Mr Pitt… for whom Elaine worked in-between stints at Pendant Publishing and J. Peterman.

I've been making my own shepherd's pie for years, trading on traditional methods depending on whatever produce looks good at the Farmer's Market or what happens to be in my pantry. But my pal Ian seemed like the natural person to ask for an authentic recipe, since he not only hails from London but has been making this dish 'since the Blitz'. I'm going to share it with you exactly as he emailed it to me:

> *Hey Kid, This is the only recipe considered my specialty and it's fed hundreds! I used to feed all the out-of-work actors who would hang around my house. Very simple to make.*
>
> *Using ground beef or turkey, brown it in a pan mixing in onions or garlic cloves, along with cooked vegetables (a variety is good), it doesn't matter which ones, anything that comes to hand. Peel and boil regular potatoes, and then mash them with*

lotsa butter. Take the browned meat and pour into a pie dish (depending on how many folk you are feeding). Cover this mess with the mashed potatoes making whirls on top of the mash and brush with a little milk (you will get a nice brown crust if you do this) and pop into the oven to warm up for about 20 minutes. It was a survivor dish at a time when we were just starting out.

P.S. It kinda sticks to the ribs.

★Great Grandmother Aspen's Ginger Cookies

My dad grew up on these family delicacies, but they are so muscle-wrenching to make that my mother finally flat-out refused to make them. So my advice is to enlist a lot of extra help when preparing this huge batch. This is the exact recipe from a century ago, transcribed from great-grandmother's own handwritten recipe card with which she signed off, 'Good Luck!' Remember: yesteryear's lard is today's Crisco!

½ lb lard (1 cup packed down)
1 cup brown sugar
2 cups New Orleans Molasses
2 heaped tsp ginger
2 heaped tsp cinnamon
2 tsp baking soda dissolved in a little vinegar
Pinch of salt
7 cups flour (approximately)
1 cup boiling water
Powdered sugar

Preheat oven to 375° Farenheight.

Put lard and sugar in boiling water and let dissolve. Add molasses, spices, baking soda with a pinch of salt and mix.

Add enough flour to roll out, about 7 cups. Roll soft and thick, cut with a rather large round cutter. Place on greased cookie sheet and bake 10 minutes or until done (test with toothpick until it comes out smooth). When cooled, sprinkle tops with powdered sugar. Makes 6 dozen plus.

★CC's 'If I Make Elvis' Peanut Butter Fudgy Wudgys Will The King Come Back?' Brownies

Worried about dessert or just want to make a yummy snack? Here's one from my good pal, Carol Connors. Elvis Aaron Presley was her first love and in honor of his memory and renowned passion for peanut butter, she concocted this recipe. And she makes it every January 8, in honor of his birthday. But first let me tell you a little bit about the spirited siren of the deep (she's a scuba diver) and you'll appreciate her personal recipe even more. You may have seen her on Victoria Beckham's *Coming to America* special as 'the Beverly Hills Dolphin Lady'. Thanks to her love of wildlife, Carol's reinvented herself to a whole new generation of fans.

Back in the late 1950s, music mogul Phil Spector made CC a star when she crooned *To Know Him is to Love Him* as the lead singer of the pop trio, The Teddy Bears. She went on to become an acclaimed songwriter and even received two Academy Award nominations for her work on the music for Disney's *The Rescuers* and the universally iconic theme for *Rocky*. Whenever I'm doing a marathon and they start playing that music, I know that the other racers are conjuring up images of Rocky Balboa dashing up the steps of the Philadelphia Art Museum, but I'm usually chuckling about some funny email or phone call from CC!

The most hysterical memory by far was her Kitty Kat Tea Party, held at her lavish hillside estate. I was invited into her inner circle of feline fanatics because I owned an Abyssinian cat akin to her own precious pair, Music and Nlyrics. Here she had gathered her coterie of cat-lovers that included funny lady Rhonda Shear, music legend Marilyn McCoo, actresses Renee Taylor (*The Nanny*), Kate Linder (*The Young and the Restless*), Charlene Tilton (*Dallas*) and Deanna Lund (*Land of the Giants*). Barbi Benton was not available…she was bunny hoppin' at the Playboy Mansion. Chef Bruno of the swank *L'Hermitage* catered a five-star tea party in honor of CC's kitties and all the ladies came clad in some form of feline attire…Rhonda even had whiskers! 'These scones are cat-tastic!' one would exclaim. Or, 'Mmm, this tea is brewed to purrr-fection'. I am not making this up. Sounds silly, but it was a meow-ing good time, trust me.

> 4 squares Baker's unsweetened chocolate
> 1 cup butter or margarine
> 2 cups sugar
> 4 eggs, beaten
> ¾ cup sifted flour
> 1 tsp vanilla
> 1 x 6 oz bag of chocolate chip morsels
> A LOT of peanut butter (at least one heaped tablespoon)
> Powdered sugar to sprinkle

Preheat oven to 325° Farenheight.

HOLLYWOOD INSIDER EXPOSED!

Melt chocolate and butter together over hot water. Cool slightly. Gradually add sugar to eggs, beating thoroughly. Blend in chocolate mixture, then stir in the flour. Add vanilla and chocolate chip morsels. Finally, stir in at least a heaped tablespoon of peanut butter. (CC uses a super crunch variety, 'cause her Elvis was such a super star.)

Spread in a greased 9-inch square pan.

Generously sprinkle the remaining morsels on top of batter.

Sing it a little song, swivel your hips, cross your fingers and bake for about 30 minutes. Remove and cool in pan. You'll Love 'Em Tender…well, at least soft and chewy. Sprinkle powdered sugar on top or frost, if you prefer.

When cool, cut into squares and dig in while wearing your blue suede shoes.

★Sexy Cindy's Fabulous Fem-Bot No-Bake Cookies

My voluptuous friend Cindy Margolis (known as 'The Most Downloaded Woman on the Internet' and one of *Austin Powers*' original Fem-Bots) went from nine months pregnant back to supermodel shape in seemingly no time, shedding the nearly 60 pounds she'd gained in between. 'The hardest challenge was understanding that my body didn't get out of shape overnight, so I had to stop expecting it to get back into shape overnight. I hung up a little sexy bikini in my gym as my motivation.' She also wisely perceives that 'Being healthy is not just for you, it's also a gift you give your family. If you do things you like to do anyway and incorporate them into your daily routine then being fit and healthy becomes a part of who you are'. I should point out that it was after this, and turning 40, that Cindy finally relented and obliged Hugh Hefner's request to pose nude for *Playboy*. She wanted to inspire mature gals to love their bodies and obviously plenty of people loved Cindy's: it was one of their best-selling issues!

That said, it doesn't mean this delicious creature doesn't like to indulge her naughtier cravings once in a while. I asked her for one of her special 'guilty' recipes and she immediately responded with this one, explaining, 'I first made these for my son's Kindergarten Holiday parade and they were the hit of the school. You know me, Martha Stewart I'm not! But these cookies are so easy and so quick. They are my "go to" plan when Nicholas says to me at 7:30 in the morning, "Oh, Mom, I need some cookies for class today!"'

Bring to a full boil for 1 minute in medium saucepan:

2 cups sugar
4 tbsps Hershey's cocoa
¾ stick margarine
½ cup whole milk

Remove from heat and stir in:

1 tbsp peanut butter
2 tsps vanilla, until creamy.

Mix in 3 cups uncooked oatmeal and quickly drop by teaspoonfuls onto waxed paper. Let cool and enjoy.

Cindy knows how to put the yummy in mummy!

My Best Friend

A lot of people assume that my circle of friends must be made up of movie stars and moguls. While I certainly do have an eclectic coterie of famous faces, most of my very closest comrades are people who live their lives outside of the spotlight, if not in different walks of life altogether. When I'm not on the Hollywood clock, the last thing I want to do is be surrounded by more showbiz schmooze, name dropping and biz blab. My best friend, Glenn (or as my malaprop-prone father is still apt to misaddress him, 'Gary'), is so far away from the celebrity beat that I still can't quite figure out what the hell it is he does. Something financial. And he's very, VERY successful at it. I'm not a money/numbers/math person. Glenn and I are as different as night and day, chalk and cheese, or Patty Duke and her twin cousin Cathy on *The Patty Duke Show*.

When we met in 1985, neither one of us could ever have guessed we'd be embarking on a lifelong friendship that made us closer than any brothers I know (with all apologies to the Farrelleys, Coens and Baldwins). I was conniving to put myself in closer physical proximity to someone I was dating on Manhattan's Upper West Side, so I applied for part-time jobs all up and down Columbus Avenue. I got an offer to be one of the first fashion consultants at the brand-new, soon-to-open Tommy Hilfiger store. (Tommy was a relative unknown at the time, very hands-on, even though his line was owned by the foreign company, Murjani.) Fashion consultant was a fancy word for minimum-wage-earning sales clerk, but it afforded me the location I was looking for and some free clothing…even though at the time the garments were—in my opinion—extremely ill-fitting and poorly made. It would prove to be a challenge to sell clothes that made me look like I was wearing denim and khaki garbage bags, but I DID manage to once win the monthly Tommy Award for highest-sales. Even Tommy's siblings Ginny and Andy couldn't touch my figures. Too bad it never occcurred... The toughest part of my job was the constant folding required for the displays. I have many talents, but folding and ironing are not among them. Lucky for me, there was a sweet-as-pie kid working his way through college who happened to be an excellent folder. His name was Glenn and I soon coerced him into doing all my dirty work. Our friendship was born.

> Ginny Hilfiger went on to become a designer, herself, which is certainly better for her than a career in retail. One time, she followed Dustin Hoffman out of the store when he browsed, but left without making a purchase. She stuck her tongue out at him and yelled 'Meanie!' as he strolled down Columbus Avenue. That's no way to win a Tommy Award!

We started running around New York City in our off-work hours having all the misadventures that 20-somethings had in the 1980s. Our nights usually started at Cottage East Chinese Restaurant because they had an early bird 'all you can drink' wine special. They lost money on us, but we dined on Sesame Chicken at least three times a week. (One Saturday night, we'd over-indulged and returned to my apartment to take a quick 'disco nap', but wound up passing out, missing our big night out altogether.) We'd encourage and console each other through various love affairs, make-ups and breakups and even went on a memorable double blind date that was such a disaster we STILL laugh about it. He knew my cabaret act, *Easily Influenced*, so well…every joke, every song, every inflection…that he could have understudied me in a heart beat. If he could sing, of course.

You probably won't be surprised to learn I didn't last too long at Tommy's…just two months. But Glenn and I remained inseparable and, even when he got his first job working on the floor of the American Stock Exchange, we still found time to gab on the phone several times a day. And that was before mobiles!

We'd spend holidays with each other's families and never seemed to stop laughing. He even rode in the ambulance with me when my mom suffered a heart attack on Halloween Night 1986. A few hours later he had us both laughing in her hospital room. As our respective careers began to flourish, we were able to cut back on the visits to Cottage East and branch out to nicer establishments. Our regular hangout was the colorful eatery owned by Broadway legend, Chita Rivera. Her look-alike sister, Lola, was the hostess and we must have had a million meals (and a *zillion* cocktails) there over the course of a couple years. It was not uncommon to see lots of theatrical folks there, like Liza Minnelli and Elaine Stritch, and Glenn even had his own hysterical run-in with a famous cabaret crooner while on a trip to the Men's Room. We helped celebrate Peter Allen's birthday at a suite in the Waldorf Astoria and drafted two other pals to help us transform into dead-ringers as the [Joan] Crawford family for Halloween—wire hangers, bruises and all. Glenn was the perfect Alfred Steele to support my version of Joan. He's always been there for me, LOL. I'm sure if I needed a kidney and he matched, he wouldn't hesitate to donate. And it goes both ways…in fact, when he was in the hospital for an emergency appendectomy (thank God he didn't listen to *my* medical advice—I told him it was a stomach-ache and to take an antacid), he may not have needed any organ or tissue donations, but I did manage to smuggle in some illegal balloons and bottles of beer. He was the first person I knew personally who'd run a marathon and I thought he was nuts. 'Why would anyone run that far if they didn't have to?' I remember asking. Now, who's the nut!?

When I decided to make the move to Los Angeles, I was worried how our friendship would survive. Glenn came with me on the long drive across country and it was a tame version of *Thelma and Louise*, all 3000 miles (with a not-so-quick detour to see the Grand Canyon). He helped me get settled into my new Hollywood digs and of course check out the local nightclub scene. Daily phone calls and, with the advent of the internet, emails kept us in constant contact on our assorted capers and sexploits, and we'd visit each other as often as possible. He surprised me by turning up at my 30th birthday bash at Mezzaluna Ristorante. I was actually singing with a jazz combo when he walked in the door. And it was perfect: he was my 30th guest! He'd rented a convertible and we had so much fun tooling around LA and introducing him to all my new friends.

✯ ✯ ✯ ✯ ✯ ✯ ✯ ✯ ✯ ✯ ✯ ✯ ✯ ✯

> If the Mezzaluna Ristorante sounds familiar to you, it is in fact the same establishment that was the setting for the beginning of the terrible true-crime tragedy that was the alleged OJ Simpson double-murder of his ex-wife and her friend, Mezzaluna waiter Ron Goldman. My cousin Keith was the manager, and Nicole Brown Simpson's boyfriend and I worked there for a short time. (As did titian-haired vixen, Laura Leighton aka Sydney from *Melrose Place*. She's now married to former *Melrose* co-star Doug Savant, who plays Tom on *Desperate Housewives*. Whenever I see them around town, we always reminisce about those early days). Nicole was a beautiful person, fun friend and devoted mom. The memory of that entire soap opera is still quite surreal.

✯ ✯ ✯ ✯ ✯ ✯ ✯ ✯ ✯ ✯ ✯ ✯ ✯ ✯

A decade later, determined to have a memorable 40th, I again celebrated with Glenn: this time at his incredible East Hampton manse, where his neighbors include Jerry Seinfeld and Martha Stewart. We were joined by my parents and longtime friend, Marie, and had a blast. He and his partner, Dan, were by now living the high life and enjoying the fruits of their workaholic lives in NYC with this great estate, a gorgeous mid-century modern pad on Central Park West and a condo in Miami. But you know what? He's the exact same sweet guy who did all my folding for me back in our salad days. Flying around on private jets and hobnobbing with the elite hasn't changed the boy from Brooklyn.

As a single guy without kids, it's reassuring to know that I have been lucky enough to form my own family of friends—I know that Glenn and I will be pals 'from womb to tomb' as the saying goes. I often tease him that in our old age when I'm ready to retire from Hollywood, I'll be moving into the guest house in East Hampton. (How very *Grey Gardens*!) You can bet we'll still be laughing.

To be continued…

A Day in the Life

I'm often asked what my typical day is like. While I am definitely a regimented creature of habit, there are no two days that are exactly alike and it is never 'typical'. I am constantly assuring folks that it is far from being all glitz and glamour. Of course it has some spectacular moments…many of which I've described in these pages, but take my word for it: life ain't all Klieg lights and red carpets.

Because of the different global time zones of my various outlets, my days start early. Even though my alarm is set for 4:10am, it rarely goes off. My inner clock usually makes sure I wake ahead of that annoying buzz…and also before my loyal Lois, who sleeps curled up at my feet. She and I trot off to the kitchen to put the coffee on and our day gets underway. On the rare occasions that the alarm *does* go off, it's the equivalent of hearing a gun fire at the beginning of a race: GO GO GO!

I sit down at the computer with my first cuppa and an energy bar, taking a deep breath as I open the morning email. Because of the never-ending cycle of news, there is seldom a hiatus from the onslaught of tips, leads, press releases and announcements that jam my Inbox—especially because of my four decades of connections in so many different areas of the industry. I sift through them, still rubbing the sleep from my eyes and try and work out their priorities.

HOLLYWOOD INSIDER EXPOSED!

By the time I finish watering the lawn or doing a load of laundry, I'm ready to put my mind to all-things showbiz.

After a careful combing of the news headlines, I begin to follow up on my sources...fact checking and seeking out first-hand accounts to put my own stamp on my reports. I start emailing my producers with the topics I'd like to cover so they can gather the accompanying graphics and footage to illustrate my reports. Of course, any last-minute breaking news results in on-the-spot revisions...which can be frustrating if I'm particularly attached to a certain story, but is always a pulse-pounding perk of my position.

★ ★ ★ ★ ★ ★ ★ ★ ★ ★ ★ ★ ★

> Global Gossip Never Sleeps! Millions of people wake up to my reports every day, so I have to be ready for 'em. Tuesday broadcasts for Ireland's *The Afternoon Show* start at 7:50am for me, then on to New Zealand's *Sunrise* twice a week at 10:40am. For Australia's *Sunrise*, every weekday, I'm on call throughout the show which is 11am–2pm for me...except in summer when that moves to 1pm–4pm. Oh, yeah and *Weekend Sunrise*! Those hours have limited my ability to cross to the UK's *GMTV* which would require me to be in the studio 11pm–1:30am. There are some days when I'm brushing my teeth, half-wondering if I'm just waking up or getting ready to go to bed. And remember, Australia is a day ahead so my Sunday is their Monday. It can all get very confusing with dates and time zones, so I have giant calendars everywhere. Tardiness isn't a trait suited to live television.

★ ★ ★ ★ ★ ★ ★ ★ ★ ★ ★ ★ ★

So by 6am local time, I usually have solid first drafts of my scripts and can turn my attention to another under-reported aspect of my career: staying healthy and in top shape. I take Lois for a walk around the neighborhood so she can make sure all the other local dogs know who's boss (keeping an eagle eye out for any wild coyotes that have strayed down from the hills—we've had a few scary encounters) and then I pack up my briefcase and bags for the day and head to the gym. The valet at the club learned his first Yiddish word when I told him I'm *schlepper*…I am always dragging around garment bags, duffle bags, grocery sacks, props and assorted other stuff. This is often the most precious time because it not only generates energy-producing endorphins to power me through the challenges of the day, but it is a chance for me to focus on my health and fitness goals. I generally spend an hour doing cardiovascular work on the treadmill or pool running and then do weight and agility exercises with my trainer. With all the celebrities that pop into my club on a regular basis and the constant access to phone and email messages, I'm never out of touch from the latest showbiz updates. In fact, one time in the middle of a workout I got a frantic call from one of my producers needing me to hustle downtown to the Lynnwood Correctional facility and await the incarceration of Paris Hilton. The hairdo I was sporting on that day's worldwide coverage was not created by gel or mousse…it was dried sweat! As luck would have it, we trounced the competing TV outlet because their on-air divas insisted on hiring a car service to chauffeur them and their hair and makeup people rather than get into their own automobiles—and the driver took them to the *wrong prison*! (I can't fathom the routine luxury of a hair and makeup person, let alone a driver. I'm far too no-frills for that.)

A protein shake or juice is my midmorning meal and then I grab a fast shower before heading into the studio. By now there are invariably adjustments to be made to my roster of stories and another dozen-plus emails to sort through. I implement all my revisions, slap on some powder and jump into the chair to start my broadcasts. I do at least three live reports every weekday and often, depending on the scale of the day's celebrity news, several other

HOLLYWOOD INSIDER
EXPOSED!

pre-records for other news outlet broadcasts. It's pretty nonstop. I always have lunch at my desk (turkey or chicken caesar wraps are my usuals). By the time I finish up at the news bureau or satellite station, I have a pretty clear idea of the major stories I want to recap for my afternoon writing for magazines, columns and blogs. I jump into the car and head for home.

On busy broadcast days, people often marvel at how I can turn on the enthusiasm for retelling the same, latest Britney/Lindsay/Brangelina story ad nauseam. A lot of the credit goes to the reception I'm getting on the other end of the air or radio waves. If the folks I'm talking to are interested and communicative, it never ceases to make it exciting for me to relay and comment on the news at hand. I'm fortunate not to be called upon merely as a talking head spouting out facts, but a conversationalist who is expected and encouraged to offer insight as well as info. Every live report is a new chance to inform, enlighten and/or entertain. I'm reminded of a 1980 quote by the divine Academy Award winner, Dame Celeste Holm (whom I had the good fortune to meet on Oscar night 2007): 'My favorite show is always the one I am doing. All you have is now…do the best you can and enjoy it'. Good advice, eh?

Quite possibly the greatest thing I did for myself in 2007 was finally acquire a personal assistant to help me take care of the household while I'm in the field. My talented comedienne friend, Deven Green (a cult-favorite for her brilliantly executed series of videos on YouTube; in fact I'm proud that one in which I guest-starred in a self-parody, debuted at number 63 of all Comedy Videos; watch out Will Ferrell) made me see that you don't have to be Madonna to merit having someone around to help you out with life's little daily problems. For a lifetime, I'd been too self-controlled to allow anyone else (even partners) to give me a hand with many of the simple demands of daily living and, honestly, I am the busiest person I know.

So Deven introduced me to her friend, Kaore. I quickly found a few days a week to make use of his competent assistance and that allowed me not only some occasional precious worry-free time to myself, but the ability to work more effectively. He's a great guy and I'm finding him more and more indispensable every day. The best bonus is how he and Lois have gotten to love each other.

So once I get home and indulge in a tail-wagging reunion with the pooch, I settle back into my home office and tackle my correspondence. Lots of emails come in every day from viewers and I'm always diligent about giving them the attention they deserve. I read and respond to all my mail. Whatever other paperwork is on my desk is attended to and then I finish up the afternoon with my writing. The sun sets and I'm pooped…ready to unwind by preparing myself a special dinner or meeting some friends out for a casual meal somewhere local and comfortable. Dinner, whether alone or shared, is a treasured time of day for me. Many people assume I must be out, drinking in the Hollywood nightlife but I'm fortunate that my network of sources, connections and tipsters is such that I am able to have eyes and ears all over town without having to go out *physically* on the prowl for news. At least one night a week, I'm called upon to attend a film screening as preparation for my celebrity interviews. Consequently, if someone suggests taking in a movie as a social outing, I usually try and convince them to opt for something else. Bowling, anyone?

Since I'm such an early riser, people ask me all the time what time I go to bed and the honest answer is, 'As soon as I can'. I just love climbing into bed with some great literature (I'm an avid reader… every room in the house has books, and I have several going at all times. Different rooms, different vibes, different genres of books) until I drift off to sleep. I gave up my membership at a 24-hour gym when I kept finding myself on the treadmill at 3am.

Of course this routine gets disrupted at least once a week by having to go out and shoot an assignment, file a story, attend a screening or interview celebs on a red carpet or at a press junket. That's always a stimulating opportunity to mix it up, meet other colleagues and get creative. I've always gotten along great with camera crews, and some of my happiest work experiences have been out working on stories with the guys and gals behind the camera. I'm always baffled when I hear about on-air talent who give their crews a hard time. Not only are they the people who have the ability to make or break your storytelling ability, but wouldn't you rather go out and enjoy being part of a team to create something, rather than make it an unpleasant struggle? Maybe it's being the youngest of five kids that has always instilled in me a team mentality. And red-carpet events are bladder-busting war zones unless you get along with your crew.

If you really want to cling to the illusion that red-carpet arrivals are a glamorous affair, you should skip ahead a page or two because I'm about to dispel that myth right now. Only media stars like Mary Hart, Conan O'Brien or Diane Sawyer can enjoy these scrums because they have climate-controlled holding areas with a full hair and makeup staff to attend to them until it's time for the cameras to roll. For the rest of us, well…here's basically how it works:

You get into your monkey suit hours before the arrivals begin, to claim your designated spot on the red carpet, making sure you have all your notes and essentials (sunscreen, breath mints, powder, ear piece, bottled water, throat lozenges, energy bar, charged cell phone, etc). Liaise with crew and start hauling equipment. Arrive at the location, go through security and trudge all your wares to the venue. Find your marked spot on the carpet which is usually about one square foot, just big enough to squeeze in with your cameraman standing on a crate over your head ('Careful not to shoot my thin patch from up there, Shane!'). As other journos arrive to fill in the other spots that square foot begins to shrink smaller and smaller until you are packed in like a sardine. You are subjected to hours of endless, mindless blabber from these other journalists, which mainly consists of complaints, outrageous braggadocio and/or prying questions about how they can possibly use other people to their own personal advantage. It can be horrific. The only bright spots are when you actually bump into people you like. Running into my mates from CNN, BBC, *Inside Edition* and *Sky News* or the boys from Boxx Communications are examples of this. That's when it begins to feel festive.

By the time you've completely perspired through your tuxedo, that's when the stars begin to dribble in. The first ones to arrive are usually the ones most desperate for attention. The up and comers, wannabes or has-beens. Since I actually enjoy chatting with these people (and it's a welcome diversion from the elbow lodged into my ribcage by the pushy teenage pageant winner representing Brazilian cable TV who has wedged herself into my space), I get warmed up with these folks. But the closer it gets to show time, the busier it gets on the arrivals line and publicists scout out your affiliation to determine whom they do and don't want their celebrity clients to stop and talk to. That's when the fighting begins and it's all out war.

'Cate! Russell! Meryl! Jake! Tom! Julia! George! Angelina! Matt!' I scream until I'm hoarse. You have to do whatever you can to get their attention. At the very least you want them to look toward your camera. Ideally, you want to lure them to your microphone for a chat. I'm fortunate that I know most of these people and can yell out some clue to alert their recognition. This goes on like a black-tie riot until the last of the stars has been pushed into the venue. But that's not the end. Then you have to pack it all up and either move on to the next venue (usually an after-party, press conference or banquet) or head back to the studio and begin the editing process to prepare your packaged reports.

HOLLYWOOD INSIDER
EXPOSED!

★ ★ ★ ★ ★ ★ ★ ★ ★ ★ ★ ★ ★ ★ ★ ★

Tom Cruise is by far the most exciting red carpet arrival. He is notorious for showing up and spending plenty of time in and amongst the fans, posing for pictures and signing autographs for adoring fans. No fool, he. Not only does that make him seem like a generous, accessible 'man of the people', it also delays him from having to make his way down the long, red aisle of reporters crowded behind the velvet ropes all waiting to ask him potentially embarrassing and/or unwanted questions about his mysterious personal life. At the *Collateral* premiere, he had given so much time to the throngs of fans that he only had a few minutes to chat to press to get inside the theater in time for the premiere. When he finally got to me, I only had time for one question so I wanted it to be something funny and offbeat, maybe a little naughty. Remember he'd dyed his hair silver for that role? I asked him, 'So, Tom. Love the white hair. But does the carpet match the drapes?' He stumbled for a moment. He either didn't get the joke or decided it was safer to play dumb. After a couple of stuttering seconds he covered with, 'Oh, yeah, I love the red carpet'.

★ ★ ★ ★ ★ ★ ★ ★ ★ ★ ★ ★ ★ ★ ★ ★

That may all sound somewhat exciting, but take it from anyone who's done it more than two or three years in a row: it's tough work.

The press junkets to help promote new movies, DVD launches or TV premieres are considerably easier…at least on the feet (unless it's a stinkpot film—then it's a case of trying to make a silk purse from a sow's ear). And at least when you show up at the location, there is almost always a comfortable waiting area, hair and makeup staffers to help you look as presentable as the talent you're about to interview and plenty of refreshments. I'm just about the only reporter I know who doesn't go ape over the thought of free food and beverages. I've always found buffet-style eating to be kind of gross and, frankly, the last thing I want to do before sitting down to have a one-on-

one conversation with Natalie Portman or Sir Michael Caine is worry about having garlic breath or a piece of spinach wedged between my front teeth. I'll eat when I get home, thanks!

> The nicest stars at press junkets, in my experience, are: Geoffrey Rush, Catherine Zeta Jones, Tom Cruise, Nic Cage and Hilary Swank. For red-carpet good manners, you can't beat Dame Julie Andrews, Doris Roberts, Eric Bana, Wentworth Miller, James Denton and Kate Walsh.

Hanging out with other journalists at these affairs is considerably more pleasant than being out on a media line. I'm fortunate to be designated as an international reporter rather than domestic. My foreign colleagues are not only vastly more interesting, well-read and fun to be around whereas most of the American staffers are 'big fish in their [local] little ponds' and this can make for inane and often insufferable conversationalists. Most of the publicists agree and always welcome the international press days for their projects as opposed to the egos of the American talking heads. Even most of the stars prefer the diversity and originality of the foreign press corps. Sad, but true.

> Barely legal, world-weary Ellen *(Juno)* Page has an uncanny knack for making an interviewer who's trying to have fun seem tragic. Her nonplussed reactions to lighthearted questions left me feeling like a silly old fart. She still has a lot to learn from Jodie, Angelina or Meryl that it's okay in an interview to be smart, serious AND still have some fun!

HOLLYWOOD INSIDER
EXPOSED!

Post interview is when you have to collect all your tapes and begin the review, log and edit process. From screening to prep to interview to final cut, that entertaining little four-minute segment you see probably entailed hours and hours of hard work!

It can all be highly amusing, intensely interesting and a challenging adrenaline rush…but don't ever be fooled by the finished product you see on your telly. It's labor intensive and whenever I hear, 'Oh, that looks like so much fun!' I can't help but be proud of knowing I've done my job well.

On Location

Many folks assume I must constantly be flying around from one amazing locale to the other, filing stories from exotic locations and making frequent visits to my assorted international outlets. *Au contraire*, aside from the aforementioned press junkets and red-carpet events, most of my time on camera is spent in the studio sitting in front of a green screen with a chroma-keyed background. As for visiting my mates overseas, I don't get the opportunity nearly enough. After all, the whole point of having a 'Hollywood Guy' on the team is having him in Hollywood!

> ★ ★ ★ ★ ★ ★ ★ ★ ★ ★ ★ ★ ★ ★ ★
>
> After years of sitting in front of the venerable Hollywood sign, I'm happy that our producers and cameramen have teamed up to generate some more interesting, iconic showbiz landmarks for my background. The corner of Hollywood and Vine, the Venice Beach boardwalk, Mann's Chinese Theater and Santa Monica Amusement Pier have been among the most colorful… and popular.
>
> ★ ★ ★ ★ ★ ★ ★ ★ ★ ★ ★ ★ ★ ★ ★

In the early days of my presenting career, because so much of my reporting content revolved around my expertise in the field of fitness, most of my location shooting was relegated to gymnasiums, health clubs and spas. I broadcasted frequently from classes which I actually taught, with many of my real-life students participating as a

supporting cast. They became quite media savvy over the years. From my trademarked treadmill class, The Brains and Brawn Workout, to celebrity-studded affairs like Spinning with the Soap Stars, I learned early on not to worry about being sweaty on camera. I got to teach lots of stars over the years, including Ashley Judd, Kristen Davis, Margaux Hemingway, Craig Bierko, Helen Hunt, Carol Kane, Alfre Woodard, Belita Moreno, Lauralee Bell and Annette Bening. I also was on the receiving end of some instruction, like my boxing lesson from Michelle Phillips…martial arts with Victor Webster…pet fitness with Betty White…and even fitness fashion with the late, great Florence Griffith Joyner. I did one shoot at the classy Beverly Hills Country Club, which I'd joined courtesy of the sponsorship of the delightful Nancy Sinatra. I'd hoped to cultivate my tennis and golf games, but was unsuccessful at both. I'm better off sticking to running. The club was visually appealing but the hysterics of the management made for an unpleasant morning of filming, and consequently I decided to terminate my membership. Like pulling aside the curtain of the Wizard of Oz, sometimes it's a big disappointment to see what goes on behind the scenes.

Of course, the biggest demand for almost all of my jobs is to give tours of famous local sites. I can't tell you how many times I've been chased off the Walk of Fame by security guards! But one of my most memorable segments there, was interviewing a disabled Vietnam vet who had been homeless for many years and actually lived ON that famous street. He spent his days crawling along the Boulevard, maintaining and polishing the often neglected and marred stars, cemented into the sidewalk. He was eventually hired by the city of Hollywood to perform that job, and thereby able to afford a place to live. It was quite an inspiring story and I learned a few helpful cleaning tips, to boot! Whenever viewers ask me for advice on planning their trips to our city, I point them to the very helpful and thorough website www.hollywoodentertainmentdistrict.com There you can find info on many of the great landmarks like the (supposedly haunted) Roosevelt Hotel, where the first Academy Awards were held…Mann's Chinese Theater (whose hand and foot prints will fit yours?)…Musso & Frank's Restaurant…the Petersen Auto Museum…La Brea Tar Pits…and of course the Kodak Theater.

And then there all the offbeat places we love to laugh at, so I've been frequently on the receiving end of experiencing micro-dermabrasion, botox injections and hyperbaric oxygen chamber treatments at beautician Maria DeSio's Beverly Hills clinic…getting an all over spray tan or wax job (but I draw the line at Jackie Stallone's 'rumpology' psychic readings of my buttocks or the Beckham-inspired 'Boyzilian'. Yowwie!)…checking out the thrones of the rich and famous in luxury Porta-Potties…donating some clean patch of skin to the ink of a new tattoo at the famous Purple Panther Parlor on Sunset Boulevard…ghost hunting at the Hollywood Forever Cemetery…judging the yummy mummies at the annual Mrs California Pageant at Knott's Berry Farm…having my face cast in plaster, or sitting on the lap of Hunky Santa at the Beverly Center. It's a tough job, but someone has to do it.

For the Aussie comedy show *Fat Pizza*, we stormed the Scientology Celebrity Center—though we found no sign of Tom Cruise—and explored Runyon Canyon and dog park, where I often go trail running. Lots of stars take their pooches up there for a hike and it's not uncommon to run into the likes of Jake Gyllenhaal, Johnny Depp, Eriq LaSalle, Mary Stuart Masterson or kd Lang with their four-legged best friends. And everybody seems to have a morbid fascination with the spot on Sunset Boulevard, outside the notorious Viper Room, where River Phoenix died.

Whether it's been for *The Bermuda Sunrise Show*, BBC News or Australia's *The Great Outdoors*, audiences everywhere have a

fascination with Hollywood and it's my privilege to be a combination ambassador/tour guide. From my favorite Mexican hangout, El Coyote (where Sharon Tate reportedly ate her last meal before the horrific Manson murder spree) to the Santa Monica Promenade and Harry Winston's jewelers on Rodeo Drive, it's great to show viewers my own back yard. Wolfgang Puck and his staff at Spago are always gracious hosts to me and my camera crews, displaying their elaborate and delicious offerings and even letting me ham it up in the kitchen… frolicking among the pizza ovens and giant walk-in refrigerators.

For over a year, I produced and hosted *New with Nelson*, which was a series of upbeat, interstitial 'how to' segments seen on a continuous 24-hour loop, by tens of thousands of Southern Californians in the Ralph's Supermarket chain. It was an incredibly fun and informative way for me to discover the best that SoCal has to offer and to learn some handy new skills such as how to make sushi rolls, install a dimmer switch, cut tiles, make candles, landscape and interior design, learn pet care tips (from my own super-handsome, charismatic, Emmy-winning veterinarian Jeff Werber aka Lassie's Vet), portrait painting with Billy Dee Williams, and exercise advice for infants and toddlers. Ed Begley Jr and Alexandra Paul have been eco-passionate long before it was *de rigueur* and we shot a lot of great episodes in their homes, focusing on everything from alternative energy to water conservation to composting. It was a great gig and seen by anyone who set foot in a grocery store. For a long time after that, people would tell me I looked familiar but they couldn't figure out why. I usually just responded with a wink and said, 'Will that be paper or plastic?'

Fashion is always a hot topic, too, although I have absolutely no expertise or credentials in the design area. All I can offer is my opinion and, fortunately, that seems to be enough when I'm dishing who's beautifying the Hollywood awards' scene and who's looking like The Corpse Bride (yes, I mean you, Helena!). But I've done live commentary from the Beverly Boulevard couture house of Cantu & Castillo during the Emmy Awards...countless interviews with my naughty neighbor, the indomitable Mr Blackwell, whose biggest claim to fame is his bitchy annual Worst Dressed List (you can imagine the anxiety I have about what to wear when he comes over for dinner!)... and I always have fun with the divine Tiara Hallman, who lets me run around her *It's a Wrap* wardrobe boutique and try on the cast-off clothing of the showbiz power elite. Charlie Lapson supplied my fabulous on-air wardrobe for several seasons of television and he has a great talent for giving advice and guidance on style-related issues. He's best known these days for his fabulous handbags, wallets and accessories for men and women that attract a wide array of stars like Marcia Cross, Antonio Banderas, Jennifer Aniston, Jessica Alba, Kirsten Dunst and Rod Stewart. I'm so proud of him.

★ ★ ★ ★ ★ ★ ★ ★ ★ ★ ★

> It hadn't occurred to me that the non-stop, repetitive loop of me dispensing helpful hints might get irritating if you were the checker who had to stand there and listen to it over and over and over during your shift. One day I was fumbling with my coupons as I was paying up and the disgruntled cashier couldn't help but grumble, 'You should go home and work on your hardwood floors'. I looked up from my discount clippings and saw my image on the video screen, cheerfully varnishing some flooring. After that, I switched to another supermarket chain!

★ ★ ★ ★ ★ ★ ★ ★ ★ ★ ★

Producing a serious story on 'medical miracles' for the magazine show *Extra!*, I found myself spending some interesting hours in the offices and laboratories of the famous Cedars-Sinai hospital. I met a man who'd been cured of advanced Parkinson's Disease thanks to the way his body responded to the implantation of stem cells that have actually been grown in a lab, from samples of his *own* brain cells. I interviewed the brilliant, enthusiastic scientist behind the groundbreaking, experimental procedure and got to see not only how it all worked, but the living proof in the gentleman it saved. For a kid who never enjoyed science class, I was completely enthralled. Of course, by the time the *Extra!* editors finished cutting the story to suit their tabloid-style format, it was less a story about this controversial, cutting-edge success story and more of a sensational titillation as to whether or not it was something that could have helped celebrities like Michael J Fox, Muhammad Ali or Christopher Reeve.

One of my best-loved locations is my own living room. I've shot so many documentaries, TV specials and even a wacky celebrity pajama party with chocolate body paints (messy and fattening, but delish comedy) in my home that my neighbors have given up wondering why camera crews are always coming and going. In fact, the night of Princess Diana's unexpected and tragic death, I was having an al fresco dinner party with some other journo friends when the call came in with the news. ABC Television sent over a satellite truck to park in my driveway and we all broadcast to outlets around the world from my living room, until the wee hours of the next morning. I can't believe we never blew a fuse. Lighter moments have included my niece Merryn joining me for Christmas carol duets and *Sunrise* host Melissa Doyle dropping by for a *Desperate Housewives* tribute to peek through my curtains at the 'hunky gardener' mowing the lawn.

Locally, I've shot tons of TV and film set visits which can always be amusing and never fail to give me a rush of excitement when I'm wandering around a studio set. That's when you really feel like you're a part of the amazing, century-plus history of Hollywood…walking across the same soundstage where Bette Davis filmed *Dark Victory*, crossing the street that is now Wisteria Lane for the *Desperate Housewives*, but I remember better as *The Munsters*' Mockingbird

Lane…and, my favorite, 20th Century Fox. (the New York City street set is so authentic you'd swear you were in Manhattan), and of course the Griffith Observatory made famous in *Rebel Without a Cause*. And always try the studio commissaries whenever possible. Usually the best food in town and great star-gazing potential!

Because of the natural beauty all around Southern California, there are bounties of outdoor locations that are fun to shoot. The Santa Monica mountains and canyons, the caves and cliffs of El Matador beach and the nearby Temecula and Paso Robles vineyards. One great Malibu excursion was for the annual summertime Doodleromp, to which I was invited by beautiful Barbara Eden. She was excited to find out I worked for Australian television, because she was the proud owner of an Aussie-bred labradoodle named Djin-Djin (like her dog on the sitcom). We went to the event and frolicked with 150 doodles of all shapes, sizes and colors and got to see their dog show and meet the breeders. At the end of the shoot, Shane my cameraman confided to me that 'doodle' is Aussie slang for a private part of the male anatomy, so there was added (albeit unintentional) hilarity from all the Americans gushing statements like 'I love doodles!' and 'I can't wait to come home and play with my doodle!' Whatever the name, I was so enchanted by these friendly, affectionate creatures that I convinced my parents to adopt their big, black beauty, Logan, and it's a match made in heaven. Thank you, Jeannie.

Universal Studios is always an entertaining venue for segments: the *Jaws* and *Mummy* rides, famous set pieces and costumed characters like Shrek and Beetlejuice. The Amphitheater is also a great concert arena and I've attended memorable concerts there with Mariah Carey and Keith Urban. But the penultimate Universal experience was getting to go behind the scenes and interview the hottest Australian import in showbiz history: The Wiggles!

I was first made aware of the Wiggles by Merryn when she was only

HOLLYWOOD INSIDER EXPOSED!

two or three years old. I was wearing a yellow shirt, so she told me I looked like Greg, the Yellow Wiggle. When they came to LA for part of their triumphant US tour, I went to the Amphitheater to shoot a hilarious segment where I pretended to audition for their ensemble.

They were all such upbeat, fun, good sports and we all worked together beautifully—along with Captain Feathersword, Dorothy the Dinosaur and Wag the Dog, of course. It was most definitely a mutual admiration society as they all knew me from watching my Aussie TV reports, so—once I learned a few dance moves—they invited me to stick around for the show and join them onstage in one of their big musical production numbers. How could I refuse? 'Lights, Camera, Action…Wiggles! Welcome to our TV Show! Lights, Camera, Action…Wiggles! Everybody let's go!' There I was being a back-up dancer to The Wiggles in front of a sold-out crowd of 3000 screaming kids. It was great. I've stayed in touch with the fellas over the years and they even bestowed upon me a Golden Wiggle Bobblehead in my likeness, proclaiming me an honorary Wiggle. You can keep your Oscars, Emmys and Golden Globes—that prized possession has a very important spot on my trophy mantle.

A little out of town is Las Vegas. I'd never been much for casinos and that insane desert heat, but when our *Sunrise* executive producer, the wunderkind of brekky TV Adam Boland, called to ask me to join the presenting team there for a week of live broadcasts I jumped at the chance. At that point, I'd only chatted with them via satellite so it would be a real pleasure to spend some time with the cast and crew *in person*. Unfortunately, Melissa Doyle was on maternity leave but I had a blast getting to hang out with Kochie, Nat, Grant and Monique and become special pals with producer Paula Crawford and makeup artist Lizzie Tagla. That was way better for me than pirate shows, Tom Jones or the roulette wheels.

✯ ✯ ✯ ✯ ✯ ✯ ✯ ✯ ✯ ✯ ✯ ✯ ✯ ✯ ✯ ✯ ✯

Another memorable moment at Universal Studios was for *TV Guide Television*. They host an annual 5k race that winds through the lot, so participants can run past the Bates Motel from *Psycho*, the marketplace from *Spartacus*, the Parisian square from *The Hunchback of Notre Dame* and the swashbuckling town in *The Pirates of the Caribbean*. I had a cameraman filming me run the route from a golf cart in front of me. That was a challenge…not only did I have to narrate an entire tour while running, I had to breathe in all the dust from the cart directly in front of me. Oh well, the price you pay for entertaining television.

✯ ✯ ✯ ✯ ✯ ✯ ✯ ✯ ✯ ✯ ✯ ✯ ✯ ✯ ✯ ✯ ✯

We did something similar from Disneyland and this time Mel got to join us, as did several *Sunrise* viewers. That was my first live experience with the *Sunrise* family audience and they were all simply brilliant. What fun we all had spending a week together in the Magic Kingdom, sampling not only all the rides but the restaurants and shops as well. I also formed a special bond with the Sophia Loren-esque newsreader from Adelaide, Rosanna Mangiarelli. Va va va voom! You can't help but feel like a kid when you're posing for pictures with Mickey and Minnie Mouse and a very special day was when Dame Julie Andrews appeared on the show, making Kochie's childhood dreams come true before our very eyes.

The only controversial moment came when I was doing a live report having something or other to do with Pamela Anderson's breasts, while standing beside Belle from *Beauty & The Beast*. The poor girl didn't know how to react to such scandalous banter when they're all under strict supervision to maintain that squeaky clean image. I told her to cover her ears.

★ ★ ★ ★ ★ ★ ★ ★ ★ ★ ★ ★ ★ ★ ★ ★ ★ ★ ★

The first experience of meeting and spending some time with those viewers was significant and special. When one gets engaged in a TV dialogue on the airwaves, it can be easy to forget about all the countless people generously giving you their attention from their living rooms or kitchens or offices. Whenever someone sends me a personal photo, letter or keepsake, it's always a treasure. I love getting to glimpse into their lives just as they get a glimpse into mine. One loyal *Sunrise* family pen pal, Trish from Sydney, sent me a personalized mouse-pad which I use at the studio. That way, right before I run on camera I am always reminded of who I'm really there to talk to. It's a wonderful way to keep it real. For me, the true magic of television isn't getting to see myself on a little monitor wearing a fancy shirt or sitting under some bright lights talking about TomKat, it's about being welcomed into someone's private routine. Whether it's while they stretch for their morning run, have a last cup of coffee before work or get their kids ready for school.

★ ★ ★ ★ ★ ★ ★ ★ ★ ★ ★ ★ ★ ★ ★ ★ ★ ★ ★

Two other close-to-Tinseltown locations of note: visiting Liberace's over-the-top Palm Springs residence, still adorned with piano-themed furnishings, mirrors, gilt and paintings of the man, himself. And, one of the best: Tippi Hedren's Shambala Preserve. I've gone there a few times and I can only say that it is a definite job perk to get to take tea in Tippi's tent overlooking the elephants and tigers. She's a class act and beautiful lady. If only her daughter Melanie possessed half her grace and charm.

Still on American soil, but a little further off the mainland was my Hawaiian adventure for *Sunrise*. This time Adam called me with a prized assignment in advance of the show heading there for a week-long remote: Monique and I would go there ahead of time and shoot whatever interesting segments we could find that would later be cut into the show for commercial bumpers and special cutaway clips of interest. Sweet! Mon and I *rendezvous*'ed there, along with her assigned cameraman, Frankie, who is just one of the most fun guys to work with in all of television. I hired a local cameraman, Gene, a real *Kamaaina* who helped me locate some of the most fascinating, undiscovered treasures of the beautiful Hawaiian isles. While Monique walked amid the lava flows, I got an emotional private tour of the Pearl Harbor Memorial with two surviving WWII veterans. I also checked out some of the surf sites, golf courses, fish markets and luaus. I got some lessons in fire-twirling and lei-making, and joined Monique for a hula class. Eat your heart out, Shakira. My favorite shoot was flying over to Kauai to tour the exotic locations used in movies like *Indiana Jones* and *Jurassic Park*. In true Indy style, I even got to reenact one of his rope-swinging exploits across a river. Of course, when I did it there were no alligators snapping at me from below!

★ ★ ★ ★ ★ ★ ★ ★ ★ ★ ★ ★ ★ ★ ★

> In January '08, I spent two days in the freezing temperatures outside Heath Ledger's SoHo loft, filing live reports on his tragic passing. The shock and subsequent outpouring of emotion made for a highly charged story. I was proud and pleased to report from the scene.

★ ★ ★ ★ ★ ★ ★ ★ ★ ★ ★ ★ ★ ★ ★

Okay, now to get out my passport and take you overseas…

For *GMTV*, we did a side-splitting 'fish out of water' story wherein I was given a Cockney Challenge to become a true East-Ender. This began with a lesson from a dialect coach not only to perfect the accent, but to learn the essential Cockney rhyming slang I'd need. For example, 'Apples and pears' instead of 'stairs' or 'Adam and Eve' for 'believe'. After being dressed in my overcoat and cap, I was whisked off to an outdoor market place to begin my training as a vendor. I successfully changed pounds and pence while hawking various fruits and vegetables. Then it was to a Pie & Mash Shoppe where I was treated to the questionable delicacies that included eating jellied eels. Suffice it to say that I would be an extremely thin person if I had to make a steady diet of this fare. Off to the dog races from there, where the punters taught me to place bets. I finished the day at a charming pub where I pulled draughts and joined the assembled late-night crowd for a raucous sing-along of olde favorites. *Cor Blimey*, it was fun.

The Afternoon Show decided I should make my first visit to Ireland as part of their second season finale and it was a surprising treat to discover what a gorgeous and cosmopolitan city Dublin is. Maybe I'd been too influenced by Frank McCourt's *Angela's Ashes* to know beforehand, but my producers Gavin and Siobhan were the best tour guides a guy could ever ask for and introduced me to some of their best and brightest attractions. From the old world charm of Trinity College and the sublime Georgian architecture to the first-rate restaurants and contemporary elegance of Bono's Clarence Hotel, Dublin is a metropolis that successfully straddles the centuries of its history. Their art museum was amazing, and a home-cooked meal at Blathnaid's house and a running excursion on the University of Dublin's lush, green campus were especially memorable. The Guinness wasn't bad, either.

An amazing Irish adventure awaited me when I returned again in April 2008. Siobhan outdid herself as the Hostess with the Most-ess and assigned to me her most talented young producer, Aidan, for two of the most enjoyable shoots ever. After co-presenting the Friday episode (always fun to be side by side on set with the team rather than being a disembodied head inside a TV monitor!)…working through two cooking segments and an interview with their Eurovision contestant, Dustin, it was off to Belfast for a visit to the Harland & Wolff shipyard where the *Titanic* was built. From there, it was all the way back south to County Cork to have a private guided tour along 'The Titanic Trail' with historian Michael Martin. As you know from the 'Ships Ahoy!' chapter, this was a dream of two lifetimes for me!

Aidan and I next moved on to the west coast for a story on Paul Fallon's innovative company, Irish Running Tours. Going on a guided run through some of the most enchanting, dramatic landscapes imaginable was an incredible treat. I got a simultaneous workout, some sightseeing and made new friends. I must have a bit of Irish luck, because the weather wasn't merely cooperative…it was breathtaking. I was sorry to leave the Emerald Isle, but my liver wasn't!

My first visit Down Under for Australia's Seven Network stands out as one of my greatest work-related adventures ever. It was decided that I would surprise our morning show hosts live on the air in the Sydney studio, by popping out from behind the set when they would ordinarily throw to me over the satellite feed. It worked like a charm and I came armed with all sorts of Hollywood souvenirs to dole out.

I was very privileged to get a private trek to the top of the Sydney Harbour Bridge on an absolutely stellar, crystal-clear day. The breathtaking views and interesting tour guide made it less scary, since I'm not a huge fan of heights. I got to try out some of the local tastes, including emu pizza, and Vegemite (definitely an acquired taste). May I say, the local wines were awesome. I got up close and personal with koalas, emus (Nasty! No wonder they eat them.), wombats and kangaroos. I also got a lesson in sheep-shearing which reminded me that I definitely chose the right career path…I wasn't cut out for farming.

Then, it was into the Outback with producer Fiona for a tour of the bush. I was outfitted in appropriate attire that would have made Paul Hogan proud (I later interviewed him and showed off my R.M. Williams boots) and did a bit of horseback riding. As a guest of honor at a local dog track, one race was named for me and I got to present the winning entrant's owner with the gold cup (in between bites of a meat pie). I got some instruction in the sport of bowls, the perfect method for 'throwing shrimp on the barbie', checked out the rides at Luna Park, made an ass out of myself trying to surf at breathtaking Bondi Beach, walked the red carpet at the famed Sydney Opera House and worked alongside the popular Aussie boy band Human Nature. What a beautiful land! And how wonderful it is that it's such an enormous country…no matter how many visits I make over a lifetime, there will always be new things to see and experience.

But the biggest crowd pleaser for the audience was also a heck of a lot of fun for me. Our sports guru, Mark 'Beretts' Beretta, arranged for me to join the champion Sydney Swans footballers for a practise session in their home stadium. Amazing. Decked out in my red jumper and knee socks, I got to take a mark over Leapin Leo Barry and score a goal against Jared (Crouchie) Crouch, who wound up becoming a good mate of mine. I don't think coach Paul Roos has much to worry about if I ever end up on an opposing team. More likely he'd be in trouble if I played *with* the Swannies!

I can often feel disconnected from the ensemble aspect of my shows, being all alone in a Los Angeles satellite studio. But these opportunities to spend face to face time with my colleagues from both sides of the camera, as well as the viewers who enjoy my work, make the gargantuan scope of global reporting into a family-friendly small world I treasure every day.

Beauty & the Blogs

I've explained how I've come to accept being constantly reminded by viewers who meet me that I'm 'shorter in person'. <shrug> Maybe they all have big screen TVs. But when you enter the blog-o-sphere of public opinion, it becomes more than critical… it can get downright vicious. I was warned a long time ago by my presenting peers not to troll through the wicked whimsies of web chat about television personalities, lest I be offended or hurt by what they'd have to say. But who among us can resist the occasional urge to Google oneself? Just be prepared for what you might find.

Since you've read this far, you know I'm not one to be cruel or make unsubstantiated judgments, but in a democracy where we celebrate freedom of speech, everyone is allowed to express their feelings…regardless how vitriolic. The three personal attacks my image most routinely faces are my teeth, weight and tan. I can only imagine what they'd say if I appeared on television being pasty, pudgy and with rotting choppers.

Teeth. *'Fake/toothy/blinding.'* Well, I've never had braces, never had a cavity and I have the exact same smile as my mother… whom we used to jokingly call 'Old 88' and 'Piano Mouth' because she had such a dazzling set of ivories. I figure if you see my teeth, it

must mean I'm smiling. And as an oral hygiene freak, I'm going to assume that 'blinding' is an indication that they're sparkling clean! I've had the same dentist for twenty years (he's a marathon runner, too), visit him regularly and am known in our office corridors for my daily jaunts to the men's room to brush and floss.

Weight. 'Cancer patient/sickly/man-orexic.' These jibes all seem so unwarranted and angry that I can only assume they're written by overweight homophobes. I'm the healthiest person I know and also one of the biggest eaters. My Body Mass Index and Body Fat Percentage are both normal (not low), so maybe I'm a rare exception to the rule that the camera adds ten pounds. In a town where you can never be too rich or too thin, I'll just take it as a compliment.

Tan. It always cracks me up when bloggers have a go at my 'fake tan/ skin the color of Highlander caramel' (whatever that is). Although I wear sunscreen, I do catch some rays when I'm out on training runs…otherwise, the only color that isn't my own comes from the studio lighting and the anti-shine powder I am required to wear to combat the gloss of my naturally oily skin. My great-grandfather was a Cherokee Indian, so I can credit him for my skin tones and cheekbones.

✯ ✯ ✯ ✯ ✯ ✯ ✯ ✯ ✯ ✯ ✯ ✯

I'm frequently asked why I don't have a MySpace, LinkedIn or Facebook account. Between all my various blogs, columns, personal websites and other writing exploits…I can't imagine maintaining *another* site. So thanks for the invites, but I won't be signing up for any new ones in the near future.

✯ ✯ ✯ ✯ ✯ ✯ ✯ ✯ ✯ ✯ ✯ ✯

Twice I've been flattered to appear on the cover of Livia Mercer's Australian monthly *The Beauty Review* (the first man, in fact) on the subject of skin care and 'man-scaping'. I don't know that I have too many tips or secrets to share beyond the ordinary advice to cleanse, hydrate and get as much sleep as possible. I remember reading a quote from Joan Crawford recommending one should 'water the face like a flower' and that always stuck with me. I dated a makeup artist for a few years and got to know a lot of the best and worst when it comes to products, and I have a very short list of what I like:

Moisturizers. Maria DeSio's Oxygen-infused moisturizer is refreshing, clean and restorative. Chanel makes an excellent tinted moisturizer I'll use if I'm going to be on camera for a long location shoot. The prescription cream Glyquin is strong, but effective on unwanted little age spots or freckles.

Shaving. I have a tough beard and a heavy five o'clock shadow usually emerges well before noon. Combined with sensitive skin, shaving can be really tough on me and I hate it. Those metro-sexual, baby-faced complexions you see on stars like Leo DiCaprio, David Beckham and Jake Gyllenhall could explain why you see them so often sporting facial hair. I strongly recommend the shaving system from Eyre Biobotanics, a Victoria-based company I discovered while broadcasting to Australia. A lemon-myrtle oil in an ingeniously designed dual pump bottle preps the whiskers for a close, soothing shave.

Cleansers. Eyre also makes a great jojoba organic scrub I use at least once a week. But otherwise, I'm an old-fashioned soap and water guy. Both Maria DeSio and Chanel make invigorating post-cleansing toners, but I don't consider them to be an absolute necessity.

HOLLYWOOD INSIDER
EXPOSED!

Cosmetics. I'm probably the most no-frills on-camera person I know. Famed stylist Jose Eber once told me, 'There's no such thing as a bad hair day in Hollywood. Anything goes'. So I don't put a lot of time or effort into getting ready to go on the air. I'm used to being self-sufficient in that aspect, so it always amazes me when I go somewhere and have a make-up artist. It seems like they put SO much on your face and it takes so long. If I'm hanging out in a make-up room, I want to be drinking coffee and gabbing, not sitting under a smock getting my face painted. As long as I have a clean, healthy complexion, I'm happy with a little dusting of Bobby Brown Medium Powder and then let me get on with it. I've always been content with Chap-stick or Vaseline on my lips, but I do admit to a recent penchant for Jo Malone's excellent lip balm.

★ ★ ★ ★ ★ ★ ★ ★ ★ ★ ★ ★

> A great quick-fix for an unexpected zit is to cover it with a little dab of Milk of Magnesia before you go to bed. In the morning, it should be practically dried up completely.

★ ★ ★ ★ ★ ★ ★ ★ ★ ★ ★ ★

Keep it all clean—-skin, teeth, diet—and you won't need hours in the makeup chair, either. And if some nasty blogger has a problem with that, click over to another web page, pronto!

Friends On-Camera and Off

Every day I get to work and hang out with so many big-hearted and talented pros on both sides of the cameras... even if it's just a pre-segment chat during the commercial breaks. Naturally, those who appear on screen with me are the ones I'm most frequently asked about. 'What's she *really* like?' 'Is he as funny in person?' 'Do they get along with each other or is it all an act?' I thought I'd devote a few pages to tell you about some of my best television buddies, so you can decide for yourself if the personae fit with the people. But I will tell you straight off the bat what they all have in common: they're great role models, talented colleagues and compassionate friends. Even if most of 'em have funny accents!

Sunrise, Australia

Melissa Doyle—What you see is what you get with our sweet and gorgeous Mel. She's girly and giggly, generous and sentimental. She's a compassionate listener and thoughtful friend. I can't say enough nice things about her and she's also a lucky lady to have a husband and kids who adore and appreciate her. She loves shoe shopping, champagne and George Clooney. Over our years together, whether

it's in person, on the air or by phone and email, she's become like a sister to me. Quite simply: I adore her!

David Koch—This guy is brilliant. Like my dad, he has an incredible head filled with knowledge and information on a vast array of subjects. He also has the charisma and natural inquisitiveness that make him a good interviewer whether he's chatting with a movie star, world leader, the man on the street or kids. His great devotion to Dame Julie Andrews is genuine and he sure can tell a cracker of a joke.

Natalie Barr—The first time I met her, I was immediately struck by her natural poise and beautiful film-star looks. But she also has a delicious wit that belies her professional onscreen presence. Her tall, lithe swell-egance would make her a designer's dream to dress.

Mark Beretta—My mate Beretts is in the right job as a sports personality because he's a great sport with a terrific personality. He is affable, good-natured and charming. Personally, I would have voted for him to win on *Dancing with the Stars*. I think he could probably do anything he set his mind to, which is why I keep nagging him to train with me for a marathon. He's younger than I am, but I'd still like him to be my 'big brother'.

Simon Reeve—A gentleman and a scholar. While I don't get to interact with him often on the air, we communicate via email several times a week—and in person, we get on like gangbusters. He possesses a rare self-assurance that allows him to laugh easily, be outgoing on-camera, no matter the situation, and be ebullient with his friends, family and colleagues. His partner, Linda, is a living doll and they are a dream duo.

Grant Denyer—This guy has so much inherent talent, it sparkles right out of him, which is why such a broad cross-section of Australian TV viewers have embraced him. He's playful and sweet, much to the adoration of his fans.

Samantha Armytage—My *Weekend Sunrise* pal is a vivacious Virgo and has a delightful, flirty sense of humor just under the surface of her professional demeanor. The sly little smile of hers looks like she's keeping a secret and I bet if Alfred Hitchcock were around to get a look at her, he'd turn her into one of his cool blonde leading ladies.

Mike Amor—Our Los Angeles bureau chief is one of my great buddies, at work and at play. I tease him that he is our own 'Clark Kent', and he's always been a supportive colleague and friend. He and Simon are also the natty dressers in our extended 'family', and both have a collection of neckties that would rival Saks Fifth Avenue's Men's Department. In one of life's great twists, he happened to marry one of my best friends, Tracy, whom I've been close to almost as long as I've lived in Hollywood.

GMTV, UK

Lorraine Kelly—What a warm, hysterical lady she is. With her sultry Scottish brogue, LK has a brilliant sense of humor combined with a childlike curiosity about people, places and things that make her the perfect presenter for brekky telly. She's fab fun to play with off-camera, too, and we've stayed in constant contact since

my GMTV days. Whether we're just chatting about silly celebrity antics, struggling to rollerblade down the Venice boardwalk or mixing margaritas, she's great company.

Andrew Castle—This handsome charmer is a superb conversationalist and good-hearted fellow. He interacts beautifully with whomever he is chatting to, be it a guest or co-presenter. I haven't met him in person yet, but we're mates via satellite and email. His tongue-in-cheek(y) style proves he's got brains as well as brawn.

The Afternoon Show. Ireland

Blathnaid Ní Chofaigh—The flame-haired whirling dervish has more energy than any other daily presenter I've ever met. She's also a generous and gracious hostess off-air. Her mind operates on all cylinders and she's one of those rare talents who can multi-task while displaying relaxed and attentive grace under the fire of live TV. She can converse simultaneously in Gaelic and English, while listening to her IFB (Interruptable Fold Back aka communication earpiece) and reading the teleprompter at the same time. She's truly amazing and great fun.

Anna Nolan—Not many reality stars (she was one of the UK version of *Big Brother*'s most popular competitors) can segue to a hosting position with such seeming natural ease, but this Lynda Carter look-alike has a calm presenting style and smart approach to the diverse subject matter that is thrown at her.

Sheana Keane—She's a spirited little lady and deft conversationalist with a saucy sense of humor. A curvy dynamo in amazing physical shape, I'm hoping to convince her to meet up with me for a marathon in '09. I know she'd have me laughing the entire way.

Sunrise, New Zealand

Carly Flynn and James Coleman—I haven't met these two yet; our relationship is thus far relegated to our chats over the airwaves. But during the commercial breaks when we can banter back and forth freely, they both strike me as bright and lighthearted pros. We have an easy chemistry for conversation…which I've learned never to take for granted. I'm hoping a visit to their beautiful country will be in my near future and meeting them face-to-face for some quality social time is a top priority.

> When I started with *Sunrise* New Zealand in October 2007, I was by then well used to understanding the Aussie accent and vernacular and I was assured by a NZ staffer that I'd have an easy time with the Kiwi accent and would find it 'much more refined'. From the first moment I was introduced as 'Nillsson Esspin', I knew I'd be adding a new one to my aural repertoire!

And Lest I Forget—

Rebecca Loos (*Power Lesbians*)—notorious in the United Kingdom for her scandals as a reality star and the alleged mistress of soccer star David Beckham, Rebecca surprised me with her professionalism, clever banter and good manners. She's as witty as she is pretty and not at all like the vituperative vixen proclaimed in so much media.

Laura Csortan (*The Great Outdoors*)—From pageant queen to game show hostess, it might surprise you that fresh-faced and funny

HOLLYWOOD INSIDER EXPOSED!

Laura is more like the girl next door than she appears on camera. She's certainly the lady you'd most want to go sailing with during the day and nightclubbing with after dark.

Sonia Kruger (*Dancing with the Stars*)—Though she'll forever be known to the world as *Strictly Ballroom*'s Tina Sparkle, sparkling Sonia is as talented and statuesque as her TV image. Don't be fooled by that dazzling smile and curvy figure, she's a smart cookie, too.

Richard Quest (*CNN*)—My colorful mate Richard is smart as a whip and one of TV's greatest finds. He makes any story he's reporting an adventure for the viewer. His enthusiasm and energetic approach to all areas of media and current events place him deservedly high in the stratosphere of news stars. He also happens to be a hell of a lot of fun to be around.

Heather Hartt (*TV Guide Television*)—A close friend and colleague, even though she's relocated to Toronto. Heather is loyal, loving and another closet brainiac. She's an alum of the Sorbonne, mon dieu! She's a first-rate hostess and so much fun to spend time with.

Janet Charlton (*The Gossip Show*)—I've known JC since her days as *Star* magazine's star gossipista, when she became one of the best-known faces in the world of celebrity dirt. She always impressed me with her vigor for her work and prudent research and fact checking. She's one of my fave people to gab on the phone with and always surprises me with new anecdotes about famous folks.

Mike Walker (*National Enquirer Uncovered*)—the granddaddy of modern tabloid reporting. Back when I was on the gossip circuit and doing showbiz stories for shows like *Inside Edition* and *Geraldo Rivera*, Mike was always a friendly and noncompetitive guy. It's not always easy to meet generous, polite fellows in his line of work, so he stood out.

Turning Points

Did you ever see *The Turning Point*…the 1977 movie with Shirley MacLaine, Anne Bancroft and Mikhail Baryshnikov? What a fun, campy bitchfest it is. This chapter has nothing to do with that film, title similarity aside, but I just felt the sudden urge to give you a recommendation for your movie library.

Life's turning points, however, are sometimes only understood in hindsight. I wrote previously how the Hugh Grant/Divine Brown story was one of those obvious career-changing moments for me, but what about some of the less apparent ones? The incidents, happenstances and encounters that some higher power writes into the unfolding events of your life the way a great writer weaves a plotline into a story? Sometimes they can be so left of center, so improbable, they would seem absurdly unreal if they hadn't actually happened. When one has a fork in the road, it's clear that something life-changing will go along with the chosen path, but when it's something hidden behind other layers of life it can make all the more impact…and excitement. These are some of mine.

The high school play. I was grossly overweight at nearly 200 lbs. Too heavy even to participate in gym class, which only made dieting all the more difficult. In lieu of social or physical activities, I poured myself into my studies and acting. While the former had its obvious benefits (including being my class Valedictorian), the latter offered limited potential for a 'fatty', no matter how much talent I had. When I lost out on the lead in *The Boy Friend* and was cast in a small supporting role as the OLD MAN it was precisely the incentive I needed to finally take charge of my bulging body. With Dad's medical supervision, I embarked on a nine-week super diet and shed 60 pounds by opening night. I may have been playing the funny geezer, but I was a skinny one! And for the final musical production before graduation, *Once Upon A Mattress*, I was rewarded with the romantic leading part of Sir Harry. To this day, no matter what my weight fluctuation, I still see that chubby adolescent when I look in the mirror and am ever-vigilant to keep on top of my health and body composition. The only thing harder than losing a lot of weight is *knowing* you have a lot of weight to lose. That personal understanding and subsequent empathy have always been key motivating factors when I'm helping others achieve their fitness goals.

Taking my first aerobics class in 1987. After leaving a job with the soap opera *Another World*, I accepted I'd put on some extra pounds and needed to get into the gym. I joined the nearby New York Sports Club and dove into a busy schedule of aerobics classes and finally got good enough to work my way into the front row. One of the best instructors told me he'd been offered a lucrative position teaching at a Tuscan health spa but was going to turn it down to concentrate on his acting career. 'Are you crazy?' I asked. 'I'd love to have an all-expenses paid three-month trip to Italy!' He suggested I get certified and take the job myself. So that's just what I did. Within the month, I was saying 'tonificare a la piscina, signore' ('toning by the poolside, ladies') and guzzling cappuccinos between every meal. Tooling around the breathtaking Tuscan countryside and making new international friends was not only an enriching cultural experience, but when I later returned to the USA I had a fun, new job skill. I attacked this new career as a fitness instructor with great enthusiasm.

Of course that would ultimately lead me to the Princess Diana/Step Aerobics connection which would land me my first presenting job, but it can all be traced back to being in the right aerobic class at the right time. It also facilitated my patented workout program, 'The Brains and Brawn Workout' (a combination treadmill class and book club), which gained me a lot of global exposure in the fitness world, and connections with many interesting personalities in the literary and publishing industries. All because I wanted to visit Italy. That's why I always encourage young people to get out there and see the world before they settle down. Who knows what career-making, life-changing opportunity awaits?

Accepting a funny nickname. In the late '90s, I was a regular contributor to one of LA's coolest radio stations which played dance music you couldn't find anywhere else on the dial. It had a cult following amongst the young, club demographic but not a mainstream ratings success. In their struggle to find a format that would result in a financial boon to match their community popularity, the Station Manager was repeatedly re-casting the morning show teams. As their entertainment reporter, I survived every cut and stayed with the station until they finally, sadly, were sold altogether. But it was the last DJ, Boomer Servantez, who nicknamed me 'The Groove-y Gossip Guy'. It was enough of a gimmick to propel me to other industry jobs after their radio signal was forever silenced. I think of them all with great affection whenever I hear one of those oldies play. And, I might add, I still love doing radio. It's fast, it's fun and you don't have to worry about shaving or what your hair looks like.

Being a tabloid target. I was living through some lean freelance times and some personal sadness in late 2003. It was one of those periods when counting my blessings was a real daily challenge. It seemed to get a little worse when a friend from the UK alerted me to the fact that an online gossip site there had written a mean-spirited item about me in an attempt to create some scandal where none existed. It turned out to be the biggest favor ever inadvertently given to me and a great example of instant karma. Before the end of business hours that day, I had a book offer from a major Manhattan publisher. By the end of the week, I had a literary agent brokering a deal and, within a month, contracts signed and an advance in the bank. October 2004 saw the publication of *Let's Dish Up A Dinner Party!*

Interviewing a Legend. I explained what a marvelous training ground *Nelson's World* was for me as an interviewer. But even with nearly 200 hours of live celebrity chat under my belt, it was a moment during my work for *TV Guide Television* that I had the epiphany that I was doing precisely the right thing with my life. What a wonderful, rewarding revelation it was to be cognizant of it at the time. From that moment, I was able to forge confidently ahead with that job and all the ones to follow. That defining interview was with a certain TV icon who could never have imagined the positive impact our conversation would have on me: the incomparable Dick Van Dyke. I went to visit him on the set of his long-running show, *Diagnosis: Murder*, and he was completely gracious with his time and talents. This was to be part of a bigger story I was putting together on the subject of ageism in Hollywood, but this great song-and-dance star spoke so eloquently and interestingly about his own struggles against this youth-driven industry, that we made it a solo spot. He was self-effacing, good natured, witty and oh-so-bright. While I had prepared questions ahead of time, a light bulb went off while we spoke and it became a real give-and-take, spontaneous conversation…and the

model for all the hundreds of celeb chats I've done in the years since. I remember calling my Executive Producer from the car on my way home from the studio, high as a kite from my encounter with Dick. I still rely heavily on what I call 'the goose bump factor': when I get the chills and the hairs on my arm stand up, I know it's a winning interview.

★ ★ ★ ★ ★ ★ ★ ★ ★ ★ ★ ★ ★ ★ ★

Multi-Emmy winner Doris Roberts (*Everybody Loves Raymond*) is another outspoken crusader in the fight against age discrimination. As rambunctious as her character Marie Barone and as ubiquitous on the publicity beat as another camera-loving septuagenarian, astronaut Buzz Aldrin, she definitely makes the case that life can begin at 40—and so can a dynamite career.

★ ★ ★ ★ ★ ★ ★ ★ ★ ★ ★ ★ ★ ★ ★

Attending a Hollywood premiere with Carol Lynley.

Pat Boone

Carol and I, 1977

It's been a while since 'CHiPs', but Erik Estrada still knows how to work a pair of handcuffs!

With sexy Seven Network's Rosanna Mangiarelli, after we wrapped our location shoot at Disneyland.

Glenn and I with my folks in Bermuda, 2008.

Carol Connors and Cindy Margolin are beautiful bakers!

I don't have to dream of Jeannie...here's the real thing, bubbly Barbara Eden!

The indomitable and always glamorous Jackie Collins!

Fabulous Fergie back when she was a single songstress!

Running the Firenze Marathon! Molto bene!

You can take John Schneider out of Hazzard County, but you can't take Hazzard County out of the Dukes!

"Sex & The City" siren Kristen Davis and I go wayyy back!

Two of my great-nieces, Michaiah and Az

On set with Anna & Blathnaid for Ireland's 'The Afternoon Show'.

With fellow political junkies, the Dentons...James & Erin.

I can tell you firsthand, Tom Cruise is the undisputed King of the Red Carpet.

One of my many appearances on "Soap Talk" with Lisa Rinna and Ty Treadway.

Photo courtesy of Disney ABC Cable Networks Group

What did I tell you? Jeff Goldblum is the No 1 Most Spic-and-Span Star!

Jeff Goldblum and Kevin Spacey. As interviewees, JG was one of the best...KS, one of the worst!

Run Nelson Run!

Crossing the finish line at the San Francisco Marathon.

Don't let the smile fool you, the Catalina Eco-Marathon was the hardest event I've ever run!

The Right Place at the Right Time

The best, most incredible showbiz stories sometimes unfold right before your very eyes when you least expect it. I bump into celebrities all over the place…waiting by the carousel at baggage claim, running on the beach or stopped at a red light. All for the (overpriced) cost of a lunch at the swanky Four Seasons Hotel in Beverly Hills, I got such a heaping first-hand helping of scoop that I dined out on it for ages. And wound up getting quoted, as I often do, in *The New York Post*'s mecca of gossip: their world-renowned Page Six column. Another perfect example of being in the right place at the right time. I am a firm believer in good old-fashioned English and communications skills, but all the preparation in the world can't guarantee you good luck…then the backup of a strong education becomes vital for making the most of opportunities when fate steps in.

I had time to kill at the hotel before attending a press tour for the acclaimed movie *Juno*. The lunch they were serving the journalists was a menu of fatty foods I try to avoid: fried chicken, french fries, mac n' cheese. So I opted instead to hit the star-studded dining room off the Main Lobby. I never mind eating alone, especially if there's a floor show like the one I was about to encounter. (Between the luxurious

spa, high-end guest suites, publicity junkets, conferences, screenings and happening bar scene at this hotel, there is never a shortage of star power to be found. Just riding the elevators or standing at the Valet Parking stand is a class in Celebrity 101!)

I sat down at a table directly across from music legend Carlos Santana who obviously didn't believe it's impolite for men to wear a hat indoors. At first I wasn't sure if it was Edward James Olmos or Tony Orlando, but the conversation quickly confirmed it was the legendary guitarist. He was surrounded by a not-very-impressive entourage of cell-phone wielding sycophants who never stopped talking to each other and to whoever was on their phones. Carlos was very mild mannered and quiet, just sort of nodded and went along with things until finally taking his leave. As soon as he left the table, the three remaining people went into a frenzy of simultaneous talking over each other and into their phones, trying very deliberately to be overheard, to show everyone else in the restaurant how important they were as Carlos' 'people'. However, Carlos might want to reconsider his reps because they were loudly spilling all the details of his upcoming gig in an effort to show off their authority to other diners. Here's what shocked me, and I'm sure Carlos would be mortified they were shouting about it publicly: HE'D MIME HIS GUITAR PLAYING! The exact words of his rep to someone on the other end of the phone: 'You can't afford him to do a live riff. It would cost you thousands and thousands and thousands [of dollars]. We have over 50,000 hours of audio and you need less than 30 seconds. You don't have to worry about rights or clearance from Arista [his record label]. We have our own unpublished music, otherwise you couldn't afford it.' Not only was this fellow obnoxious, to be so rudely conducting his business in a public place, he was idiotic to expose such personal details of his client where there were so many eyes and ears surrounding him. He went on to discuss how Carlos could just play along to one of the prerecorded riffs. I was pretty surprised to find out that the great guitarist would ever fake his riffs. You can bet when I reported this, news of the great Santana playing 'air guitar' made international headlines.

So while they're still blabbering on, who stumbled in but self-proclaimed supermodel/reality star, Janice Dickinson. She was wearing what looked to be a riding outfit with super-tight cream colored pants and high boots. That footwear, combined with a pair of ridiculous oversized black sunglasses explains why she was tripping (it was too early for cocktails!). She charged in one direction and two minutes later reappeared and charged out the other way, yelling at a waiter, 'He knows I'm here. He knows I'm here.' Never saw her again. I thought she was lost or disoriented until a source of mine reminded me that she had a paternity dispute with Sylvester Stallone back in the 1990s (they were briefly engaged back then and she claimed her daughter, Savannah, was Sly's child, but DNA tests proved otherwise and their romance—not surprisingly—crashed and burned). Then it all made sense: I knew Stallone was in the hotel at that very moment: in an upstairs suite doing press interviews for his umpteenth *Rambo* movie. Was Janice trying to find Sly or avoid him? The former couple was about to—the very next day—make headlines again over her claims that he once injected her full of steroids against her will. Since his own 2007 run-in with Australian authorities over the question of illegal performance-enhancing human growth hormones, Sly eschews Aussie media, so I may never find out for sure.

Then after all this, like some kind of slapstick tabloid sitcom… three heavies enter, pushing porn's paralyzed publishing mogul Larry (*Hustler*) Flynt in his wheelchair. Apparently, he's a luncheon regular there, and they wheeled him to a corner table and all sat down for lunch. One of the security guard/assistants in the dark suits tucked a napkin into his collar, but Larry had no trouble whipping out, holding

HOLLYWOOD INSIDER
EXPOSED!

and gabbing into his own cell phone. I felt like I could have sat there picking at my Chicken Caesar Salad all day, watching the drama unfold. But…I had work to do.

> ★ ★ ★ ★ ★ ★ ★ ★ ★ ★ ★ ★
>
> It should be noted that publicist Lizzie Grubman, whose 2001 plea-bargain on a 26 felony count indictment made her a celebrity herself, represents Janice and denies her presence at the hotel that day. But after all my many years of expert star-spotting: if that wasn't the real Ms Dickinson, she should be flattered that a leggy Beverly Hills wannabe has so perfectly replicated her look…and manner. She fooled me.
>
> ★ ★ ★ ★ ★ ★ ★ ★ ★ ★ ★ ★

However, it wasn't over when I paid my tab and left the table. On the way out, who do I see but Hollywood heartthrob Blair Underwood with a woman (his wife, Desiree, me thinks) taking what looked to be a business meeting with two gentleman in suits. It was during the Writers' Strike which must have been bringing out the creativity in everyone because, as I walked by she was giving the guys a hard sell on Blair. 'Well, you know…Blair wrote a book!' (I looked it up and he indeed wrote two: *Casanegra* and *Before I Got Here*). Maybe he was looking to take advantage of the strike and work out a writing deal of his own? During the strike, union members were rampantly exploring other options (children's books, novels) while actors-who-write, such as Ed Burns, concentrated on other avenues of literary creativity. Ed, for example, is in business with Deepak Chopra's son, Gotham, on publishing a series of graphic novels through Chopra's India-based Virgin Comics Company (will there be an ultimate movie version of the series à la *The Dark Knight* or *V for Vendetta*?).

Not a bad way to spend forty-five minutes, eh? Sure beats sitting around having fried chicken with a bunch of other journalists, if you ask me. Never be afraid to dine alone; take a book along for company, but chances are, at least in Hollywood, you'll have much more juicy storylines just by keeping your eyes and ears wide open. What's in Britney Spear's shopping cart? What did Niecy Nash leave behind in the bathroom? Did you spot one of the Baldwin brothers in the steam room? How'd Diane Lane take her tea? Did you notice how Scarlett Johanssen behaved when she barked out her frappuccino order to the barista?

> ★ ★ ★ ★ ★ ★ ★ ★ ★ ★ ★
>
> I inadvertently scared poor Diane Lane when I interviewed her by saying how much my trainer loved her, when he told me he'd 'cut off my arm for her'. She visibly blanched and I guess I don't blame her.
>
> ★ ★ ★ ★ ★ ★ ★ ★ ★ ★ ★

Of course, if you choose your timing wisely there can be opportunities to craft for the purposes of storytelling. At the beginning of 2008, word got out in the media that Scientology spouse Katie Holmes would be running the famed Boston Marathon, one of the most elite sporting events in the world. To participate, it's necessary to first qualify with an impressive finishing time in another certified marathon course. A few exceptions are made for entrants who are doing special charitable fundraising in conjunction with their participation. This was reportedly how Katie was circumventing the qualifying process.

My neighbors jokingly refer to me as 'Nelson Aspen: Super Citizen' because of my intense commitment to justice and fair play. Whether it's a game of Scrabble, paying taxes or enforcing the '10 Items or Less' policy at the supermarket checkout line, I'm a fiend for playing by the rules. When I got wind of Katie and Boston, I was incensed. Letting Paris Hilton out of jail was one thing, but this case of star-privilege was quite another! A chronic writer of Letters to the Editor, I dashed off a statement and fired it off to my network of sports journos and the most popular runners' websites and blogs. It read: 'There are plenty of marathon runners who dream of qualifying for Boston…in fact for many it's a lifelong dream and even with the "charity lottery", it's a very slim shot at attaining. If the report about Katie Holmes is true, it's a particularly annoying example of celebrity rule-bending when there are so many thousands of folks pounding out the training miles to benefit charities at the same time. This example of favoritism will prove to be a very unpopular decision for the Boston Marathon organizers within the racing community they covet. I wonder if she'll ignore the 'no headphone' rule as she did in the NYC Marathon?'

Gotta love the internet. That shot around the world faster than I could run 5k, and by the end of the day Katie's rep issued a simple statement: 'Katie Holmes will not be running the Boston Marathon'. Maybe she never intended to. But the kernel of a story, combined with a passionate opinion, made for a great headline feature. Like any other good storytelling, you need to have a beginning, a middle and an end—even if the end is a question mark.

There is Nothing Like a Dame

Being the youngest son of a youngest son of a youngest son, I grew up in a world filled with elders. It wasn't until my nieces and nephews came along that I began to encounter people younger than myself. But by then, I was already working as a child actor and accustomed to the company of adults. A chubby little grown up. I also happened to have two very influential grandmothers who each lived to the ripe old age of 99…and were as interesting and enjoyable as anyone half their age. Neither ever learned how to drive a car or use a computer, but were living history books of the twentieth century. They not only taught me the intricacies of playing Yahtzee or Gin Rummy, but how to make the perfect chocolate or pineapple upside down cakes. I still know their World War One songs like 'There once was a lonely country gink, a way out west where the hop toads wink…' and 'Down by the Weeping Willow'. Gram was adventurous, outgoing and verbose. Mom Mom was nervous, soft spoken and gentle. It was never a chore to be around them, even when I was a moody adolescent. Perhaps it was those 30-plus years I got to spend with them that made me appreciate the feisty fun of being around mature ladies. What follows are some recollections of several showbiz gals I've had the good fortune to know during my career.

★Betty Garrett

Like Jessica Tandy, I think Betty is one of those rare gems that kept getting prettier with age. Born in 1919, she made a big splash in the lavish MGM classic musical *On the Town*, as Frank Sinatra's love interest: the wise-cracking cab driver, Hildy. (She told me she never tires of watching the reruns because 'we had so much fun with that and when I watch it, it recreates the fun time'.) Her film career stalled when her husband Larry Parks was investigated for possible links to Communism during Hollywood's post-war Blacklist era ('My only regret is that Larry didn't get to see this time where it's all being brought out in the open and people are seeing it for what it was. Which is literally, a witch hunt.'). But Betty was a talented trouper and went on to become best known for her TV roles as Archie Bunker's ukulele-strumming, feminist nemesis Irene on *All in the Family* and landlady Edna Garrett to *Laverne & Shirley*. I met her in the late 1990s shortly after she'd written her interesting autobiography, *Betty Garrett and Other Songs: A Life on Stage and Screen*. She is a stunning example of someone for whom age seems to have no boundaries...full of vitality, wit and inherent curiosity for new and wonderful things. I could talk to her for days. She's done it all and is still hungry for more.

The last time I ran into her was when we'd both been booked to host on-air pledge drives for Public Television. I was flattered that she remembered me and we settled right back into conversation. I'd been paired with famous fashion designer Bob Mackie (remember all those outrageous creations he did for Cher?) and she with veteran film star Nina Foch. But we pretty much abandoned our designated co-hosts when it came to off-camera chit chat.

> On B-movie star Ronald Reagan becoming President of the United States, Betty commented: 'I loved the idea that an actor could be President, but I think they picked the wrong actor'.

★Gwen Verdon

It was no mean feat for Renée Zellweger to win me over as Roxie Hart in the movie version of *Chicago*. I'd been weaned on the original Broadway cast album starring the 'real' Roxie, Bob Fosse's wife, muse and show biz legend: the leggy, raspy, redheaded Gwen Verdon. I knew every song from her recordings of that show as well as her triumphant *Sweet Charity* and *Damn Yankees*. In her post-dancing years, she became a familiar character actress on TV's *Magnum: P.I.* and the big screen's *Cocoon* (dancing with Don Ameche) and *Marvin's Room*, earning a Best Supporting Actress Oscar nomination. It was during the summer of 1990 that I first encountered her in person.

Every weekend, I'd take the jitney bus from Manhattan out to West Hampton, where I spent the days teaching aerobic classes to the wealthy vacationers and the nights partying with the locals. Good times. It was the height of Madonna's 'Vogue' craze and I incorporated a bit of that stylized choreography into my exercise routines. Gwen would routinely take the callisthenic and stretch classes that followed mine and I immediately noticed whenever she'd be observing me from the back of the studio.

She still sported her carrot-topped hairdo and always wore a lavender sweat suit. I couldn't help but want to show off a bit for the famous star and seeing her always energized me to give my class an extra-tough workout.

One Saturday, she approached me as I was packing up my gear in between classes. In that daffy, distinctive voice she asked me if I lived in the city. When I replied that I did, she asked if it would be all right to get some private coaching from me on how to 'Vogue'. I was stunned. How the heck could I teach Gwen Verdon *anything* about dance?

Of course, it took no time at all before the student became the master. I showed her once and that was all it took. But she wanted to try out some of my classes and put her new skills to use. I was nervous: my routines were notorious cardio-blasts and all I could think of was the outrage of the theatrical community and the headlines that would scream, 'Beloved Broadway Legend Murdered by Aerobics Instructor!' Hey, it could happen. I'd just worked with Douglass Watson, patriarch Mac Cory on the soap *Another World*. He'd been a professional dancer in his youth, but his ticker tired out soon after a group exercise class (not one of mine!!).

I acquiesced and all my singer/dancer/actor/fitness friends turned up to see the famous star appear at the New York Sports Club. She arrived about ten minutes before start time, hips thrust forward and toes pointed out in a jaunty dancer's gait, and her dance bag slung over one shoulder. It was the first time I saw her wear anything other than her favorite purple sweats. She was in a form-fitting black leotard and tights and when she leaned up against a stationary bicycle outside the workout studio, you could still see how she earned her nickname, 'The Superior Posterior'. She was as svelte and provocative as when she struck that iconic pose for the poster of *Sweet Charity* in 1966! The face was lined, but the physique and wide-eyed sexy innocence were still there. No wonder 'whatever Lola wants, Lola gets'.

Class got underway and, for about twenty minutes, Gwen kept up with the 20-something regulars in the front row. After showing off her newly acquired 'Vogue-ing' prowess, she drifted to the back of the room to catch her breath and finish out the rest of the routine. I think we both felt a great sense of accomplishment…and relief.

It wasn't long after that I relocated to Hollywood and Gwen generously referred me to her commercial rep at the William Morris Agency. I only ever saw her one more time after that, at the LA premiere of the musical revue *Fosse*, which she co-created. Stunning Valerie Pettiford performed several of Gwen's most famous numbers (ironically, I knew Valerie from when we both worked on *Another World*. I think they should have renamed that show *Another Small World!*).

If you want to see a glimpse of the great Gwen Verdon I appreciated so much, check out her work in the film version of *Damn Yankees* and I bet you'll be smitten by the magic in her movement. My pal Glenn now resides in an apartment on Central Park West directly adjacent to hers, so I always think of her when I enter that building. A great lady of the stage and of the world.

★ Dorothy Loudon

I was so excited. I'd just left school to move into my first apartment, smack dab in the middle of Hell's Kitchen. It was the most run-down, roach-infested neighborhood in pre-revitalized Times Square, but to a nineteen-year-old actor it felt like Park Avenue. I started auditioning for anything and everything, and my first success came being cast in something called *Dorothy Loudon's Musical Comedy Showcase*, a revue of musical numbers by twenty young performers hand-picked by the Tony-winning star of *Annie*, *Noises Off* and *Sweeney Todd*. I was singing *I Love a Piano* and the romantic *They Were You* from *The Fantasticks*. I loved our rehearsals with Dorothy…she was such a ham. You could just tell she wanted to perform every song herself. She rarely directed or coached; she was much more likely to take the stage herself and say 'Here, let me show you how to do it'.

There was, I soon discovered, a very troubled side to the talented toast of Broadway, though. She would often make rambling, middle-of-the-night phone calls to her cast and most of us (myself included) were too polite or scared to hang up and let her sleep off the demons. Legend has it that she never recovered from two major blows: the death of her beloved husband, Norman, in 1977 and being replaced by Carol Burnett as Miss Hannigan in the 1982 film version of *Annie*.

She hosted a closing night party for us in her expansive West-side apartment and for those of us who lived in six-floor walk-ups and scraped by on meager 'survival job' earnings, that kind of catered festivity was a big treat. Unfortunately, Dorothy was in an altered state by the time the party got underway and I spent the better part of the evening trying to remain inconspicuous behind a potted palm. I ate as many hors d'oeuvres as I could and nearly made a clean getaway before she managed to launch a verbal assault on me for leaving 'too early' (I was never a night owl) and in the company of our director Russ, with whom I was sharing a taxi.

Dorothy passed away in 2003, largely unremembered except by her passionately devoted theater fans. Whenever I think of her, I am reminded of how all the talent and success in the world can't be enough to make a sad person happy.

★ Laurie Beechman

Laurie was another great Broadway singing sensation, best remembered for her Tony-nominated turn as The Narrator in *Joseph and the Amazing Technicolor Dreamcoat*, Fantine in *Les Misérables* and the longest-running Grizabella in *Cats*. She died tragically at only age 44, from ovarian cancer. But her mom, sisters and I all performed together in the early days of my career and her continued friendship and encouragement, even after she'd made it, always meant a lot to me. I must have seen *Joseph* a dozen times from every perspective in the theater. Fortunately, her powerful voice and most emotional performances have been preserved on several albums and cast recordings.

★Ruta Lee

This patriotic songstress always signs her emails to me 'Ruta Toot Toot' and that pretty much sums up her *joie de vivre*. She is a pistol and one of the dearest, sprightly broads in the biz. I grew up watching her as a celebrity panelist on all the game shows and her name always adorned the marquees for touring productions of crowd-pleasers such as *Hello, Dolly!*, *The Best Little Whorehouse in Texas* and *The Unsinkable Molly Brown*. She also made great films like *Seven Brides for Seven Brothers* and *Funny Face*. You may have seen her on episodes of *Roseanne*, as the 'lipstick lesbian' lover of Roseanne's mom, Bev. She is not only a crack up and a fire cracker, she's a tireless champion for the philanthropic Thalians organization of which she serves as Chairman.

★Sally Kirkland

I have to admit, I can't recall the first time I met Golden Globe winning Sally. She seems to have always been around…a particularly *outré* character on almost every red-carpet event in recent memory. Even though she has made everyone's 'Worst Dressed' list at least twice, her new age spirit and good intentions are as genuine as her colorful, revealing outfits are outrageous. I knew she was an ordained minister (The Church of the Movement of Spiritual Inner Awareness), taught acting classes (combining yoga, performance and meditation) and held court at West Hollywood's Silver Spoon diner along with other fellow Actors Studio devotee, the late Shelley Winters. I had interviewed her on *Nelson's World* and there was a brief period when

HOLLYWOOD INSIDER
EXPOSED!

she was determined to buy the house next door to mine. I was thankful when she lost interest in it. I had a strong sense that sharing a property line with Sally would result in many years of interesting anecdotes but probably very little sleep. (Ironically, in January of 2008, she was briefly hospitalized for exhaustion. The woman *never* stops!)

The most interesting time we spent together was when I interviewed her for some TV and print stories about her controversial stance *against* silicone implants and breast augmentation. She was one of the first celebrities to celebrate and flaunt such enhancements, until the chemicals inside her began to leak and poison her…thrusting Sally into a years-long nightmare of health problems. She became a passionate advocate for banning such cosmetic procedures and even had the removal of hers filmed. No glitz and glamour there. Sally took a lifetime of passion for fashion (her mother was a famous editor for *Vogue*) and spurned it in her tireless pursuit of self-awareness. I vividly recall conducting one interview on her enormous bed, alongside her little dog Shiva. She was unabashed as she exposed her misshapen breasts and grabbed my hand to actually feel the deformities. There was no pretence or hesitation on her part, only a fierce urgency to communicate her point of view about the dangers of implants.

Brave, ballsy Sally proved to me first hand (no pun intended) that there's much more to a blonde bombshell than meets the eye.

★ ★ ★ ★ ★ ★ ★ ★ ★ ★ ★ ★ ★

> Curvy platinum-haired sexpot Anna Nicole Smith achieved with her death the eternal fame she so blatantly craved in life. Since the triumphs and tragedies of her story are well-renowned, I can only add that any time I ever saw her out-and-about around town, she was *always* smiling and light-hearted. She always gave me the impression that she was in on the joke…and loving every second of it.

★ ★ ★ ★ ★ ★ ★ ★ ★ ★ ★ ★ ★

★Cyd Charisse

Like Gwen Verdon and Leslie Caron (whom I see around Beverly Hills occasionally), the late Cyd is proof that song and dance definitely contribute to ageless beauty and vigor. The first time I encountered the leggy goddess of the silver screen (good thing she changed her name from Tula Ellice Finklea, it doesn't quite have the same ring, does it!?) was on the dance floor of the Coconut Club in Merv Griffin's Beverly Hilton Hotel. She was steppin' out with her baby, husband of sixty years, Tony Martin. The dapper duo looked elegant and Cyd was especially radiant. I'm no ballroom dancer, but something came over me and all I could think was this could be a once in a lifetime opportunity to trip the light fantastic with one of the greatest, most famous dancers in the world. I summoned up all my nerve and asked if I might cut in. Cyd beamed graciously but answered with perfect MGM Studio elocution, 'I'm sorry, but I only dance with my husband'. How could I mind a rejection so polite and so romantic?

I bumped into them not too long ago at a restaurant in Westwood and told that story to Tony, saying it still ranks as the nicest let-down I've ever had. His proud smile said it all: she may have danced with Fred Astaire and Gene Kelly, but all her best dances were saved for him alone. *Très romantique!* We miss her.

★Shirley Jones

Pretty Shirley will always be best known as the crooning matriarch of *The Partridge Family*, but diehard film fans know she played an important part in dramatic and musical big-screen works such as *The Music Man* and *Oklahoma!* She even garnered a Best Supporting Actress Oscar for her performance as a prostitute, opposite Burt Lancaster in the classic *Elmer Gantry*.

Shirley stunned the showbiz community in 1977 when, after her divorce from dashing Broadway star Jack Cassidy, she wed wacky comedian Marty Ingels. Their tumultuous marriage has endured, although most people are still a bit baffled by one of Hollywood's oddest couples. She seems to convey an aura of linen and rose petals, while he is all hand buzzers and horns. Who knows what secret chemistry they share behind closed doors? I'm betting it's a sense of humor. Shirley's the first one to chuckle at her wholesome image. 'People are always surprised to find out that I love to read true crime', she once told me. 'I love anything about serial killers!' I completely understood, being a bit of a buff on the genre myself, and joked that 'Shirley Jones and The Serial Killers' would be a great name for a punk rock band. She is as charming and warm as you'd imagine.

★ ★ ★ ★ ★ ★ ★ ★ ★ ★ ★ ★ ★ ★ ★ ★ ★ ★ ★

> Always remember that what you see isn't always what you get. I'm more surprised when stars in private are more like their public personae. It's more often a case of street angel/house devil.

★ ★ ★ ★ ★ ★ ★ ★ ★ ★ ★ ★ ★ ★ ★ ★ ★ ★ ★

★Florence Henderson

Another beloved sitcom mom is Florence Henderson aka Carol Brady. Unlike her *Partridge* counterpart, Flo only got to sing in one Christmas episode, even though she'd been a musical star when producers decided to cast her in the role that would define the remainder of her career. Carol was the oh-so-sweet, uncomplicated suburban wife and mom, rarely called upon to do more than say 'Oh, Mike', when one of their six kids had a problem. She even had the luxury of a live-in housekeeper to do all the hard work.

That groovy, saccharine *haus frau* she's been playing in various incarnations of *The Brady Bunch* since 1969 could be why Florence has always sought to show off her true colors: that of a sensual woman with a naughty sense of humor and an easy laugh. She's a fun interview precisely because she is so opposite from that milk-and-cookies image. A licensed hypnotherapist, she can also help cure your insomnia or kick that cigarette habit. That's way more than Mrs Brady could ever do.

★ ★ ★ ★ ★ ★ ★ ★ ★ ★ ★ ★ ★

> In 2007, I interviewed the surviving cast members of the ghoulish sitcom *The Addams Family* and asked them which clan would win if they were pitted against *The Munsters*. Gomez, Cousin Itt, Wednesday and Pugsley all agreed they could 'kick the Munsters' asses!' That's a family feud I'd like to see! Hmmm…'Thank you, Thing!'

★ ★ ★ ★ ★ ★ ★ ★ ★ ★ ★ ★ ★

★A Tex-Mex Trio: Polly, Lois and Heather

With apologies to my local Mexican cantina, El Coyote, it is courtesy of Sunday brunches at Marix Tex-Mex restaurant in West Hollywood that I've had a triumvirate of great dame encounters. I don't count Jennifer Aniston or Lucy Liu, both of whom are also frequent patrons, since I never chatted with them.

Back when I was a social smoker, Polly Bergen tapped me on the shoulder to bum a ciggie. I sputtered less from the tobacco and more because I recognized the great actress from her long career in films. From *Cape Fear* to *The Caretakers* to *Cry Baby* to a 'rebirth' on *Desperate Housewives*, this talented businesswoman and performer has always been one of my faves. I told her I'd give her a cigarette if she'd allow me to share a pitcher of margaritas with her. It was a memorable trade.

Another time, I found myself sitting beside one of the great leading ladies of 1970's TV movies, Lois Nettleton. She was in some mod attire of that very era...she'd obviously decided she found a style she liked and wanted to stick with it. (Do you have any friends who still wear clothes from twenty-plus years ago simply because they can still fit in them? I do and I think it's bizarre.) Again, the exchange of frozen margaritas for fascinating conversation was a wise investment.

The third in my tequila trifecta was none other than stunning Heather Locklear, whose presence with then-husband Richie Sambora had attracted the notice of everyone in the place. She was, after all, at the zenith of her *Melrose Place* fame and beauty. As an amateur cartoonist, I started working on a tablecloth portrait of Heather and Richie, surrounded by adoring diners. As I'd hoped, she noticed and they joined me and my companion Louan, sharing their pitcher of margaritas. I drew all four of us, cocktails in hand, and she enthusiastically accepted it as a souvenir. I wonder who got custody of it in the split.

★Barbara Eden

I told you about meeting Barbara and being introduced to her labradoodle, but there's more to the story. I'd been hearing about her for years from my sister, Lee. Barbara was engaged at one point to a friend of Lee's (like I weave through the Tinseltown tapestry, my sis does so similarly in Washington, DC) before she met and fell in love with her current husband, Jon. They're a great couple: it obviously pays to wait for the right soul mate, or so I keep telling myself.

> 'If gentlemen prefer blondes, then I'm a blonde who prefers gentlemen.' —Barbara Eden

On August 23, 2006, I was working out at the club when I heard the strains of 'Happy Birthday' coming out of the Spinning studio. It was, unbelievably, Barbara's 72nd! She must be a genie, because she really does look almost as impossibly cute and curvy as she did back in 1965 when she first popped out of that bottle! Some rather lecherous old fella came by and said, 'I still dream of you, Jeannie.' She cleverly fired back a muttered, 'More like a nightmare'.

I couldn't resist extending my own best wishes for her special day and, since everyone had been singing, ask her if she was aware that the familiar, bossa-nova *I Dream of Jeannie* theme song actually had lyrics. To my happy surprise, she said no. So right there in the middle of the hallway, I launched into an impromptu rendition with Barbara accompanying me on percussion. I'm such a dweeb, but it was fun and makes a great story.

Barbara is a great, down to earth gal and enormous fun. What a hoot to sing the Jeannie theme to the original Genie herself. (In my cabaret show I do a medley of unknown lyrics to famous TV themes, including *M*A*S*H*, *Bewitched*, *The Munsters* and undiscovered verses to *The Mary Tyler Moore Show*, *Petticoat Junction* and *The Flintstones*.)

★ ★ ★ ★ ★ ★ ★ ★ ★ ★ ★ ★ ★ ★ ★

> The late literary lion, Sidney Sheldon, actually created *Jeannie*, after a tremendously successful screenwriting career. He later went on to become one of the bestselling novelists of racy fiction and I interviewed him a few times in the late 1990s. He was an amazing fellow and told me the transition from sitcoms to authoring books 'was a pure accident. I was producing *Jeannie* and simultaneously writing *The Patty Duke Show*, which I also created. I got an idea which I didn't know how to put into a dramatic form, so I decided to write it as a novel.' That turned out to be *The Naked Face* which *The New York Times* hailed as the best mystery novel of the year. As for the

EXPOSED!

ingenious genie, I found out from him how he slipped such a provocative concept past the strict guidelines of early 1960s television executives. 'When I created the show, censorship was very strong. They bought the show but then someone at the network woke up and said, "Hold it! We just bought a show about a half naked woman who lives with a bachelor and keeps saying '*What can I do for you, Master?*'" Before the first episode went on the air, I had twenty pages of notes from the network censor. After that first show, it started diminishing when they saw I was just doing a romantic comedy. And then the notes stopped.' And although I was tempted to disagree with the venerable scribe, I asked him whom he thought would win a magic death match: Jeannie, or Samantha from *Bewitched*. He laughed and answered, 'I'm afraid I have to say Jeannie. Although I like Samantha a lot'.

★ ★ ★ ★ ★ ★ ★ ★ ★ ★ ★ ★ ★ ★ ★ ★ ★

★ Dame Julie Andrews

I'd never have described myself as a Julie-groupie. I was surprised how many MILLIONS of them are out there when I saw for myself after my third encounter with her…which coincided with the release of her literary autobiography, *Home*.

One of my producers inquired if I could interview JA on short notice, in New York City. I'd have a one-on-one and it would be a national exclusive. There was a caveat, however: we needed the approval of a New York-based film crew and there had been some difficulty securing the booking.

'Two Degrees of Nelson Aspen' to the rescue! Not only did I know the crew from a previous gig, their Bureau Chief started out as a production assistant on one of my most successful shoots…a decade before! She was all grown up now, and the 'head honcho'. One phone call and five minutes later, the Exclusive was secured and I was packing my bags to catch an overnight flight for the Big Apple.

Not only was it a happy reunion, but I had the pleasant surprise of being one of only three reporters granted time with Dame Julie: a colleague from GMTV and my merry mate, Richard Quest. The fab producer, Helen, had transformed an already lush suite and when JA and her small entourage arrived, it was a literal tea party! Dame Julie even brought the teabags (PG Tipps) and, in further 'small world' wonder, her daughter Emma and I had a mutual friend: my buddy Roy…her childhood crush!

I cannot gush enough about JA from start to finish. I'd seen her in action before: charming, well mannered, friendly, energetic and a consummate professional. But in this unusually private setting, there was a much greater glimpse into the person…not merely the persona. She was relaxed, in the company of friends, family and handpicked professionals whom she trusted. This was as close to seeing her 'let her hair down' as anybody's ever likely to get. Along with our natural chemistry, she and I gabbed right through the allotted time.

The interview, as it went to air, made for a highly rated episode and a YouTube debut which garnered two honors as 'Most Viewed' and 'Most Favorited' that week. But since TV dictates editing, it only lasted under five minutes. Here, as a keepsake for you *and* me, is the full chat I had with this dear lady.

Nelson: *When we think of Julie Andrews, we think of the penultimate English lady, and yet you've lived in Los Angeles for so long. What is the most English thing about you and the most American thing about you?*
JA: I love a cup of tea and for me a good English tea is something that I still do and search for. I carry my teabags with me everywhere. And the most American thing, you know…I don't know! I'd have to ask somebody else. I think that probably I've picked up on a few American phrases because I've lived there so long now. But I still feel very British in fact. And I love all things that came from Britain in the first place.

EXPOSED!

Nelson: *Is your home in Los Angeles very English? Do you have English gardens?*

JA: I do. I have a very tiny garden in Los Angeles but it is a beautiful little garden. It's got a lot of rosemary, a lot of iris, a lot of myrtle trees. Many roses. It's very charming. It has a mixture of a little English and perhaps a little French garden too.

Nelson: *And that's the name of your book…Home. Are you a homebody?*

JA: Yes, I have to make home wherever I go…whether I'm in a hotel or up in an airplane, or whatever. It has to be my space. But this word home, I hope that the reader might decide for themselves what home represents to them and to me. Is it the theater which certainly was my home for my whole childhood or is it really home? They all mean so much to me.

Nelson: *When you close your eyes and think of home, where do you land?*

JA: Well, home for me was Walton-on-the-Thames in Surrey in England and that was the home that my parents strived to buy. It was the home that we all eventually loved and the home that I was always glad to get back to after traveling as much as I did. And this book is a memoir of my early years…before Broadway. Though I do describe Broadway in the book, it's certainly before the movies and Hollywood. I just thought, maybe, I could capture a little tiny bit of the history of the theater in those days when I was a kid…when vaudeville was dying, when I was touring endlessly around England and belting out my little arias in a squeaky high voice.

Nelson: *It still kind of hurts me to think vaudeville is dead. I don't want vaudeville dead!*

JA: I don't want it to die either. There's nothing more fun, there's nothing sillier than some of the great vaudeville schtick that I used to see. There's still a lot of it embedded in the great comedians in England and in America. You don't see it as much. These days it's more reality TV and *Dancing with the Stars* and all of that.

Nelson: *But even in your most romantic leading lady roles, you've never been afraid to take a pie in the face. You've always had a knack for comedy. Did you learn that from your parents?*

JA: No, I think I learned that from vaudeville!

Nelson: *And Dick Van Dyke, your mate…such a great slapstick fellow. It's interesting when I talked to Dick Van Dyke, we talked at length about ageism in Hollywood and that seems never to have touched you. You've always been in demand.*

JA: My father was a great advocate [of fighting ageism]. At 74 or 76 he sent himself back to college to learn German. And he didn't, just didn't, allow age to be a factor.

Nelson: *Six decades in the making for you to tell this story. Why did you choose now? Why did you wait so long?*

JA: I didn't feel ready, for starters. My lovely publishers, Hyperion, were pushing me to do this for about fourteen years now and they never gave up. And finally I thought if I could write a little history about the way it was in those days, maybe that's good reason to write it. And it seemed like a good time. My family are all gone. Whatever I write, I'm free to write. I didn't want to hurt anybody. As I said, I didn't feel ready. I think it sort of had to ingest a while.

Nelson: *You write stories about the rather difficult times in your childhood, revelations about your paternity. We live in a society where any celebrity's information—How did you manage to keep a personal life through your career?*

JA: My parents were very good on all sides, my family were great. It was home, as the title of the book suggests, it was home, home mattered. My mother was great about not becoming conceited, or thinking that I had 'it' or I was better than anything. She always reminded me that there is always somebody that could do something far better than you can and to be grateful. And I am! The breaks that I've had, the good fortune that I've had…I think it's above and beyond anything anybody could have dreamt.

Nelson: *You've performed for royalty, you've been made a Dame, you have an Oscar, you were the toast of Broadway. When did you finally give yourself a pat on the back and say 'Good job, Julie?'*

JA: I don't think you ever stop learning. I don't think you ever stop saying 'What can I do? What makes it valuable to the audience when they're watching it? How can I give them the best afternoon or evening of their lives?' That's something that came to me in my 20s and I write about it in the book, when I began to know a little bit more about what I was doing and how I really could maybe make a difference to someone as they came into the theater.

Nelson: *Might there be a Julie Andrews biography film? Can we turn this [book] into a film? Who would play you?*

JA: God knows! I can't think right now. Listen, I'm just so happy I got it done. I'll just wallow in that for the moment.

Nelson: *The whole process of writing: describe what your routine was. Did you go into hiding? Did you go to a tropical island? What was the writing process?*

JA: Mostly it was in my bedroom. My daughter, my natural born daughter, Emma, is a writer. She writes with me when we write our children's books together and we've done a great many of them. She was the one who encouraged Mum to get the book out. I had done a huge extensive timeline and sort of put all my dates (as much I could remember!) together and she started to question me…ask me things. And a lot of the times we did it on a built-in camera on our computers, sometimes by phone, sometimes in person. Then she transcribed all those tapes, she put them altogether and just sent me the bulk of the words and then I began the writing process. So I had something laid out in front of me.

Nelson: *And the very difficult times you described as a youngster, does that make you strive to have more empathy for young people? And certainly, and not just even among the celebrity culture, you seem to transmit a certain empathy to young people.*

JA: Well, I do feel an empathy with young people particularly today because I think they face more choices and more difficulties than you or I ever knew, because the world is so full and so crazy, and so, so different. I don't know. I'm sure my childhood did affect the way I am, but I hope I've always had some empathy. I have brothers and sisters so maybe that had something to do with it.

Nelson: *You were one of the first celebrities to adopt children long before it became 'Brangelina' fashionable to do so. Was there a lesson you wanted to make sure your children learned? Was there one thing that you wanted to make sure your kids walked away with?*

JA: Well, I wanted to instill in them that sense of being special no matter where they're from. Everyone is special in this world. Everybody should find their individuality and the best of themselves if they can. And I was so encouraged as a child. I say in the book that I walked with giants, gentle giants, that helped me so much. I hadn't a clue what I was doing when I started and so many people taught me and helped me and encouraged me along the way. And I think I'd like to give back and do that for everybody else.

Nelson: *There are some dishy little anecdotes in here about some celebrities you've worked with. Olivier, Richard Burton, Rex Harrison. For people who haven't read the book yet and if they want to go out pick up a copy, what are some of the little tidbits that they can look forward to?*

JA: There's a lot of tales of how *My Fair Lady* was created and what it was like to be out of town with rehearsals and what the first night was like. The first night out of town, it was in a huge snow storm and people were driving down from New York in droves and the *My*

Fair Lady turntables weren't working on stage, and Rex Harrison threatened not to go on because he was so nervous about singing with an orchestra. There's a lot of that in the book. And, it was true about *Camelot*, too. We had some tremendous setbacks in *Camelot*. And thanks to Richard Burton and the entire company who loved the piece so much, the heart of *Camelot*, was so beloved by all of us. That in spite of our director having a heart attack, and Alan J Lerner who wrote the wonderful lyrics having almost a perforated ulcer, we kept going until they could come back and fashion for us a better musical.

Nelson: *It is amazing when you think of the golden age of the Broadway musical…*

JA: I was there!

Nelson: *The first songs I learned were* My Fair Lady…

JA: It was just like that—the absolute peak of the great days of the Broadway musical and I was lucky enough to come to Broadway. The things that were all around were just stunning.

Nelson: *When you go to the theater now what draws you in, what kind of shows do you go to?*

JA: Well…musicals of course, 'cause I love them and I know how hard they are. I think it was Alan J Lerner who said that 'a musical is never finished; you could go on perfecting it for ever more'. But one really succeeds if one manages to make it to Broadway. There were tons that came into Broadway and got casually tossed aside since there was so much great stuff to choose from. It's getting better again, I think, now we're coming full circle, but for a while there was so little in the musical theater….

Nelson: *It doesn't help that there are these reality stars on Broadway!*

JA: Well, I think it gives them a phenomenal education and that's not a bad thing.

Nelson: *You're famous for having friendships with celebrities like Dick Van Dyke and Carol Burnett…*

JA: Well, I've lived a long time! We're talking six decades.

Nelson: *You've kept your friends. What qualities do you look for in a friend?*

JA: Oh…fun, humor obviously. All the things you must do…decency. All my friends, all the people that I work with in film, all we have to do is meet up again, we might not meet for years and years and the minute we take up with each other again, it's like we never stopped. It's lovely to know that there are that many gorgeous people. It's an odd thing to say, I think, [but] the bigger the celebrity—the nicer they are. They've had to fight. They've had to do what they've had to do to become so famous. And my friends certainly don't pull rank. They're real people.

Nelson: *It doesn't get any more famous than Dame Julie Andrews and to be a fighter—what would surprise people to know about you? There must be something…it can't all be sweetness and light. There's a career to be steered.*

JA: I think a lot of people feel one picks and chooses one's career and certainly there are choices one makes. But so much of the time, especially when you're just beginning in this business, you are lucky if you get any chance that comes your way. It isn't that you sit back and everybody offers you this, that and the other. It isn't that you control your destiny especially at the beginning. You try to work and get it done and that's what I had to do.

Nelson: *Everybody has a favorite Julie Andrews' movie. I know Kochie's is* The Sound of Music. *But even if he didn't have a favorite Julie Andrews movie,* The Sound of Music *would still be his number one. What are some of your favorite films?*

JA: Oh, my. I have a lot of favorite films…I'm a big movie buff anyway. I love everything from *Ben Hur* to *On the Waterfront* to *The Quiet Man*—it's a wonderful movie with John Wayne and Maureen O' Hara directed by John Ford, to *As Good As It Gets*, the Nicholson

film. And just all of them! Tons of movies for different reasons.

Nelson: *I just saw* Look Back In Anger, *speaking of Richard Burton.*

JA: He was so charismatic. Sad thing is that so many people in the book are no longer with us. He was wonderful.

Nelson: *What do you credit your longevity to, not just as a public figure? You're in such terrific shape, you're beautiful. Is it the case that 'bodies in motion stay in motion?'*

JA: It might be. It might be keeping your brain as active as possible which is what my dad taught me. It may be I get a lot of help from very kind makeup men and hairdressers who really do wonderful things.

Nelson: *[imitating Eliza Doolittle] Garrn!*

JA: It's true. It all helps, believe me!

Nelson: *Will there be another book after* Home?

JA: I don't know. I thought I wrote reams and reams and suddenly there is that book and it's only that thick [indicating a thin volume]. I thought I wrote a tome. I don't know. We'll see. The reason to write it was because not many people know about those early years, not about me, not about what it was like after the war. I grew up in war, and that's all I knew. The rest a lot of people [already] knew. They knew I went to Hollywood, I did *Poppins*, *Sound of Music*…

Nelson: *Is there something you're hoping people walk away with when they've closed the book? 'I know a little bit about Julie.' What are you hoping they will feel emotionally?*

JA: Well, as an author I hope they feel satisfied. They've had a good read. Learned a little something they didn't know before.

Nelson: *I think they'll be waiting for the sequel!*

JA: Thank you.

Nelson: *Reading seems to be a dying art. I don't know that the internet is so great. Yeah, sure you can read e-books there, but that's not the same as the tactile [experience].*

JA: I'm passionate about reading and literacy. My daughter and I do an enormous amount, as much as we can, to be advocates for it. To bring the arts program into schools and just all of that. If you don't read…Helen Hayes said something 'Your parents can teach you many things, but when you open a book up you learn how to fly'. And it's true…you can have wings when you read a book and take off.

Nelson: *It's funny when I was walking here today to meet you, I walked past a bookstore and there was a biography of Julie Andrews in the window.*

JA: Was it this one or one of the others?

Nelson: *It wasn't this one. We'll have to drop this off at the bookstore and make sure they put it in the window!*

JA: There've been a few and I guess that was another reason to write this 'cause they've all been so wrong and the dates were so muddled and so many people didn't know what went on.

Nelson: *Was there a tremendous editing process or was this pretty much along the lines of what you guys put together?*

JA: I think there was a lot of editing…a lot of adding, actually. 'Could I just put one more paragraph in about this person or that person' and 'could I capture what it really felt like working with so and so' and 'could I add another paragraph please or is it too late?'

Nelson: *And lots of personal photos. How did you sort your collection?*

JA: There are so many in there, but it doesn't seem like that now that the book is finally published. But I thought the best thing I could do was show what I'm writing about so the reader would know what I was saying.

Nelson: *I love the pictures of you as a little girl. You can see the face of Maria and Mary Poppins in that little girl and yet studio executives at one point said you were not photogenic?*

JA: Not photogenic for film. Yes, that's when I was fourteen and had a big gap between my teeth and one eye was slightly in the corner and my legs were bowed and I really did understand what they meant!

HOLLYWOOD INSIDER
EXPOSED!

Nelson: Was that your awkward time…14?
JA: Teens were awkward in general.
Nelson: Is living well the best revenge?
JA: I always say survival is the best revenge. Just being here is wonderful. And best thing about it: I'm still curious. I love to know what's going on…see what's on Broadway. I've just begun a new publishing venture with my daughter. Two of my books for children are being adapted for the theater and that's wildly exciting for me. One of them is being done as a symphonic concert of a little book called Simeon's Gift. I'm going out this summer to narrate it on stage with a symphony orchestra and I'll be going out to the Hollywood Bowl, to Atlanta, to Philadelphia, Louisville…
Nelson: To Sydney and Melbourne, maybe?
JA: From your lips to someone's ears!
Nelson: We're going to get you 'home' to Australia.
JA: I'd love that. That would be so nice.
Nelson: We'll make it happen. Now, let's have some tea.
JA: I'd love to. If you'll pass the teapot.

Cool, huh? And nothing was sweeter icing on the tea cake than when I found out the next day from Helen that JA had told the crew after I'd departed that I 'was one of the best interviewers in recent memory'. Wow! You may now officially count me among the Julie-groupies!!

How reassuring it is to know that if I live as long and healthy a life as my grandmothers, when it is over I will arrive in a Heaven filled with such a dizzying array of dynamic dames. We'll be putting on razzle-dazzle revues for all eternity!

So Long for Now

I am uncertain of how to end this book since my story, I trust, is very far from over. Thanks to an inquisitive mind, the courage to ask questions and the desire to make others laugh, I shall keep plugging away at broadcast journalism as long as there are subjects to be interviewed and stories to be told.

It's been great fun sharing these personal recollections with you and I'd love to know if you were amused and entertained, so be in touch. Please, pick up a pen and write me an old fashioned *letter*, care of the Publisher's address. Too many of us have fallen into the immediate gratification and laziness of e-mail. It's not only penmanship that suffers, but the lost art of spelling, grammar and punctuation. Bookmark www.merriam-webster.com and treat yourself to boning up your English skills. Believe it or not, I've written this entire book long-hand on legal pads. (And before you jump on me, yes: I use recycled paper!)

So, how to end? To paraphrase Jo Tourneur, as played by Mary Stuart, in the final lines from my long-running, beloved soap opera *Search for Tomorrow*, I'll simply say:

'What am I searching for? Tomorrow. And I can't wait!'

First published in Australia in 2008 by
New Holland Publishers (Australia) Pty Ltd
Sydney • Auckland • London • Cape Town

1/66 Gibbes Street Chatswood NSW 2067 Australia

218 Lake Road Northcote Auckland New Zealand
86 Edgware Road London W2 2EA United Kingdom
80 McKenzie Street Cape Town 8001 South Africa

Copyright © 2008 in text: Nelson Aspen
Copyright © 2008 New Holland Publishers (Australia) Pty Ltd
Copyright © 2008 Getty Images, picture section Jeff Goldblum and Kevin Spacey,
Tom Cruise, Julie Andrews, Nicole Kidman.

All rights reserved. No part of this publication may be reproduced, stored in a retrieval system
or transmitted, in any form or by any means, electronic, mechanical, photocopying, recording
or otherwise, without the prior written permission of the publishers and copyright holders.

National Library of Australia Cataloguing-in-Publication Data:

> Aspen, Nelson.
>
> Hollywood insider : exposed! / Nelson Aspen.
>
> 9781741106985 (pbk.)
>
> Fame--Anecdotes.
> Gossip columnists--California--Hollywood--Anecdotes.

791.409793

Publishers: Fiona Schultz and Linda Williams
Publishing Manager: Lliane Clarke
Project Editor: Diane Jardine
Designer: Natasha Hayles
Production Manager: Linda Bottari
Printer: McPhersons Printing Group, Maryborough, Victoria

Front and back cover images: Michael Higgins

Academy Awards[®], Oscars[®] and Oscar Night are the registered trademarks and
copyrighted property of the Academy of Motion Picture Arts and Sciences.

10 9 8 7 6 5 4 3 2 1